ANDROID™ BOOT CAMP FOR DEVELOPERS USING JAVA™, INTRODUCTORY

ANDROID™ BOOT CAMP FOR DEVELOPERS USING JAVA™, INTRODUCTORY: A BEGINNER'S GUIDE TO CREATING YOUR FIRST ANDROID APPS

CORINNE HOISINGTON

Australia • Brazil • Japan • Korea • Mexico • Singapore • Spain • United Kingdom • United States

Android Boot Camp for Developers Using Java, Introductory: A Beginner's Guide to Creating Your First Android Apps
Corinne Hoisington

Executive Editor: Marie Lee

Senior Product Manager: Alyssa Pratt

Development Editor: Lisa Ruffolo

Associate Product Manager: Stephanie Lorenz

Content Project Manager: Heather Hopkins

Art Director: Faith Brosnan

Marketing Manager: Shanna Shelton

Compositor: Integra

Cover Designer: Wing-ip Ngan, Ink design, inc. ©

Cover Image Credits:
istockphoto.com/zentilia
istockphoto.com/thesuperph
istockphoto.com/franckreporter
iQoncept/Shutterstock.com

Library of Congress Control Number: 2012932024

ISBN-13: 978-1-133-59439-0

Course Technology
20 Channel Center Street
Boston, MA 02210

Cengage Learning is a leading provider of customized learning solutions with office locations around the globe, including Singapore, the United Kingdom, Australia, Mexico, Brazil, and Japan. Locate your local office at: **international.cengage.com/region**

Cengage Learning products are represented in Canada by Nelson Education, Ltd.

For your lifelong learning solutions, visit **course.cengage.com**

Visit our corporate website at **cengage.com**.

Printed in the United States of America
1 2 3 4 5 6 7 18 17 16 15 14 13 12

Brief Contents

Contents

Preface

Welcome to *Android Boot Camp for Developers Using Java, Introductory: A Beginner's Guide to Creating Your First Android Apps*! This book is designed for people who have some programming experience or are new to Java programming and want to move into the exciting world of developing apps for Android mobile devices on a Windows or Mac computer. Google Android is quickly becoming the operating system of choice for mobile devices, including smartphones and tablets, with nearly half of the world's mobile devices running on the Android platform. To help you participate in the growing Android market, this book focuses on developing apps for Android devices.

Approach

The approach used in *Android Boot Camp for Developers Using Java, Introductory* is straightforward. You review a completed Android app and identify why people use the app, the tasks it performs, and the problems it solves. You also learn about the programming logic, Java tools, and code syntax you can use to create the app. Next, you work through a hands-on tutorial that guides you through the steps of creating the Android app, including designing the user interface and writing the code. After each step, you can compare your work to an illustration that shows exactly how the interface should look or what the code should contain. Using the illustrations, you can avoid mistakes in creating the app and finish the chapter with an appealing, real-world Android app.

The main tool used in *Android Boot Camp for Developers Using Java, Introductory* is a standard tool developers use to create Android apps: Eclipse Classic, a free, open-source integrated development environment (IDE). Eclipse includes an emulator for testing your apps, so you don't need a smartphone to run any of the apps covered in this book. Instructions for downloading and setting up Eclipse are provided later in this preface.

What This Book Is

This book introduces you to writing apps for Android mobile devices. It familiarizes you with the development software for creating Android apps, programming logic used in the apps, and Java code that puts the software design and logic into practice. You don't need an Android device because you can run the apps you create in this book by using an Android emulator.

What This Book Is Not

Because this book is targeted to those new to developing Android apps, it doesn't cover advanced topics, such as application programming interfaces (APIs) for each platform. Instead, this book provides a launch pad to begin your journey into creating Android apps for fun and for profit.

In addition, this book isn't an exhaustive information resource. You can find a wealth of information, tutorials, examples, and other resources for the Android platform online. You should learn enough from this book that you can modify and make use of code you find to fit your needs. The best way to learn how to create Android apps is to write code, make mistakes, and learn how to fix them.

Organization and Coverage

Chapter 1 introduces the Android platform and describes the current market for Android apps. You create your first Android project using Eclipse and become familiar with the Eclipse interface and its tools. As programming tradition mandates, your first project is called Hello Android World, which you complete and then run in an emulator.

Chapter 2 focuses on the Android user interface. While developing an app for selecting and displaying healthy recipes, you follow a series of steps that you repeat every time you create an Android app. You learn how to develop a user interface using certain types of controls, select a screen layout, and learn how to write code that responds to a button event (such as a click or tap). While creating the chapter project, you develop an app that includes more than one screen and can switch from one screen to another. Finally, you learn how to correct errors in Java code.

Chapter 3 covers user input, variables, and operations. You develop an Android app that allows users to enter the number of concert tickets they want to purchase, and then click a button to calculate the total cost of the tickets. To do so, you create a user interface using an Android theme and add controls to the interface, including text fields, buttons, and spinner controls. You also declare variables and use arithmetic operations to perform calculations, and then convert and format numeric data.

Chapter 4 discusses icons and decision-making controls. The sample app provides health care professionals a mobile way to convert the weight of a patient from pounds to kilograms and from kilograms to pounds. You create this project using a custom application icon, learn how to fine-tune the layout of the user interface, and include radio buttons for user selections. You also learn how to program decisions using If statements, If Else statements, and logical operators.

Chapter 5 describes how to use lists, arrays, and Web browsers in an Android app. You design and create an Android app that people can use as a traveler's guide to popular attractions in San Francisco, California. To do so, you work with lists, images, and the Switch decision structure. You also learn how to let users access a Web browser while using an Android app.

Chapter 6 explains how to include audio such as music in Android apps. The sample app opens with a splash screen and then displays a second screen where users can select a song to play. To develop this app, you create and set up a splash screen, learn about the Activity life cycle, pause an Activity, and start, play, stop, and resume music playback.

Features of the Book

Android Boot Camp for Developers Using Java, Introductory includes the following features:

- *Objectives*—Each chapter begins with a list of objectives as an overview of the topics discussed in the chapter and as a useful study aid.
- *GTKs and In the Trenches*—GTK stands for Good to Know. These notes offer tips about Android devices, Android apps, and the Android development tools. The In the Trenches features provide programming advice and practical solutions to typical programming problems.
- *Figures and tables*—Chapters contain a wealth of screen shots to guide you as you create Android apps and learn about the Android marketplace. In addition, many tables are included to give you an at-a-glance summary of useful information.
- *Step-by-step tutorials*—Starting in Chapter 1, you create complete, working Android apps by performing the steps in a series of hands-on tutorials that lead you through the development process.
- *Code syntax features*—Each new programming concept or technique is introduced with a code syntax feature that highlights a type of statement or programming structure. The code is analyzed and explained thoroughly before you use it in the chapter project.
- *Summaries*—At the end of each chapter is a summary list that recaps the Android terms, programming concepts, and Java coding techniques covered in the chapter so that you have a way to check your understanding of the chapter's main points.
- *Key terms*—Each chapter includes definitions of new terms, alphabetized for ease of reference. This feature is another useful way to review the chapter's major concepts.
- *Developer FAQs*—Each chapter contains many short-answer questions that help you review the key concepts in the chapter.
- *Beyond the Book*—In addition to review questions, each chapter provides research topics and questions. You can search the Web to find the answers to these questions and further your Android knowledge.
- *Case programming projects*—Each chapter outlines six realistic programming projects, including their purpose, algorithms, and conditions. For each project, you use the same steps and techniques you learned in the chapter to create a running Android app on your own.
- *Quality*—Every chapter project and case programming project was tested using Windows 7 and Mac OS X computers.

Student Resources

Source code and project files for the chapter projects and case programming projects in *Android Boot Camp for Developers Using Java, Introductory* are available at *www.cengagebrain.com*.

For complete instructions on downloading, installing, and setting up the tools you need to perform the steps in this book, see the section titled "Prelude! Installing the Android Eclipse SDK" later in this preface.

For the Instructor

Android Boot Camp for Developers Using Java, Introductory is intended to be taught as a complete course dedicated to the mobile programming of the Android device or as an exploratory topic in a programming class or literacy course. Students can develop Android applications on a Windows or Mac computer using the Eclipse emulator in a traditional or online class. Offering such an exciting topic that is relative to today's huge growth in the mobile environment brings excitement to the programming classroom. The Eclipse/Android platform is fully free and open-source, which means all students can access these tools on their home computers.

Instructor Resources

The following teaching tools are available on the Instructor Resources CD or through *login.cengage.com* to instructors who have adopted this book:

Instructor's Manual. The electronic Instructor's Manual follows the book chapter by chapter to assist in planning and organizing an effective, engaging course. The manual includes learning objectives, chapter overviews, ideas for classroom activities, and abundant additional resources. A sample course syllabus is also available.

ExamView®. This book is accompanied by ExamView, a powerful testing software package that allows instructors to create and administer printed, computer (LAN-based), and Internet exams. ExamView includes hundreds of questions corresponding to the topics covered in this book, enabling students to generate detailed study guides that include page references for further review. These computer-based and Internet testing components allow students to take exams at their computers and save instructors time by grading each exam automatically. Test banks are also available in Blackboard, WebCT, and Angel formats.

PowerPoint presentations. This book comes with PowerPoint slides for each chapter. They're included as a teaching aid for classroom presentations, to make available to students on the network for chapter review, or to be printed for classroom distribution. Instructors can add their own slides for additional topics or customize the slides with access to all the figure files from the book.

Solution files. Solution files for all chapter projects and the end-of-chapter exercises are provided.

Prelude! Installing the Android Eclipse SDK

Setting Up the Android Environment

To begin developing Android applications, you must first set up the Android programming environment on your computer. To establish a development environment, this section walks you through the installation and setup for a Windows or Mac computer. The Android Software Development Kit (SDK) allows developers to create applications for the Android platform. The Android SDK includes sample projects with source code, development tools, an emulator, and required libraries to build Android applications, which are written using the Java programming language.

The Android installation is quite different from a typical program installation. You must perform the following tasks in sequence to correctly prepare for creating an Android application. Before you write your first application in Chapter 1, complete the following tasks to successfully install Android SDK on your computer:

1. Prepare your computer for the installation.
2. Download and unzip the Eclipse Integrated Development Environment (IDE).
3. Download and unzip the Android SDK package.
4. Install the Android Development Tools (ADT) Plugin within Eclipse.
5. Set the location of the ADT within Eclipse.
6. Set up the Android emulator.

Preparing Your Computer

The Android Software Development Kit is compatible with Windows XP (32-bit), Windows Vista (32- or 64-bit), Windows 7 (32- or 64-bit), Windows 8 (32-, 64-, or 128-bit), and Mac OS X (Intel only). To install the basic files needed to write an Android application, your hard drive needs a minimum of 400 MB of available space.

Downloading Eclipse

Before downloading the necessary files, create a folder on the hard drive (C:) of your computer named Android. Next, you must download and unzip the software in the C:\Android folder. Windows Vista and Windows 7 automatically unzip files, but if you are using Windows XP, you will need to first download an unzip program such as WinZip at *download.com*.

The preferred Java program development software is called Eclipse. Eclipse is a free and open-source IDE. To download Eclipse:

1. Open the Web page *www.eclipse.org/downloads* and look for the most recent version of Eclipse Classic as shown in Figure 1.

Figure 1 Eclipse Downloads page (*www.eclipse.org/download*)

2. Select the most recent version of Eclipse Classic. If you are downloading to a Macintosh computer, click the **Windows** list arrow and then click **Mac OS X (Cocoa)**. If you are downloading to a Windows computer, click **Windows 32 Bit** or **Windows 64 Bit** based on the system on your computer.

3. After downloading the Eclipse package, unzip the downloaded eclipse file into a subfolder of the Android folder at C:\Android on your local computer. The unzipped file contains the contents of the Eclipse development environment (Figure 2). You may want to create a shortcut on the desktop to make it easy to start Eclipse.

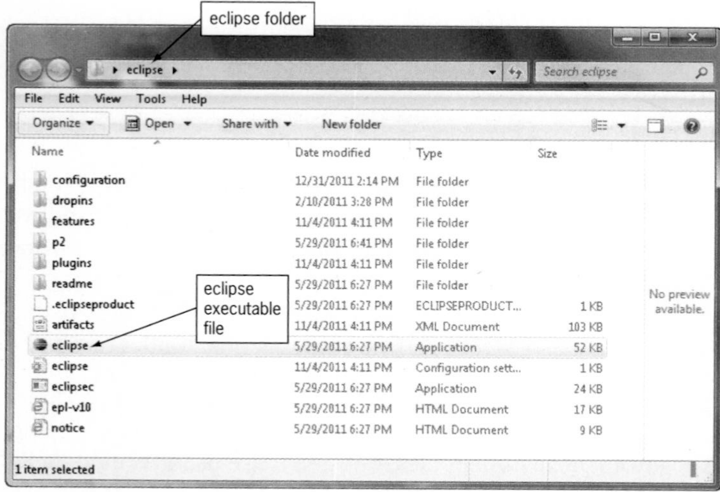

Figure 2 Contents of the Eclipse folder

Downloading the SDK Starter Package

After unzipping the Eclipse package, the next step is to download the Android Software Development Kit (SDK), which is a collection of files and utilities that work with Eclipse to create Android applications. The SDK starter package includes only the core SDK tools, which you can use to download the rest of the SDK components such as the latest Android platform. To download the Android SDK:

1. Go to the Android developers Web site at *http://developer.android.com/sdk.*
2. Download the latest SDK for your computer's platform (Figure 3).

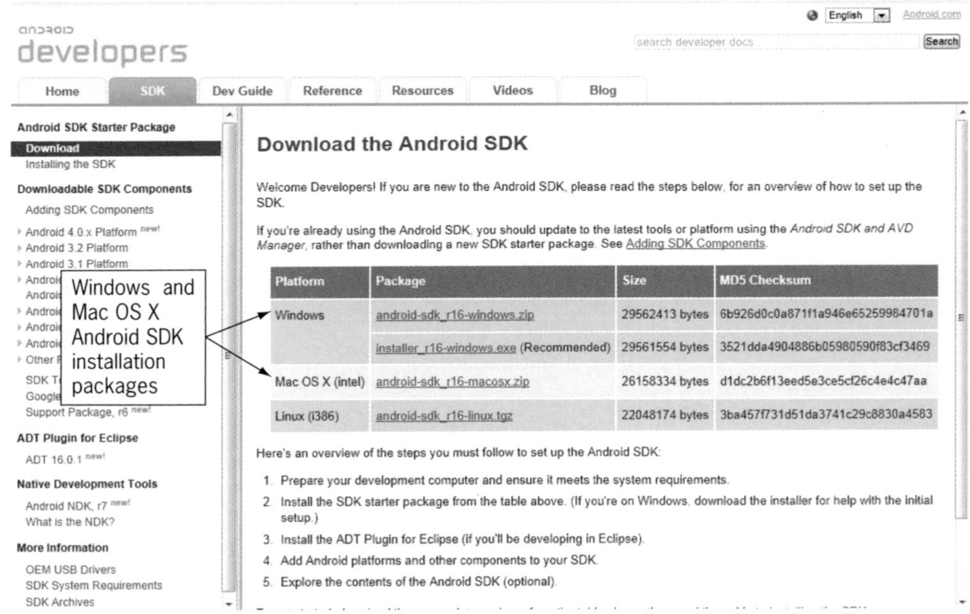

Figure 3 Android SDK download site (*http://developer.android.com/sdk*)

3. After downloading the SDK, unzip its contents into the C:\Android folder.

Setting Up the Android Development Tools in Eclipse

After you install Eclipse and the Android SDK, the next step is to install the ADT (Android Development Tools) plug-in from Eclipse. The ADT plug-in for Eclipse is an extension to the Eclipse IDE that creates Android applications, debugs the code, and exports a signed application file to the Android Market. To download the Android Development Tools:

1. In the Android folder on your computer, open the **eclipse** folder and double-click the **eclipse.exe** file to open Eclipse. (If an Open File - Security Warning dialog box opens, click the **Run** button.)

2. In Eclipse, click **Help** on the menu bar and then click **Install New Software** to open the Install dialog box.
3. Click the **Add** button in the upper-right corner of the dialog box.
4. In the Add Repository dialog box, type **ADT Plugin** for the Name and the following URL for the Location: ***https://dl-ssl.google.com/android/eclipse/*** (Figure 4).

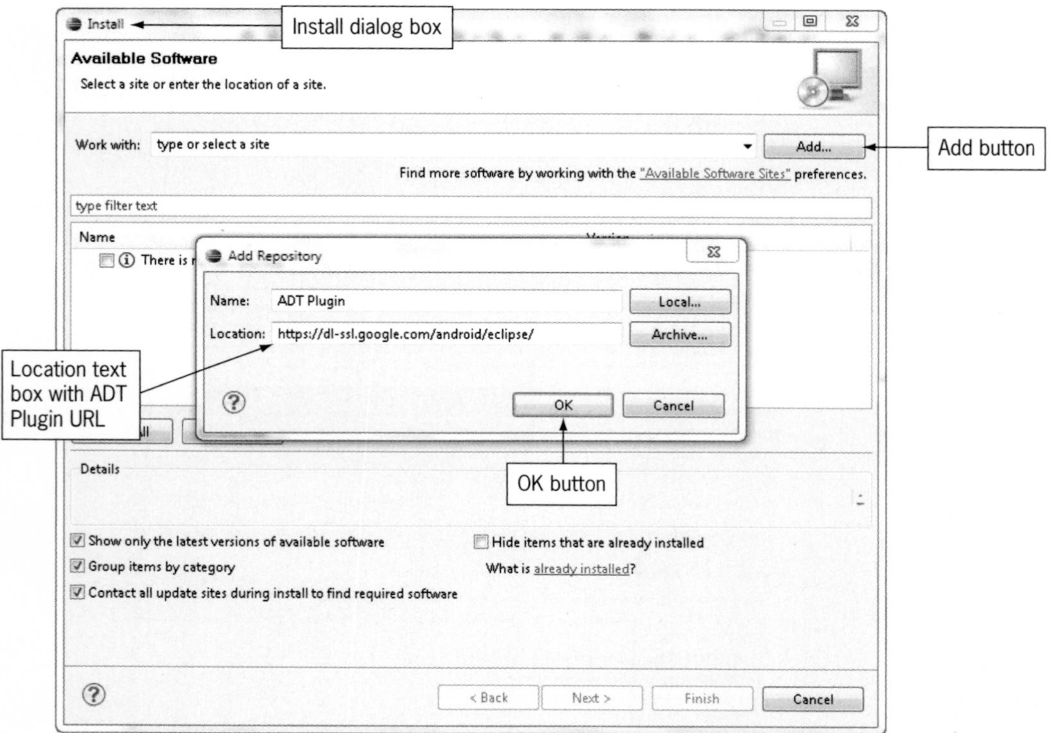

Figure 4 Install dialog box in Eclipse

5. Click the **OK** button.
6. In the Available Software dialog box, select the **Developer Tools** check box and then click the **Next** button.
7. In the next window, click the **Next** button.
8. Read and accept the license agreements, and then click the **Finish** button. If a security warning appears indicating that the authenticity or validity of the software can't be established, click **OK**. When the installation is finished, restart Eclipse.

Configuring Eclipse with the Location of the ADT Plugin

After successfully downloading the ADT plug-in, the next task is to modify your ADT preferences in Eclipse to use the Android SDK directory. Next, you install the repositories for Android 4.0 SDK, Google API, and the emulator.

1. In Eclipse, click **Window** on the menu bar and then click **Preferences** to open the Preferences dialog box.

   On Mac OS X, click **Eclipse** on the menu bar and then click **Preferences**.

2. Select **Android** in the left pane. To set the SDK Location, type **C:\android\android-sdk-windows** to enter the path to the installed files (Figure 5).

   On Mac OS X, set the SDK Location to **/Library/android**.

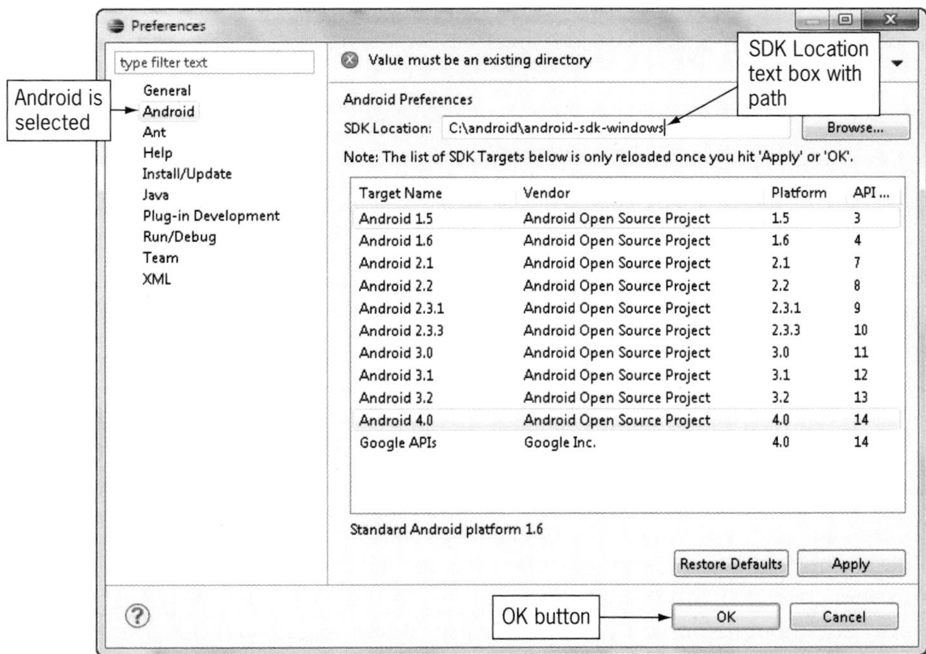

Figure 5 Setting the SDK Location in Eclipse

3. Click the **OK** button. To install the repositories for the Android 4.0 SDK, click **Window** on the Eclipse menu bar and then click **Android SDK Manager** to open the Android SDK Manager dialog box.
4. Click **Android 4.0 (API 14)** to select it, and then click the **Install packages** button.
5. In the next window, click **Install** to install the Android 4.0 SDK in Eclipse (Figure 6). The installation may take some time to complete.

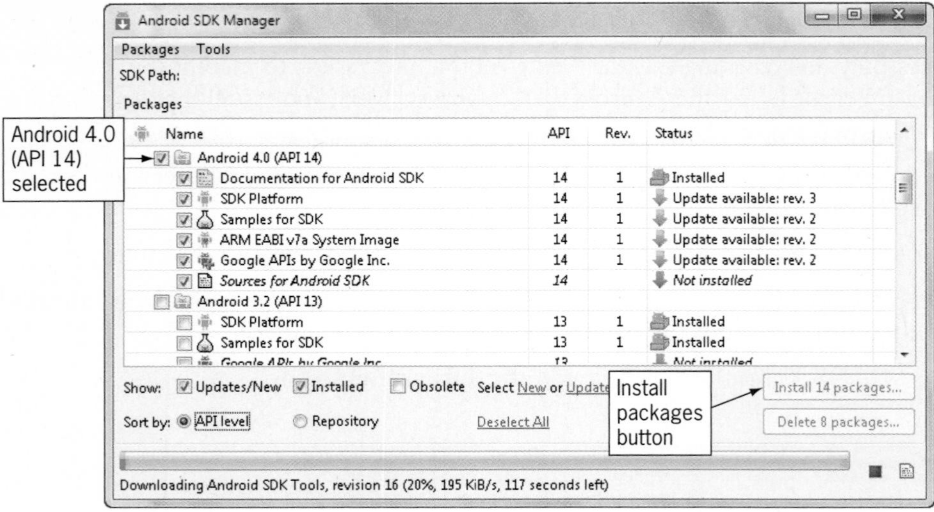

Figure 6 Installing Android 4.0 using the SDK Manager in Eclipse

Setting up the Android Emulator

The Android SDK includes a phone and tablet emulator that allows you to develop and test your Android applications. Android mobile devices come in many shapes and sizes and must be tested on a host of emulator layout sizes to verify the configuration and usability. Each Android device configuration is stored in an Android Virtual Device (AVD).

The Android SDK and AVD Manager within Eclipse provide multiple emulators for test-driving your application without using a physical device. When you run an Android app, it runs in an emulator so you can interact with the emulated mobile device just as you would an actual mobile device. You can simulate touching the screen of the emulator with the pointing device on your computer.

To use the emulator, you first must create one or more AVD configurations. In each configuration, you specify an Android platform to run in the emulator and the set of hardware options and emulator skin you want to use. When you launch the emulator, you specify the AVD configuration that you want to load. In this book, the Android 4.0 Ice Cream Sandwich version emulator is used, although based on your actual Android device, you can add multiple emulators to test the devices on which you plan to deploy your apps.

You must name the emulator that you set up to use to deploy your Android apps. By selecting an emulator, you choose the skin, or resolution, that the Android emulator displays. To specify the Android 4.0 emulator:

1. In Eclipse, click **Window** on the menu bar and then click **AVD Manager** to open the Android Virtual Device Manager dialog box.
2. Click the **New** button to open the Create new Android Virtual Device (AVD) dialog box.

3. To name your Android emulator, type **IceCream** in the Name text box.
4. To target your Android app to appear in the Android 4.0 version, select **Android 4.0 – API Level 14** in the Target list (Figure 7). You can select newer Android versions, but most devices are not using the newest platform.

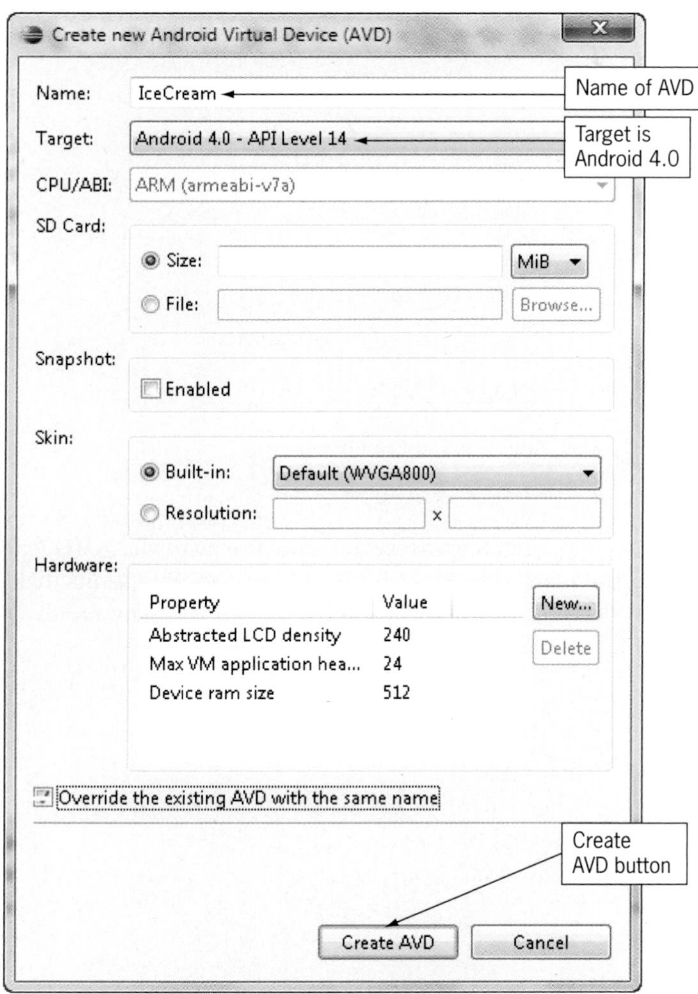

Figure 7 Create new Android Virtual Device (AVD) dialog box

5. Click the **Create AVD** button. The Android Virtual Device Manager dialog box lists the AVD Name (IceCream) for the Android 4.0 target device (Figure 8).

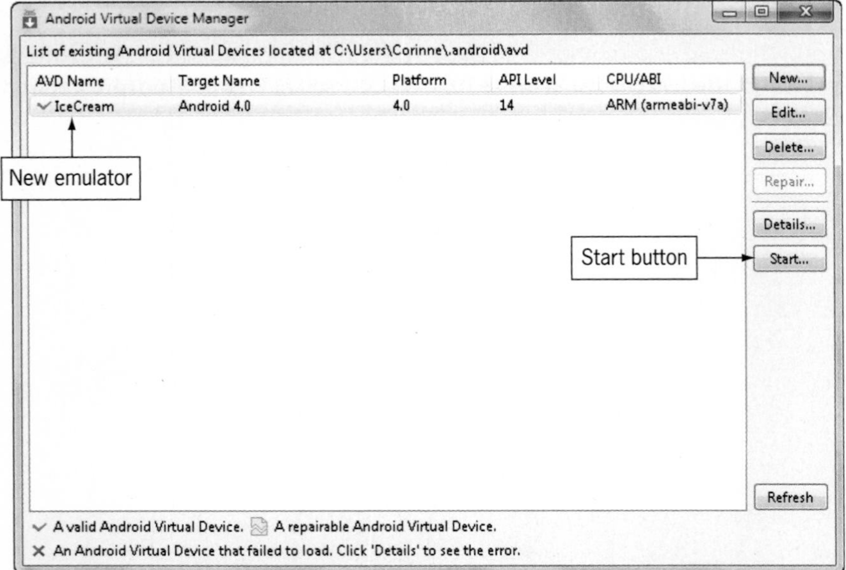

Figure 8 Android Virtual Device Manager dialog box

6. Your AVD is now ready to use. To launch and test the emulator with the AVD, click the **IceCream** emulator and then click the **Start** button. If a Launch Options dialog box opens, click the **Launch** button. After a few moments, the Ice Cream Sandwich Android 4.0 emulator starts (Figure 9).

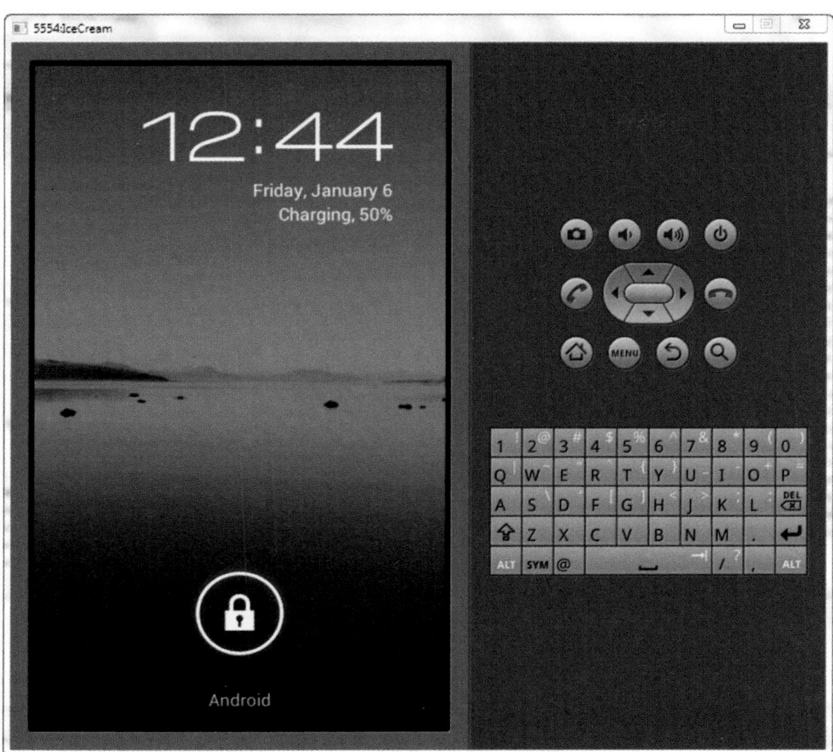

Figure 9 Android emulator

7. Close Eclipse by clicking **File** on the menu bar and then clicking **Exit**. Close all other open windows. You are now ready to create your first application.

Acknowledgements

Android Boot Camp for Developers Using Java, Introductory: A Beginner's Guide to Creating Your First Android Apps! is the product of a wonderful team of professionals working toward a single goal: providing students with pertinent, engaging material to further their knowledge and careers. Thank you to the folks at Cengage—specifically Acquisitions Editor Brandi Shailer; Senior Product Manager Alyssa Pratt; Content Project Manager Heather Hopkins; Karen Annett, the copyeditor; Suzanne Huizenga, the proofreader; and Susan Whalen and Susan Pedicini, the MQA testers.

Thank you to the reviewers of this book: Sam Abraham, Siena Heights University; Marilyn Achelpohl, Galesburg High School; Jay Bohnsack, Moline High School; Arshia Khan, College of Saint Scholastica; Larry Langellier, Moraine Valley Community College; and Roseann Rovetto, Horry-Georgetown Technical College. It's because of their insights and experience that *Android Boot Camp for Developers Using Java* is a book that can actually be used in the classroom.

Writing a book is similar to entering a long-term relationship with an obsessive partner. Throughout the journey, life continues around you: teaching classes full time, presenting across the country, and attending family events at every turn. As the world continues, those closest to you allow you to focus on your reclusive writing by assisting with every other task. My husband, Timothy, is credited with learning to cook dinner, to cheer me on, and most of all for his love. Special thanks to my six children Tim, Brittany, Ryan, Daniel, Breanne, and Eric for providing much needed breaks filled with pride and laughter. A heartfelt thanks to my dear sister Shirley who has encouraged me for a lifetime. And a special thanks to Lisa Ruffolo as my developmental editor and master wordsmith who provided the perfect polish for every chapter.

CHAPTER 1

Voilà! Meet the Android

In this chapter, you learn to:

- Understand the market for Android applications
- State the role of the Android device in the mobile market
- Describe the features of the Android phone
- Identify which languages are used in Android development
- Describe the role of the Android Market in the mobile marketplace
- Create an Android project using Eclipse
- Explain the role of the Package Explorer
- Specify the use of layout and widget controls in the user interface
- Execute an Android application on an emulator
- Open a saved Android project in Eclipse

Welcome to the beginning of your journey in creating Android phone applications and developing for the mobile device market. Mobile computing has become the most popular way to make a personal connection to the Internet. Mobile phones and tablets constitute the fastest growing category of any technology in the world. Mobile phone usage has quickly outgrown the simple expectation of voice calls and text messaging. An average data plan for a mobile device, often called a **smartphone**, typically includes browsing the Web, playing popular games such as Angry Birds, using business applications, checking e-mail, listening to music, recording live video, and mapping locations with a GPS (global positioning system).

When purchasing a phone, you can choose from many mobile operating systems, including the iOS for the iPhone, Google Android, Microsoft Phone 7, and BlackBerry OS. Recently the Android phone has become the sales leader, outselling its competitors. The Android market is exploding with more than 50 million Android phones now being used worldwide. Nearly one-half of the world's mobile devices run on the Android platform.

IN THE TRENCHES

More than 25 percent of all U.S. households have canceled their landlines for the convenience of receiving only one bill from a mobile carrier.

Creating mobile applications, called apps, for the Android phone market is an exciting new job opportunity. Whether you become a developer for a technology firm that creates professional apps for corporations or a hobbyist developer who creates games, niche programs, or savvy new applications, the Android marketplace provides a new means to earn income.

Meet the Android

The Android phone platform is built on a free operating system primarily created by a company called Android, Inc. In 2005, Google obtained Android, Inc., to start a venture in the mobile phone market. Because Google intended the Android platform to be open source, the Android code was released under the Apache license, which permits anyone to download the full open-source Android code for free. Two years later, Google unveiled its first open-standards mobile device called the Android (Figure 1-1). In less than a decade, the Android phone market has grown into the world's best-selling phone platform.

Figure 1-1 Android phone

Android is the first open-source technology platform for mobile devices. Being an open-source operating system effectively means that no company or individual defines the features or direction of the development. Organizations and developers can extract, modify, and use the code for creating any app. The rapid success of the Android phone can be attributed to the collaboration of the **Open Handset Alliance** (*http://openhandsetalliance.com*), an open-source business alliance of 80 firms that develop standards for mobile devices. The Open Handset Alliance is led by Google. Other members include companies such as Sony, Dell, Intel, Motorola, Qualcomm, HTC, Texas Instruments, Samsung, Kyocera, and LG. Competitors such as Apple, which produces the iPhone, and Research In Motion (RIM), which produces the BlackBerry, do not have an open-source coding environment, but instead work with proprietary operating systems. The strength of the open-source community lies in the developers' ability to share their source code. Even though the open-source Android software is free, many developers are paid to build and improve the platform. For example, proprietary software such as the Apple operating system is limited to company employees licensed to build a program within the organization. The Android open-source platform allows more freedom so people can collaborate and improve the source code.

Many phone manufacturers install the Android operating system (OS) on their brand-name mobile phones due to its open-source environment. The open-source structure means that manufacturers do not pay license fees or royalties. With a small amount of customization, each manufacturer can place the Android OS on its latest devices. This minimal overhead allows manufacturers to sell their phones in the retail market for relatively low prices, often less than $100. Low prices on Android mobile devices have increased the sales and popularity of these devices.

One of the key features that make Android phones so attractive for consumers is the openness of the Android OS. Android has a large community of developers writing apps that extend the functionality of the devices. Users, for example, can benefit from over 250,000 apps available in the Android marketplace, many of which are free. Because the Android phone platform has become the leader in sales in the mobile market, the Android application market is keeping pace.

Android Phone Device

The Android phone is sold by a variety of companies under names you may recognize, such as EVO, Droid X, Galaxy, Echo, Optimus, Xperia, Cliq, Inspire, Thunderbolt, Atrix, Desire, Nexus, Infuse, Pyramid, and Revolution (Figure 1-2).

Figure 1-2 Android on many types of devices

IN THE TRENCHES
Android has ventured into the television market as well. Google TV integrates Google's Android operating system and the Linux version of the Google Chrome browser to create an interactive Internet television.

Android devices come in many shapes and sizes, as shown in Figure 1-2. The Android OS powers all types of mobile devices, including smartphones, tablets, netbooks, e-readers, MP4 players, and Internet TVs. The NOOK, a color e-book reader for Barnes and Noble, is based on the Android OS as well. Android devices are available with a variety of screen dimensions and many devices support a landscape mode where the width and height are spontaneously reversed depending on the orientation of the device. As you design Android apps, the screen size affects the layout of the user interface. To take full advantage of the capabilities of a particular device, you need to design user interfaces specifically for that device. For example, a smartphone and a tablet not only have a different physical screen size, but also different screen resolutions and pixel densities, which change the development process. As you develop an Android app, you can test the results on an emulator, which duplicates how the app looks and feels on a particular device. You can change the Android emulators to simulate the layout of a smartphone with a 3.5-inch screen or a tablet with a larger screen, both with high-density graphics. Android automatically scales content to the screen size of the device you choose, but if you use low-quality graphics in an app, the result is often a poorly pixelated display. As a developer, you need to continue to update your app as the market shifts to different platforms and screen resolutions.

The Android phone market has many more hardware case and size options than the single 3.5-inch screen option of an iPhone. Several Android phones such as the Atrix, Droid X, EVO, and Nexus offer screens 4 inches or larger. This extra space is excellent for phone users who like to watch movies, play games, or view full Web pages on their phone. In addition, tablets, also called slates, are now available on the Android platform. The Xoom Android tablet is produced by Google/Motorola and offers a 10.1-inch screen with a very high resolution of 1280 × 800 pixels. Amazon also has a 7-inch Android slate device called the Kindle Fire (Figure 1-3), currently available for $199. The Android tablets are in direct competition with other tablets and slate computers such as the iPad (various generations), BlackBerry PlayBook, and Galaxy Tab.

KEVIN DIETSCH/UPI/Newscom

Figure 1-3 Kindle Fire Android tablet

Features of the Android

As a developer, you must understand a phone's capabilities. The Android offers a wide variety of features that apps can use. Some features vary by model. Most Android phones provide the features listed in Table 1-1.

Feature	Description
Flash support	Flash video plays within the Android Web browser. (The iPhone does not support Flash capabilities.)
Power management	Android identifies programs running in the background using memory and processor resources. You can close those apps to free up the phone's processor memory, extending the battery power.
Optimized gaming	Android supports the use of gyroscope, gravity, barometric sensors, linear acceleration, and rotation vector, which provide game developers with highly sensitive and responsive controls.
Onscreen keyboard	The onscreen keyboard offers suggestions for spelling corrections as well as options for completing words you start typing. The onscreen keyboard also supports a voice-input mode.
Wi-Fi Internet tethering	Android supports tethering, which allows a phone to be used as a wireless or wired hot spot that other devices can use to connect to the Internet.
Multiple language support	Android supports multiple human languages.
Front- and rear-facing camera	Android phones can use either a front- or rear-facing camera, allowing developers to create applications involving video calling.
Voice-based recognition	Android recognizes voice actions for calling, texting, and navigating with the phone.
3D graphics	The interface can support 3D graphics for a 3D interactive game experience or 3D image rendering.
Facial recognition	Android provides this high-level feature for automatically identifying or verifying a person's face from a digital image or a video frame.

Table 1-1 Android platform features

Writing Android Apps

Android apps are written using the Java programming language. **Java** is a language and a platform originated by Sun Microsystems. Java is an **object-oriented programming language** patterned after the C++ language. Object-oriented programming encourages good software engineering practices such as code reuse. The most popular tool for writing Java programs is called Eclipse, an integrated development environment (IDE) for building and integrating application development tools and open-source projects.

As shown in the preface of this book, the first step in setting up your Android programming environment is to install the free Eclipse IDE. After installing Eclipse, the next step is to install the plug-in called the Android Software Development Kit (SDK), which runs in Eclipse. The Android SDK includes a set of development tools that help you design the interface of the program, write the code, and test the program using a built-in Android handset emulator. To write Android programs, you must also add an Eclipse plug-in called the Android Development Tools (ADT), which extends the capabilities of Eclipse to let you quickly set up new Android projects, create an application user interface, and debug your applications. Another language called **XML** (Extensible Markup Language) is used to assist in the layout of the Android emulator.

GTK

Eclipse can be used to develop applications in many programming languages, including Java, C, C++, COBOL, Ada, and Python.

Android Emulator

The Android emulator lets you design, develop, prototype, and test Android applications without using a physical device. When you run an Android program in Eclipse, the emulator starts so you can test the program. You can then use the mouse to simulate touching the screen of the device. The emulator mimics almost every feature of a real Android handset except for the ability to place a voice phone call. A running emulator can play video and audio, render gaming animation, and store information. Multiple emulators are available within the Android SDK to target various devices and versions from early Android phones onward. Developers should test their apps on several versions to confirm the stability of a particular platform. The first Android version, release 1.0, was introduced in September 2008. Each subsequent version adds new features and fixes any known bugs in the platform. Android has adopted a naming system for each version based on dessert items, as shown in Table 1-2. After the first version, dessert names have been assigned in alphabetical order.

Version	Name	Release Date
1.0	First version	September 2008
1.5	Cupcake	April 2009
1.6	Donut	September 2009
2.0	Éclair	October 2009
2.2	Froyo (Frozen Yogurt)	May 2010
2.3	Gingerbread	December 2010
3.0	Honeycomb	February 2011
4.0	Ice Cream Sandwich	May 2011

Table 1-2 Android version history

Getting Oriented with Market Deployment

The Android platform consists of the Android OS, the Android application development tools, and a marketplace for Android applications. After you write and test a program, you compile the app into an Android package file with the filename extension .apk.

Programs written for the Android platform are sold and deployed through an online store called the **Android Market** (*http://market.android.com*), which provides registration services and certifies that the program meets minimum standards of reliability, efficiency, and performance. The Android Market requires that you sign an agreement and pay a one-time registration fee (currently $25). After registration, you can publish your app on the Android Market, provided the app meets the minimum standards. You can also release updates as needed for your app. If your app is free, the Android Market publishes your app at no cost. If you want to charge for your app, the standard split is 70 percent of sales for the developer and 30 percent for the wireless carriers. For example, if you created an app for your city that featured all the top restaurants, hotels, attractions, and festivals and sold the app for $1.99, you would net $1.39 for each app sold. If you sell 5,000 copies of your app, you would earn almost $7,000. You can use the Android Market to sell a wide range of content, including downloadable content, such as media files or photos, and virtual content such as game levels or potions (Figure 1-4). As an Android developer, you have the opportunity to develop apps for a fairly new market and easily distribute the app to the millions of Android mobile device owners.

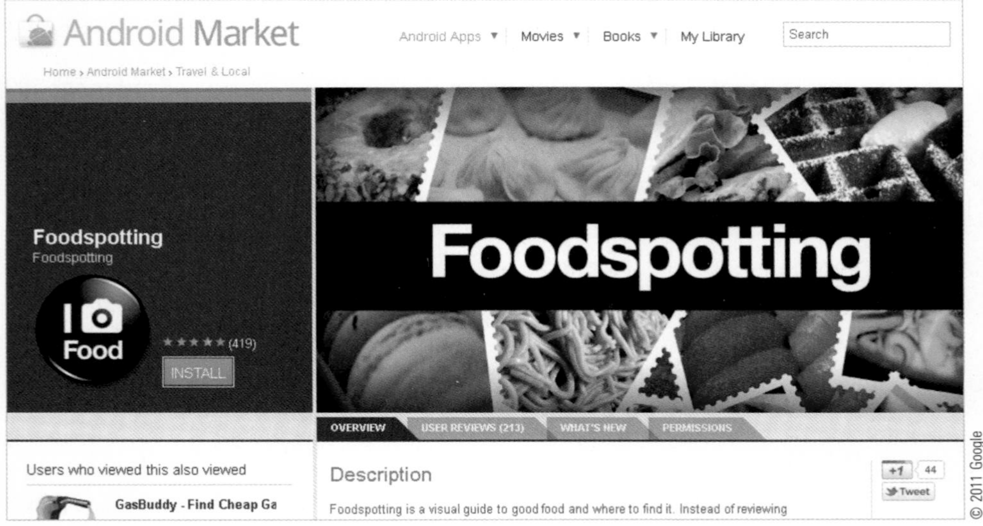

Figure 1-4 Android Market

IN THE TRENCHES

The Apple iTunes App Store charges a $99 yearly registration fee to publish an app through the iPhone Dev Center. The iTunes App Store has a much more rigorous standards approval process than the Android Market.

The online company Amazon also has a separate Appstore (*http://amazon.com/appstore*) where Android apps can be deployed and sold. The Amazon Appstore is a category listed on Amazon.com. Customers can shop for apps from their PCs and mobile devices. The Amazon Appstore has an established marketing environment and search engine that displays a trusted storefront and creates app recommendations based on customers' past purchases. The Amazon Appstore charges a $99 annual developer program fee, which covers the application processing and account management for the Amazon Appstore Developer Program. Amazon also pays developers 70 percent of the sale price of the app; in addition, you can post free apps.

First Venture into the Android World

After installing the Eclipse IDE, installing the Android SDK, and creating the Android Virtual Device (AVD) as instructed in the preface of this book, the next step is to create your first Android application. As programming tradition mandates, your first program is called Hello Android World. The following sections introduce you to the elements of the Android SDK and provide a detailed description of each step to create your first app.

Opening Eclipse to Create a New Project

To create a new Android project, you first open Eclipse and then select an Android project. As you create your first project, you provide the following information:

- *Project name*—The Eclipse project name is the name of the directory that will contain the project files.
- *Application name*—This is the human-readable title for your application, which will appear on the Android device.
- *Package name*—This is the Java package namespace where your source code will reside. You need to have at least a period (.) in the package name. Typically, the recommended package name convention is your domain name in reverse order. For example, the domain name of this book is androidbootcamp.net. The package name would be net.androidbootcamp.HelloAndroidWorld. The package name must be unique when posted on the Android Market, so it is vital to use a standard domain-style package name for your applications.
- *Create Activity*—As the Activity name, use the name for the class that is generated by the plug-in. This will be a subclass of Android's Activity class. An Activity is a class that can run and do work, such as creating a user interface. Creating an Activity is optional, but an Activity is almost always used as the basis for an application.

- *Minimum SDK*—This value specifies the minimum application programming interface (API) level required by your application.

Creating the Hello World Project

A project is equivalent to a single program or app using Java and the Android SDK. Be sure you have a blank USB (Universal Serial Bus) drive plugged into your computer so you can store the Android project on this USB drive. To create a new Android project, you can take the following steps:

1. Open the Eclipse program. Click the first button on the Standard toolbar, which is the New button.

   The New dialog box opens (Figure 1-5).

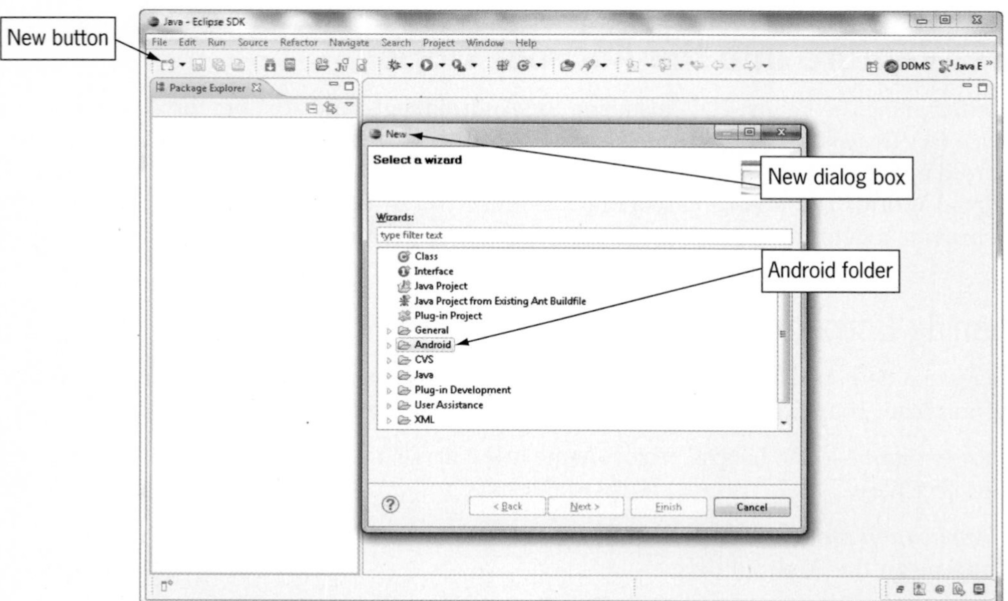

Figure 1-5 New dialog box

2. Expand the Android folder and then select the Android Project icon.

   Android Project is selected in the New dialog box (Figure 1-6).

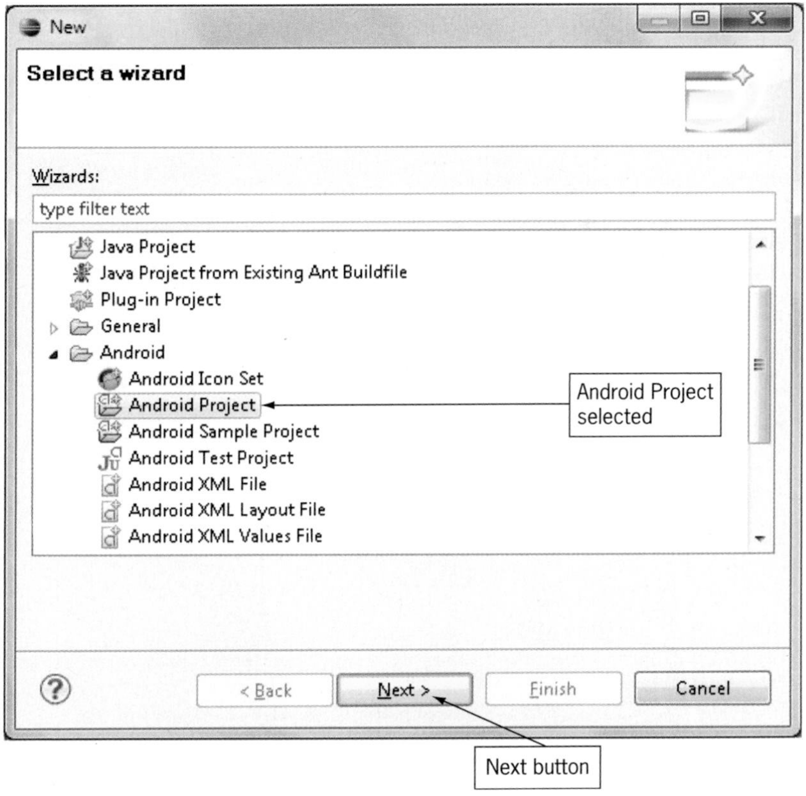

Figure 1-6 Selecting an Android project

3. Click the Next button. In the New Android Project dialog box, enter the Project Name **Hello Android World**. To save the project on your USB drive, click to remove the check mark from the Use default location check box. In the Location text box, enter **E:\Workspace** (E: identifies the USB drive; your drive letter might differ). Throughout the rest of this book, the USB drive is called the E: drive, though you should select the drive on your computer that represents your USB device.

   If you are using a Mac, enter **\Volumes*USB_DRIVE_NAME*** *instead of E:\Workspace.*

   The New Android project has a project name and a location of E:\Workspace, a folder on a USB drive (Figure 1-7).

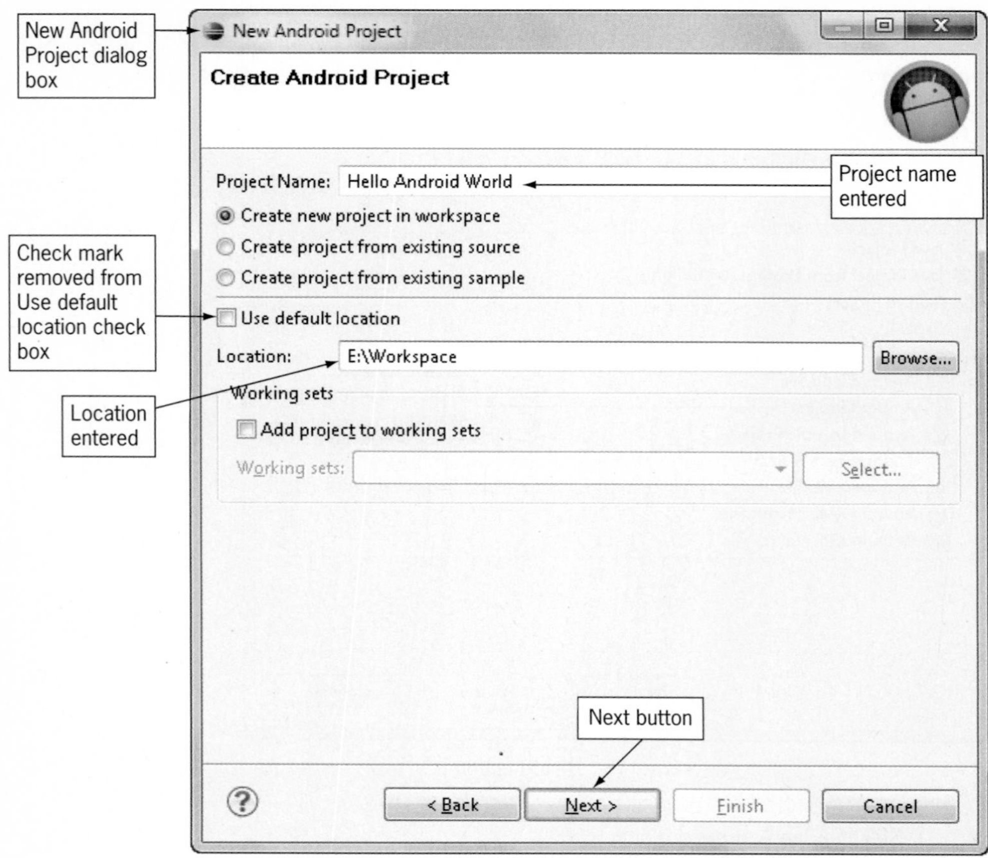

Figure 1-7 Project information entered

4. Click the Next button. To select a build target that works on most Android phones, accept Android 4.0 for the Build Target, which is selected by default. (If you are deploying to an earlier model of an Android phone, you can select an earlier version for the Build Target.) Click the Next button.

   For the Application Info, type the Package Name **net.androidbootcamp.helloandroidworld**. Enter **Main** in the Create Activity text box. Notice the Minimum SDK uses the API number of 14 from the selected Build Target of the Android 4.0.

   The new Android project has an application name, a package name, and an Activity (Figure 1-8).

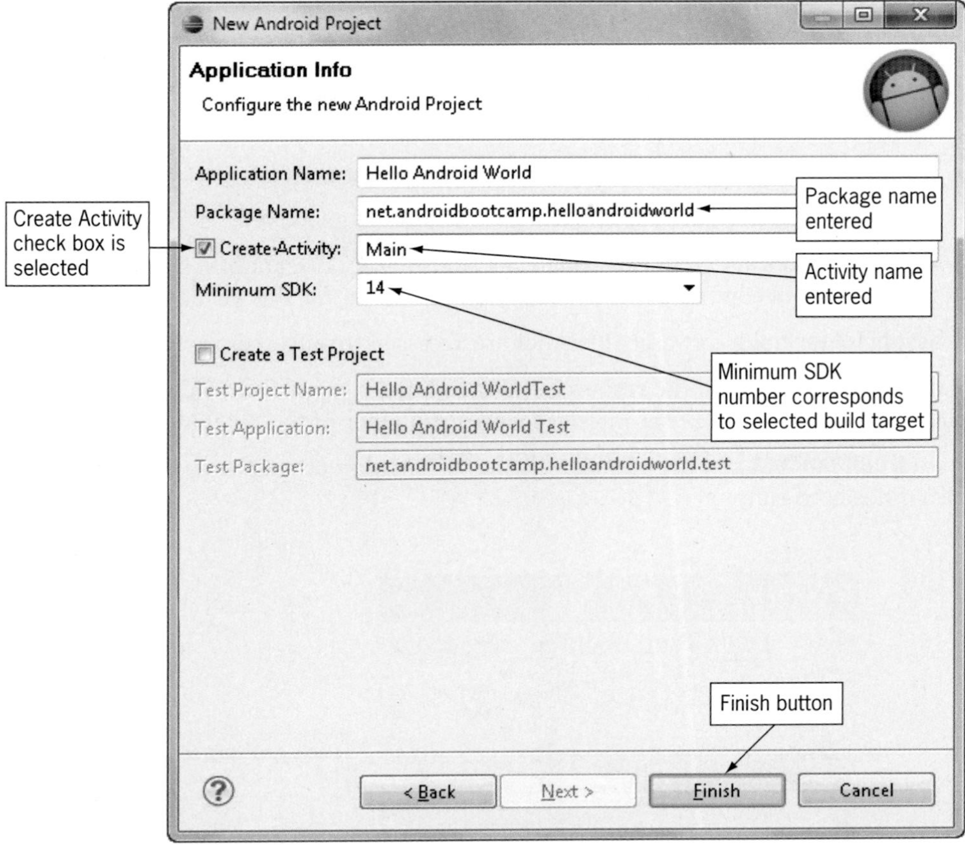

Figure 1-8 Application information entered

5. Click the Finish button.

   The Android project files are created on the USB drive. The project Hello Android World appears in the left pane.

Building the User Interface

This first Android app will display the simple message, "Hello World – My First Android App." Beyond the tools and gadgets of the Android environment, what will stand out most is the user experience—how a user feels while using a particular device. Ensuring an intuitive user interface that does not detract from functionality is the key to successful usage. Android supports two ways of building the user interface of an application: through Java code and through XML layout files. The XML method is preferred as it allows you to design the user interface of an application without needing to write large amounts of code. Both methods and more details about building the user interface are covered in later chapters.

Taking a Tour of the Package Explorer

The **Package Explorer** on the left side of the Eclipse program window contains the Hello Android World application folders. When the project folder Hello Android World is expanded (Figure 1-9), the Android project includes files in the following folders:

- The **src folder** includes the Java code source files for the project.
- The **gen folder** contains Java files that are automatically generated.
- The **Android 4.0 Library** contains a single file, android.jar. The android.jar file contains all the class libraries needed to build an Android application for this version.
- The **assets folder** holds any asset files that are accessed through classic file manipulation.
- The **res folder** contains all the resources, such as images, music, and video files, that your application may need. The user interface is in a subfolder of the res folder named layout.
- The **AndroidManifest.xml** file contains all the information about the application that Android needs to run.

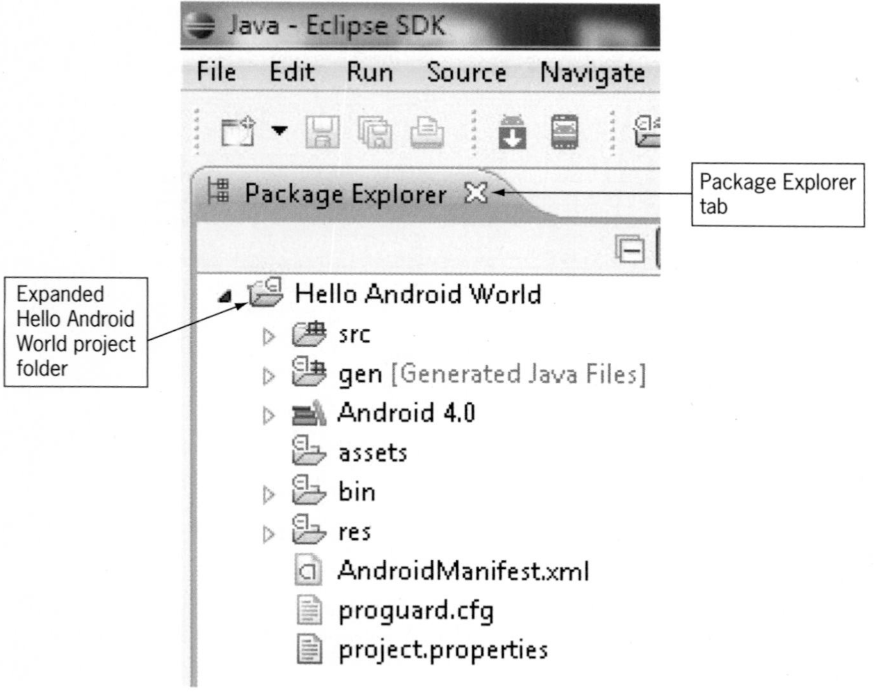

Figure 1-9 Expanded Hello Android World project folder

Designing the User Interface Layout

To assist in designing the Android user interface, the Android SDK includes layout files. You can create a layout and then add widgets to the layout. A **layout** is a container that can hold as many widgets as needed. A **widget** is a single element such as a TextView, Button, or CheckBox control, and is also called an object. Upcoming chapters demonstrate many layouts, each with unique properties and characteristics. To open the layout files, follow these steps:

1. Close any tabs that are open on the right side of the Eclipse window and minimize the Console pane that appears at the bottom of the window, if necessary. Open the Package Explorer (if necessary) by clicking Window on the menu bar, pointing to Show View, and then clicking Package Explorer.

   Expand the Hello Android World project in the Package Explorer. Expand the res folder to display its subfolders. Expand the layout subfolder. Double-click the main.xml file. To select an emulator, click the emulator button directly above the Palette, and then click 3.7in WVGA (Nexus One), if necessary. You can use many phone emulators, but throughout this text, select the 3.7in WVGA (Nexus One) emulator. Click the Zoom In button on the right side of the window to make the emulator screen as large as possible.

   The main.xml tab and the contents of the main.xml file are displayed in the Project window. The main.xml tab includes an asterisk (*) to indicate that project changes have not been saved. Note that Android placed a default TextView control in the emulator window (Figure 1-10).

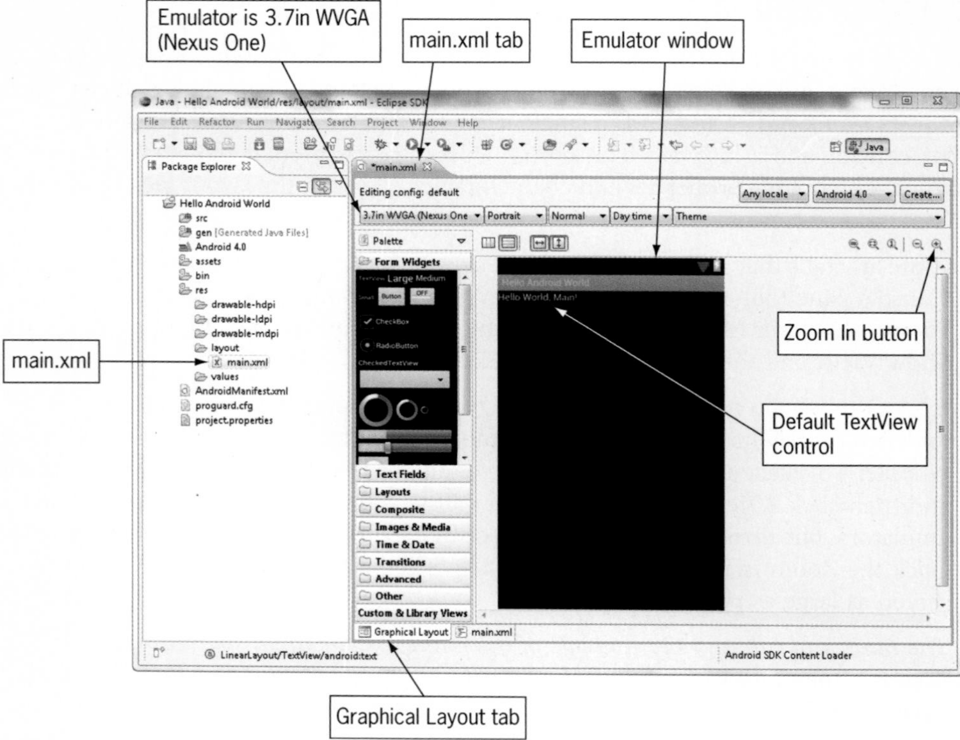

Figure 1-10 Layout displayed in the Eclipse window

2. In the emulator window, select the default TextView control, which reads Hello World, Main!.

   The default TextView control is selected and displayed in a blue selection box (Figure 1-11).

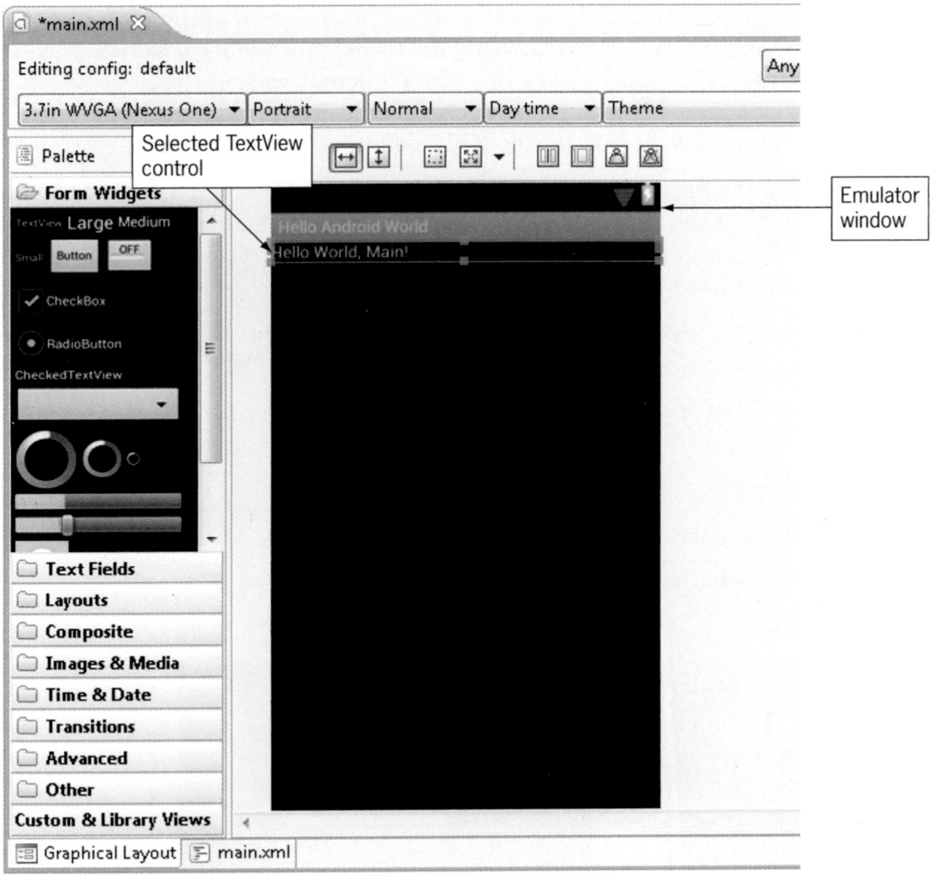

Figure 1-11 Selected TextView control

3. Press the Delete key.

   The default TextView control that Android placed in the user interface is deleted.

GTK

The default Android device shown in the Graphical Layout view when using some of the latest platforms is a 10.1-inch tablet. You can select a different device at the top of the Graphical Layout tabbed window. It is best not to target your program for the latest platform because older phones cannot run the application.

Adding a Form Widget to the User Interface Layout

The Android User Interface Layout editor displays form widgets that you place on the user interface using the drag-and-drop method. Technically, a widget is a View object that functions as an interface for interaction with the mobile user. In other words, a widget is a control such as a message users read or a button users click. The tabs at the bottom of the emulator identify the Graphical Layout window and the main.xml window, which displays the code behind each form widget. Each window displays a different view of the project: The Layout view allows you to preview how the controls will appear on various screens and orientations, and the XML view shows you the XML definition of the resource.

To display a message on the Android device, you must first place a TextView form widget on the emulator and then select the main.xml tab to open the code behind the TextView control. The main.xml coding window is written in XML code, not Java code. To add a form widget to the user interface layout, follow these steps:

1. In the main.xml tab, select TextView in the Form Widgets list. Drag the TextView control to the emulator window and drop it below the title Hello Android World.

   The TextView control is placed in the emulator window (Figure 1-12).

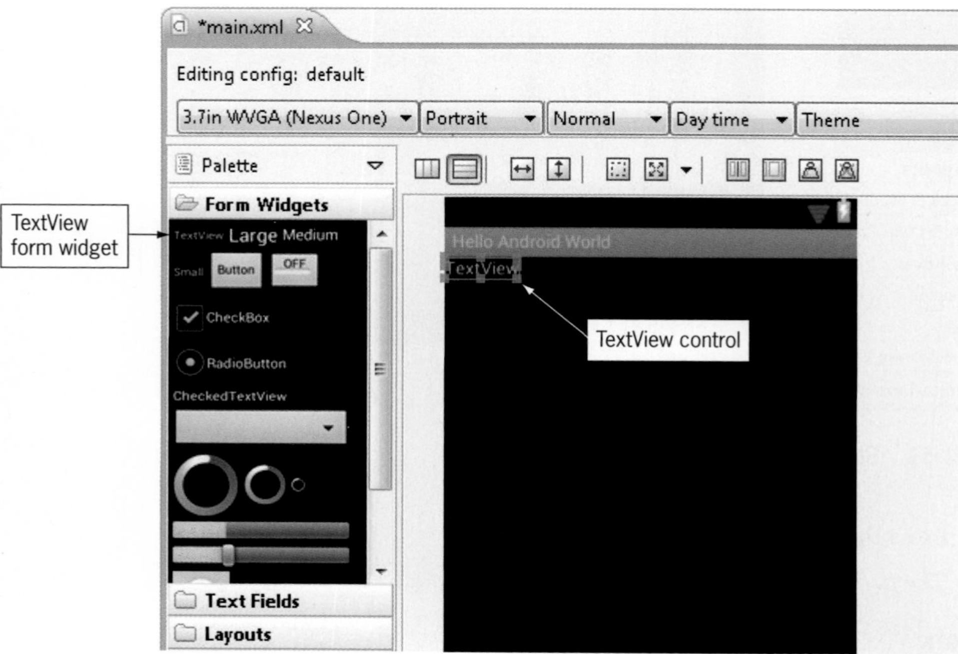

Figure 1-12 TextView form widget in the emulator

2. Click the main.xml tab below the emulator window.

   The main.xml code window is displayed. The TextView code that is associated with the TextView control contains the text android:text="TextView" /> (Figure 1-13).

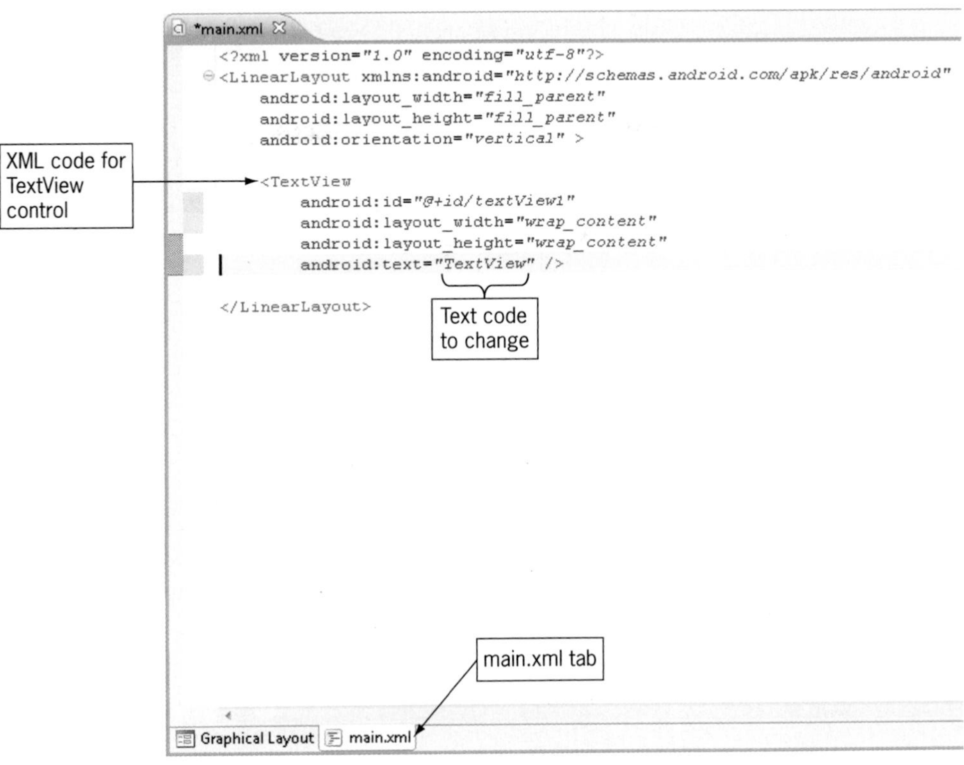

Figure 1-13 Displaying the XML code for the TextView control

3. To change the text displayed in the TextView control when the program is executed, select the word TextView in the next-to-last line of code, android:text="TextView". Change "TextView" to **"Hello World – My First Android App"**. Do not change any other text on this line of code.

   The next-to-last code line now begins with android:text="Hello World – My First Android App" (Figure 1-14).

```
*main.xml
<?xml version="1.0" encoding="utf-8"?>
<LinearLayout xmlns:android="http://schemas.android.com/apk/res/android"
    android:layout_width="fill_parent"
    android:layout_height="fill_parent"
    android:orientation="vertical" >

    <TextView
        android:id="@+id/textView1"
        android:layout_width="wrap_content"
        android:layout_height="wrap_content"
        android:text="Hello World - My First Android App" />

</LinearLayout>
```

New text entered

Figure 1-14 Changing the TextView control text

4. Click the Graphical Layout tab to display the revised text in the TextView control. Click File on the menu bar and then click Save All to update your project.

   The Hello World – My First Android App TextView control fits on one line in the emulator (Figure 1-15).

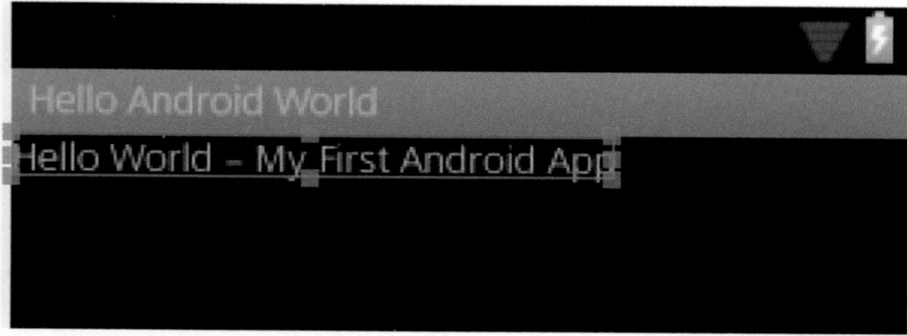

Figure 1-15 Displaying the revised text in the emulator

GTK

To deploy your app to an actual Android device instead of the emulator, you first need to install a USB driver for your device from *http://developer.android.com/sdk/win-usb.html*. On the Android device, the "USB Debugging Mode" must be checked on the Application menu. On a Mac, no USB driver installation is needed.

Testing the Application in the Emulator

Time to see the finished result! Keep in mind that the Android emulator runs slowly. It can take over a minute to display your finished results in the emulator. Even when the emulator is idling, it consumes a significant amount of CPU time, so you should close the emulator when you complete your testing. To run the application, follow these steps:

1. Click Run on the menu bar, and then click Run.

   The first time an application is run, the Run As dialog box opens (Figure 1-16).

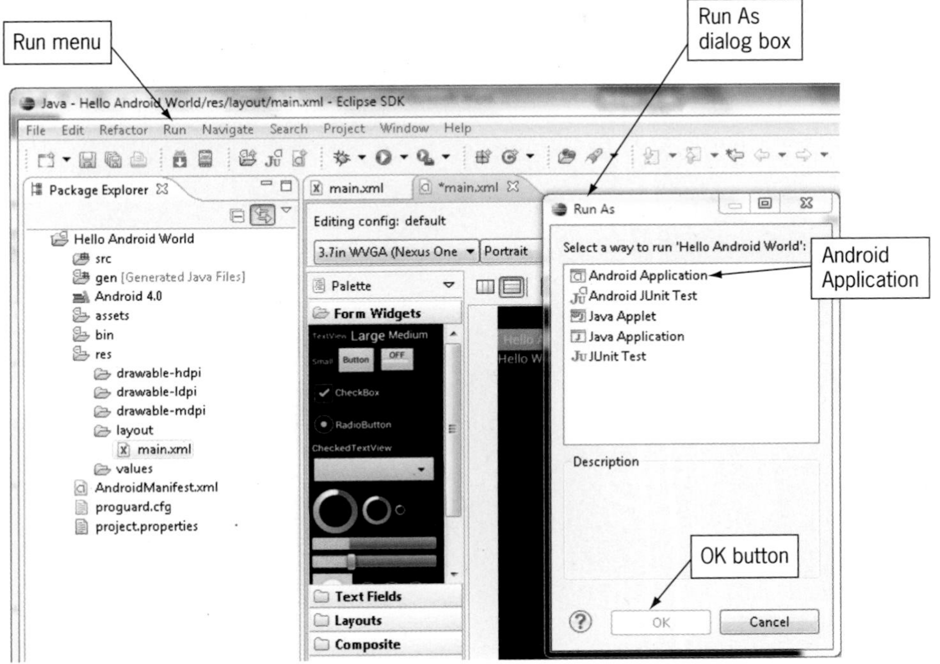

Figure 1-16 Run As dialog box

2. Click Android Application in the Run As dialog box, and then click the OK button.

   The program slowly begins to execute by displaying the Android logo and then an application window with the Android splash screen on the left. This may take up to one full minute. Next, the Android main screen appears with a lock icon (Figure 1-17).

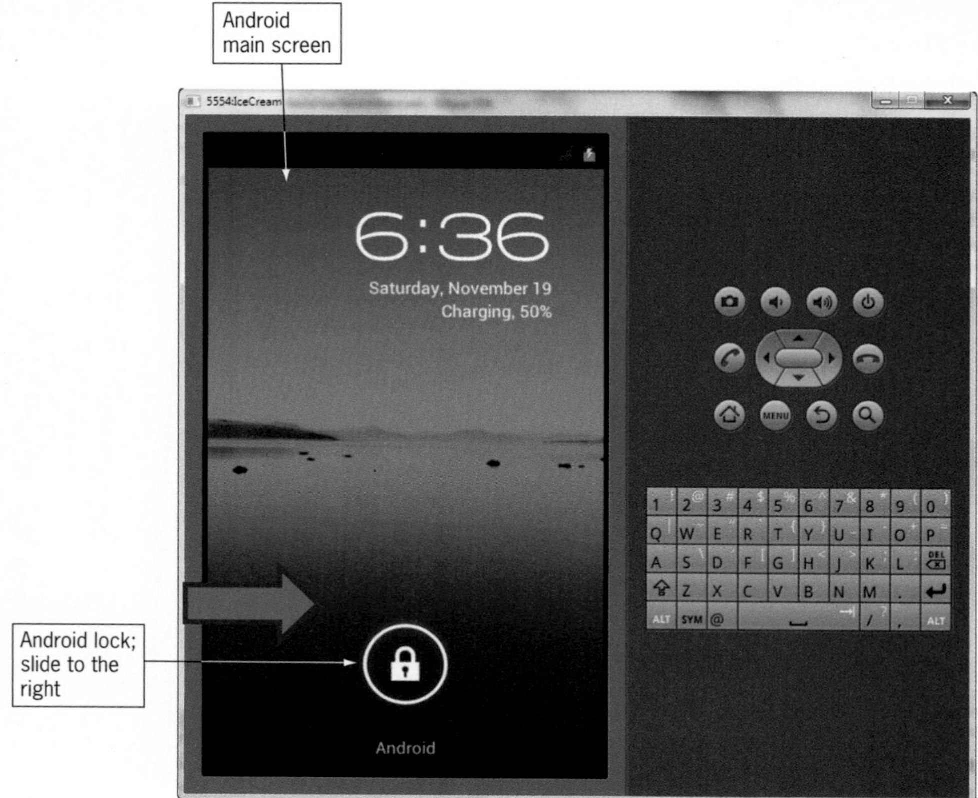

Figure 1-17 Android main screen and lock icon

3. Click the lock icon and slide it across the screen to the right until you see a green dot to unlock the simulated device.

   If you are using a Mac, drag the lock icon until it changes to an unlock icon.

   After the Android device is unlocked, the emulator displays the text message (Figure 1-18).

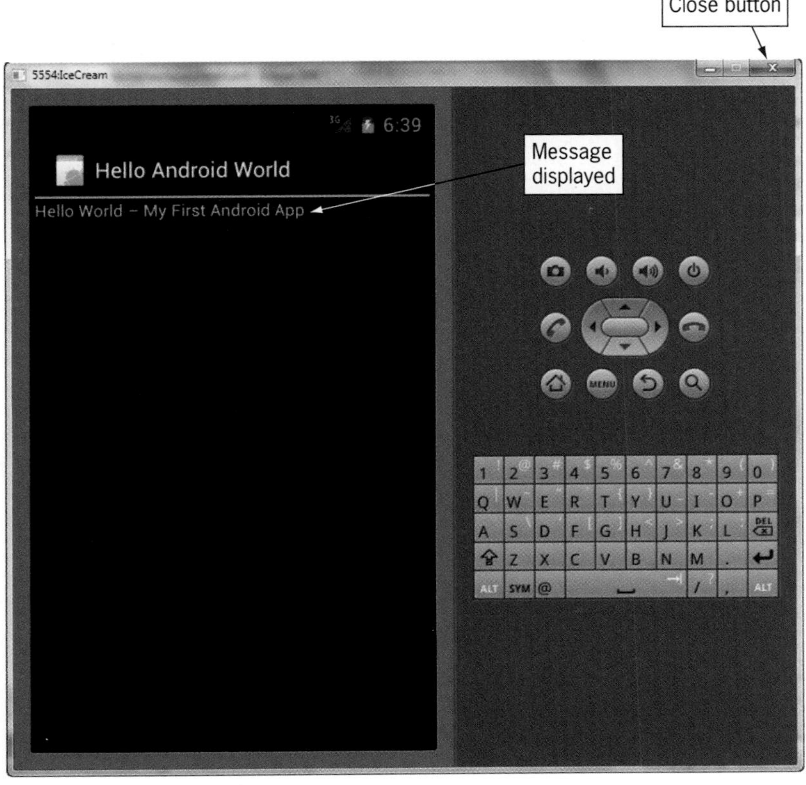

Figure 1-18 Message in the Android emulator

4. Close the application by clicking the Close button.

   The emulated application window closes. The program is saved each time the program is run. You can close Eclipse by clicking File on the menu bar and then clicking Exit if you are working on a Windows computer. Click Quit Eclipse if you are working on a Mac.

GTK

Ctrl+F11 is the Windows shortcut key combination for running your Android application in Eclipse. On a Mac, the shortcut keys are Command+Shift+F11.

Opening a Saved App in Eclipse

After you save a project and close Eclipse, you might need to open the project and work on it again. To open a saved project, you can follow these steps with Eclipse open:

1. If the project is not listed in the Package Explorer, click File on the Eclipse menu bar and select Import. In the Import dialog box, expand the General folder, if necessary, and then click Existing Projects into Workspace.

   The Import dialog box opens and in the Select an import source area, the Existing Projects into Workspace folder is selected (Figure 1-19).

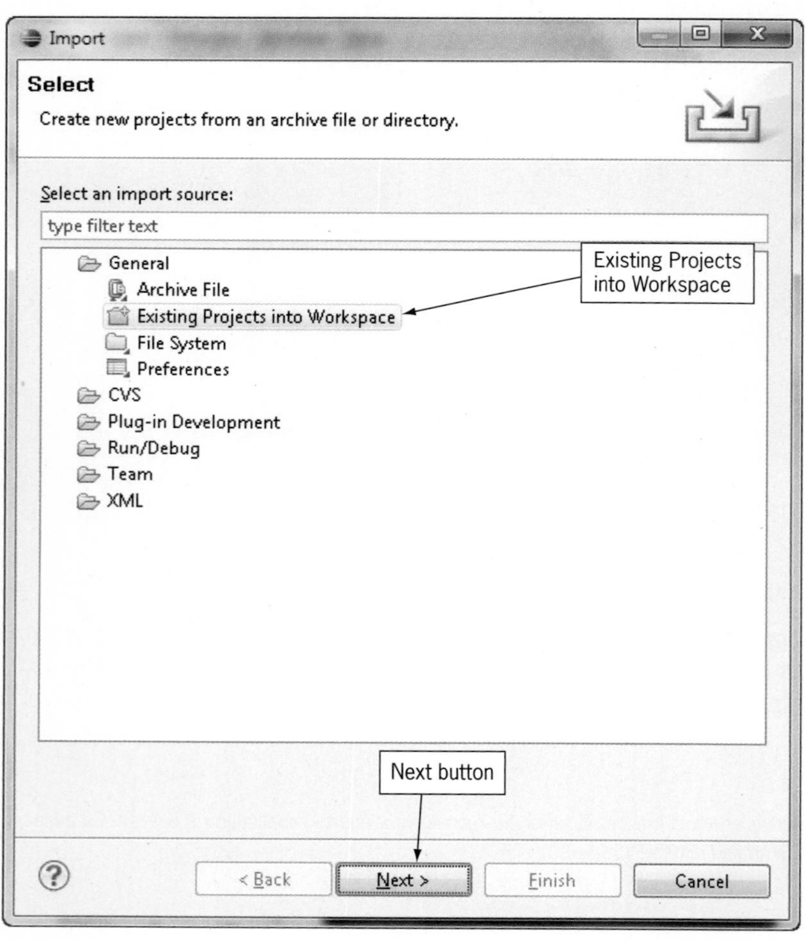

Figure 1-19 Import dialog box

2. Click the Next button. Click the Browse button next to the Select root directory text box. Click Computer and then click the USB drive on a Windows computer. (If you are using a Mac, click the USB DEVICE in the left pane of the Finder.) Click the Workspace folder. Click the OK button (or the Open button on a Mac). Insert a check mark in the Hello Android World check box, if necessary. Insert a check mark in the Copy projects into workspace check box.

   In the Import dialog box, the root directory is selected. The Hello Android World project is selected, and the Copy projects into workspace check box is checked (Figure 1-20).

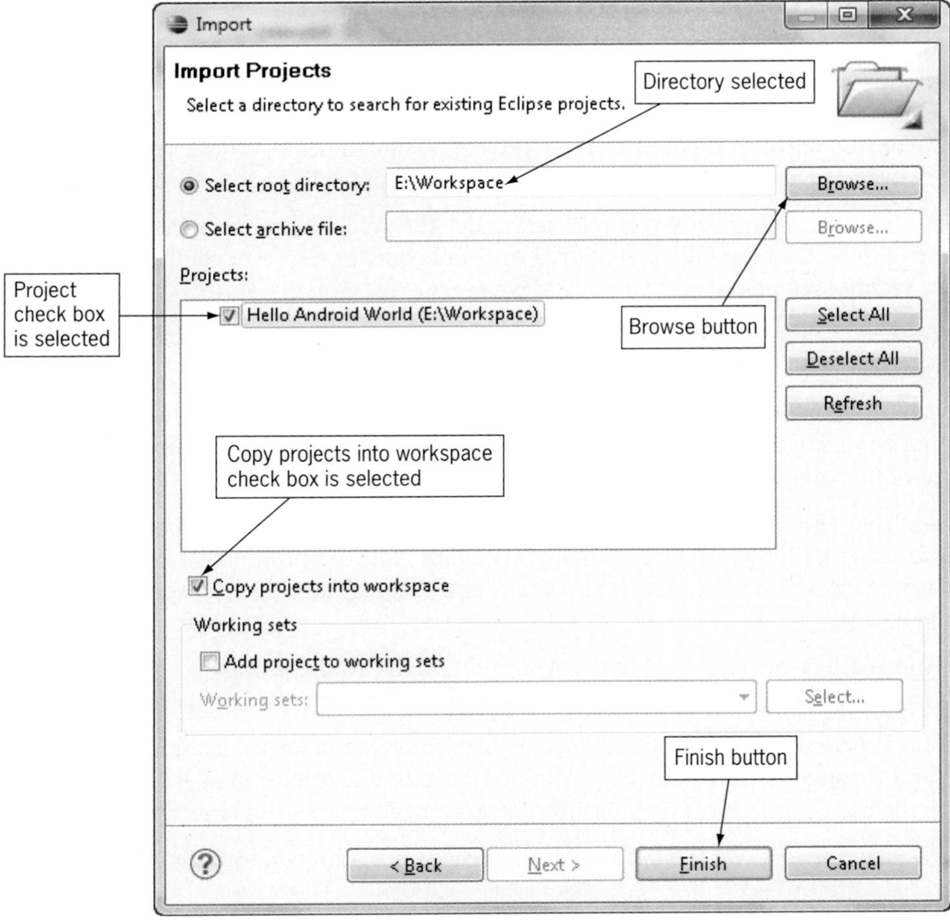

Figure 1-20 Project and directory selected

3. Click the Finish button.

   The program loads into the Package Explorer. You can now continue working on your user interface and code.

GTK

To delete a project from the project workspace, right-click the project name in the Package Explorer. Select Delete on the shortcut menu. Click the OK button. The project is still saved on the USB drive, but is no longer in the Package Explorer.

Wrap It Up—Chapter Summary

This chapter has provided an overview of the Android open-source platform, which is positioned for fast innovation without the restraints of a proprietary system. With the largest market share and its rich feature set, the Android environment allows you to develop useful, inventive Android apps. In the first chapter project, Hello Android World, you completed steps that start your journey to create more interesting applications in future chapters.

- The Android operating system is released under the Apache license, which permits anyone to download the full open-source Android code for free. Android is the first open-source technology platform for mobile devices.
- The Android OS powers all types of mobile devices, including smartphones, tablets, netbooks, e-readers, MP4 players, and Internet TVs.
- To write Android apps, you can use Eclipse, an integrated development environment for building applications, including Android apps, using Java, an object-oriented programming language.
- The Android emulator lets you design, develop, prototype, and test Android applications without using a physical device. When you run an Android program in Eclipse, the emulator starts so you can test the program as if it were running on a specified Android mobile device.
- The Android platform consists of the Android OS, the Android application development platform, and the Android Market, a marketplace for Android applications.
- Android supports two ways of building the user interface of an application: through Java code and through XML layout files. The XML method is preferred as it allows you to design the user interface of an application without needing to write large amounts of code.
- The Package Explorer on the left side of the Eclipse program window contains the folders for an Android project.
- To design a user interface for an Android app, you can create a layout, which is a container that displays widgets such as TextView, Button, and CheckBox controls, also called objects.
- After you create an application, you can run it in the Android emulator to test the application and make sure it runs correctly.

Key Terms

Android 4.0 Library—A project folder that contains the android.jar file, which includes all the class libraries needed to build an Android application for the specified version.

Android Market—An online store that sells programs written for the Android platform.

AndroidManifest.xml—A file containing all the information Android needs to run an application.

assets folder—A project folder containing any asset files that are accessed through classic file manipulation.

gen folder—A project folder that contains automatically generated Java files.

Java—An object-oriented programming language and a platform originated by Sun Microsystems.

layout—A container that can hold widgets and other graphical elements to help you design an interface for an application.

object-oriented programming language—A type of programming language that allows good software engineering practices such as code reuse.

Open Handset Alliance—An open-source business alliance of 80 firms that develop open standards for mobile devices.

Package Explorer—A pane on the left side of the Eclipse program window that contains the folders for the current project.

res folder—A project folder that contains all the resources, such as images, music, and video files, that an application may need.

smartphone—A mobile phone with advanced computing ability and connectivity features.

src folder—A project folder that includes the Java code source files for the project.

widget—A single element such as a TextView, Button, or CheckBox control, and is also called an object.

XML—An acronym for Extensible Markup Language, a widely used system for defining data formats. XML assists in the layout of the Android emulator.

Developer FAQs

1. In which year did Google purchase the company Android, Inc.?
2. What is the one-time cost for a developer's account at the Android Market?
3. When you post an Android app at the Android Market, what percentage of the app price does the developer keep?
4. How much is Amazon's annual fee for a developer's account?

5. Which three manufacturers' operating systems can be used to program an Android app?
6. Which two languages are used in creating an Android app in Eclipse?
7. What would be the recommended package name if your domain was karencodeworld.net and your project name was AndroidMap?
8. Name three widgets mentioned in this chapter.
9. What is the name of the widget that was used in the Hello Android World app?
10. Which two key combinations can you press to execute an Android app in Eclipse?
11. Which Android version is Ice Cream Sandwich?
12. Using the alphabetical theme for Android version names, list three possible future names for the next versions of Android device operating systems.
13. What does XML stand for?
14. What does SDK stand for?
15. Where are music and image files saved within the Package Explorer?

Beyond the Book

Using the Internet, search the Web for the following answers to further your Android knowledge.

1. Research a particular model of a popular Android mobile device and write a paragraph on this device's features, specifications, price, and manufacturer.
2. Name five Android mobile device features not mentioned in the "Meet the Android" section of Chapter 1.
3. What is the current annual cost for a developer's account at the Phone 7 app store called the Windows Phone 7 Marketplace?
4. Go to the Android Market Web site and take a screen shot of each of the following app categories: education, gaming, mapping, travel, and personal hobby. Place screen shots in a word processor document and label each one to identify it.

Case Programming Projects

Complete one or more of the following case programming projects. Use the same steps and techniques taught within the chapter. Submit the program you create to your instructor. The level of difficulty is indicated for each case programming project.

Easiest: ★

Intermediate: ★ ★

Challenging: ★ ★ ★

Case Project 1–1: Quote of the Day App ★

Requirements Document

Application title:	Quote of the Day App
Purpose:	In the Quote of the Day app, a famous quotation of your choice is displayed.
Algorithms:	The opening screen displays the quotation of the day.
Conditions:	You may change the quotation to your own (Figure 1-21).

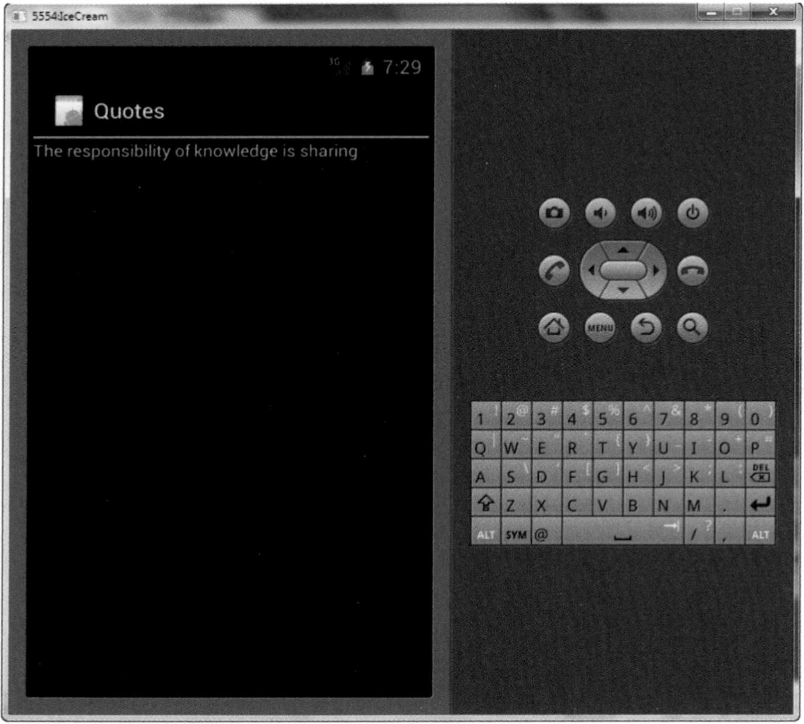

Figure 1-21

Case Project 1–2: Android Terminology App ★ ★

Application title:	Android Terminology App
Purpose:	In the Android Terminology app, three terms introduced in Chapter 1 and their definitions are displayed.
Algorithms:	The opening screen displays three different terms from this chapter and their definitions.
Conditions:	Multiple TextView controls are required.

Case Project 1–3: Business Card App ★ ★ ★

Application title:	Business Card App
Purpose:	In the Business Card app, your address and information are displayed.
Algorithms:	The opening screen displays a simple business card with your personal information. The first line should include your name. The second line should include your future dream job title. The third line should include your address. The fourth line should include your city, state, and postal code. The last line should include your phone number.
Conditions:	Multiple TextView controls are required.

CHAPTER 2

Simplify! The Android User Interface

In this chapter, you learn to:

- Develop a user interface using the TextView, ImageView, and Button controls
- Create an Android project that includes a Button event
- Select a Linear or Relative layout for the user interface
- Create multiple Android Activities
- Add activities to the Android Manifest file
- Add a Java class file
- Write code using the onCreate method
- Display content using the setContentView command
- Open a second screen using a Button event handler
- Use an OnClickListener to detect user interaction
- Launch a second screen using a startActivity method
- Correct errors in Java code
- Run the completed app in the emulator

Before a mobile app can be coded using Java, it must be designed. Designing a program can be compared with constructing a building. Before cement slabs are poured, steel beams are put in place, and walls are erected, architects and engineers must design the building to ensure it will perform as required and be safe and reliable. The same holds true for a computer app developer. Once the program is designed within the user interface, it can be implemented through the use of Extensible Markup Language (XML) and Java code to perform the functions for which it was designed.

Designing an Android App

To illustrate the process of designing and implementing an Android app, in this chapter you will design and code the Healthy Recipes application shown in Figure 2-1 and Figure 2-2.

Figure 2-1 Healthy Recipes Android app

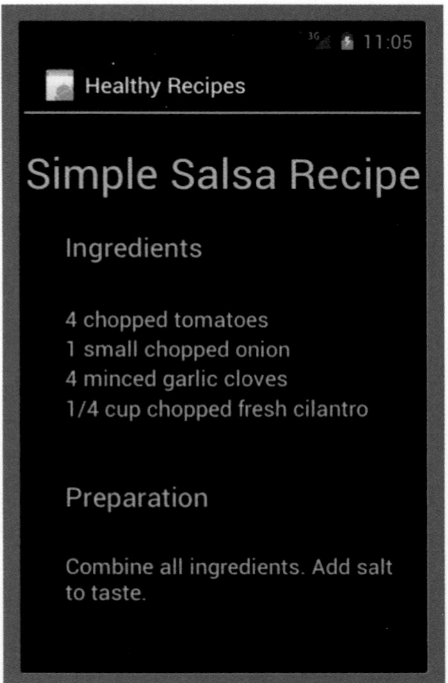

Figure 2-2 Second window displaying the recipe

The Android app in Figure 2-1 could be part of a larger app that is used to display Healthy Recipes. The Healthy Recipes app begins by displaying the recipe name, which is Simple Salsa for this recipe, and an image illustrating the completed recipe. If the user taps the View Recipe button, a second window opens displaying the full recipe, including the ingredients and preparation for the salsa.

IN THE TRENCHES

If you own a data plan phone, tablet, or slate device, download the free app called Epicurious to get an idea of how this Healthy Recipes app would be used in a much larger application.

The Big Picture

To create the Healthy Recipes application, you follow a set of steps that you repeat every time you create an Android application.

1. Create the user interface, also called an XML layout, for every screen in the application.
2. Create a Java class, also called an Activity, for every screen in the application.
3. Update the Android Manifest file for each Java class in the application.
4. Code each Java class with the appropriate objects and actions as needed.

Using the Android User Interface

Before any code can be written for an Android application, the project structure of the user experience must be designed by means of the user interface. For an Android application, the user interface is a window on the screen of any mobile device in which the user interacts with the program. The user interface is stored in the res/layout folder in the Package Explorer. The layout for the user interface is designed with XML code. Special Android-formatted XML code is extremely compact, which means the application uses less space and runs faster on the device. Using XML for layout also saves you time in developing your code; for example, if you developed this recipe app for use in eight human languages, you could use the same Java code with eight unique XML layout files, one for each language. To open the layout of the user interface of the Healthy Recipes app, follow these steps to begin the application:

1. Open the Eclipse program. Click the New button on the Standard toolbar. Expand the Android folder, if necessary, and select Android Project. Click the Next button. In the New Android Project dialog box, enter the Project Name **Healthy Recipes**. To save the project on your USB drive, click to remove the check mark from the Use default location check box. Type **E:\Workspace** (if necessary, enter a different drive letter that identifies the USB drive). Click Next. For the Build Target, select Android 4.0, if necessary. Click Next. Type the Package Name **net.androidbootcamp.healthyrecipes**. Type **Main** in the Create Activity text box.

Notice the Minimum SDK text box displays the API number from the selected Build Target (Android 4.0). If you are deploying to an earlier model of an Android phone, you can select an earlier version.

The new Android Healthy Recipes project has an application name, a package name, and a Main Activity (Figure 2-3).

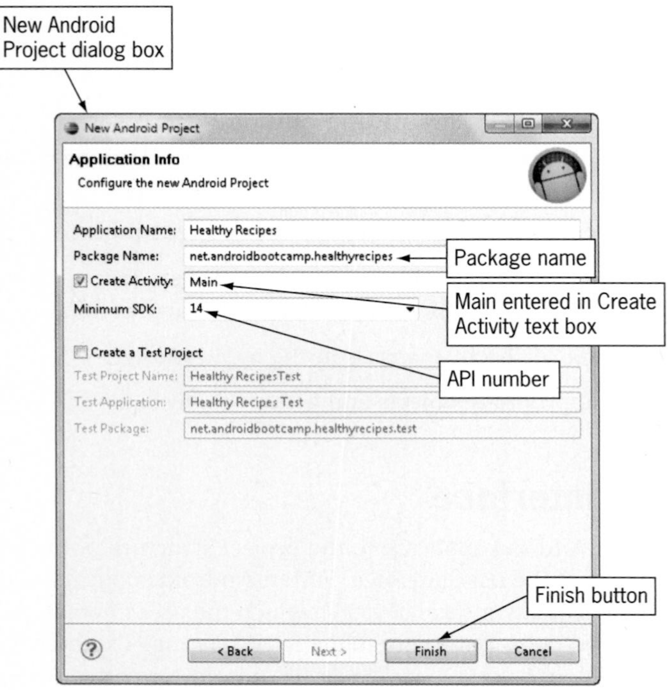

Figure 2-3 Application information for the new Android project

2. Click the Finish button. Expand the Healthy Recipes project in the Package Explorer. Expand the res folder to display its subfolders. Expand the layout subfolder. Double-click the main.xml file. Click the Hello World, Main! TextView (displayed by default). Press the Delete key.

   The main.xml file is displayed on the Graphical Layout tab and the Hello World TextView widget is deleted (Figure 2-4).

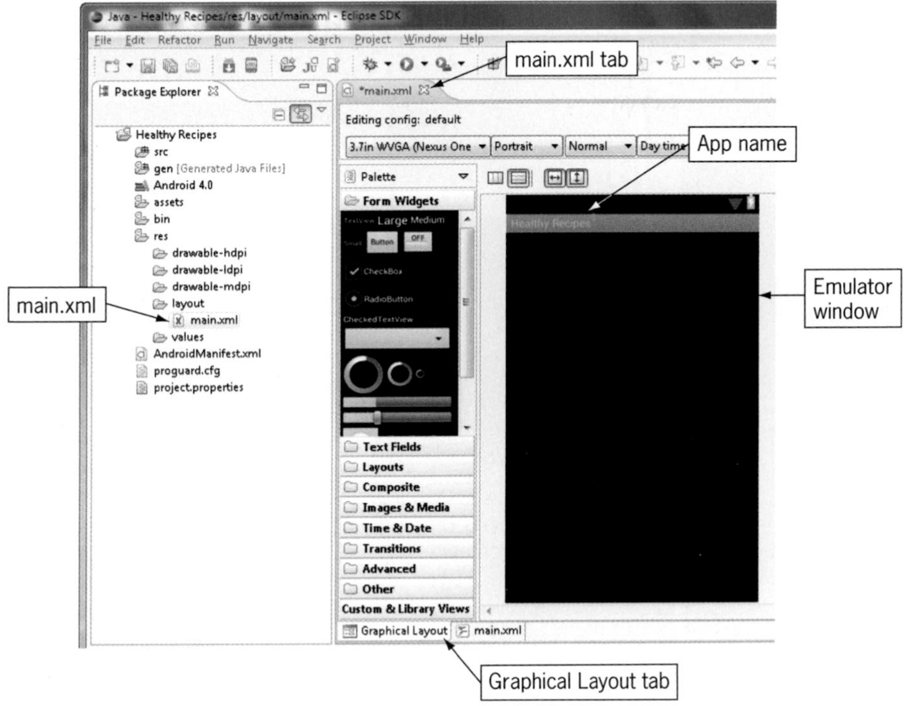

Figure 2-4 Displaying the emulator window for the Healthy Recipes project

Linear Layouts and Relative Layouts

The Android user interface includes a layout resource designer that organizes how controls appear on the app's various screens. When you click the Graphical Layout tab as shown in Figure 2-4, you display the default user interface for main.xml, which uses a resource file defined as a Linear layout. A **Linear layout** organizes layout components in a vertical column or horizontal row. In Figure 2-5, multiple ImageView controls (Android icons) were dragged onto the emulator window. By default, the Linear layout places each control directly below the previous control to form a vertical column. You can change the Linear layout's orientation from vertical to horizontal by right-clicking the emulator window, pointing to Orientation on the shortcut menu, and then clicking Horizontal. If you select a horizontal Linear layout, the controls are arranged horizontally in a single row, as shown in Figure 2-6.

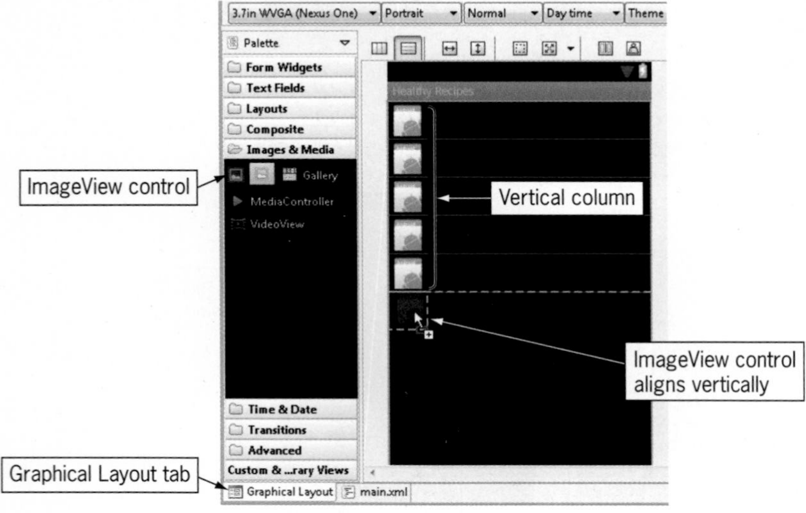

Figure 2-5 Linear layout with a vertical orientation (default)

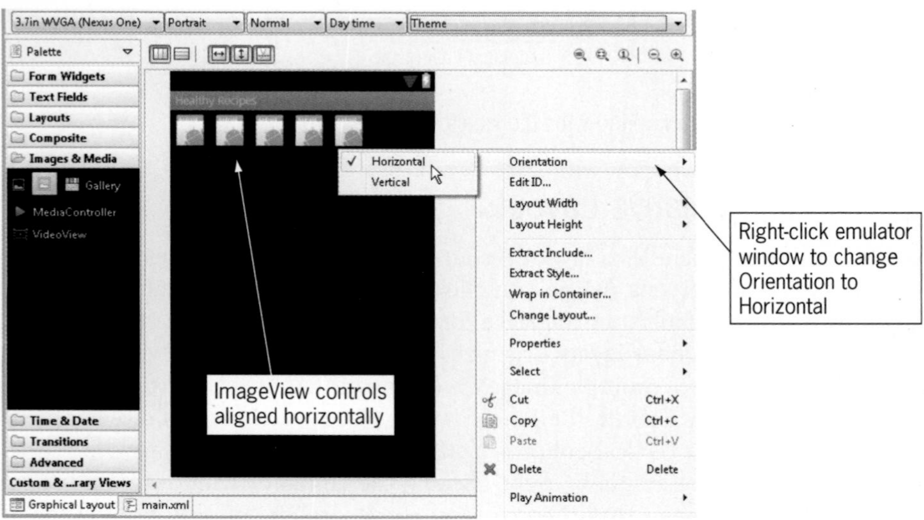

Figure 2-6 Linear layout with a horizontal orientation

Linear layouts are common for forms that display controls in a single row or column. Android user interface designers typically use another layout called a Relative layout. A **Relative layout** organizes layout components in relation to each other. This provides more flexibility in positioning controls than Linear layouts. To change the default Linear layout to a Relative layout, right-click the emulator window and click Change Layout. In the Change Layout dialog box, click the New Layout Type button and then click RelativeLayout. Click the OK button to change the emulator to a Relative layout. As shown in Figure 2-7, five ImageView controls are placed anywhere the developer desires. Using a Relative layout, you can place an ImageView, TextView, RadioButton, or Button control to the left of, to the right of, above, or below another control. Layout resources are stored as XML code in the res/layout resource directory for the Android application corresponding to the user interface template.

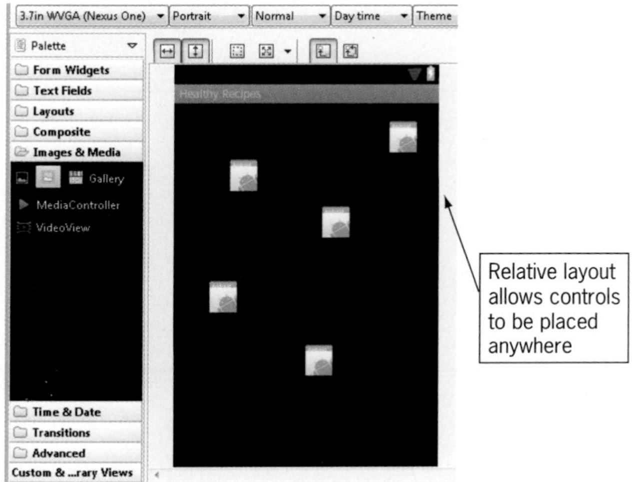

Figure 2-7 Relative layout

GTK

Other layouts you can use include a Frame layout, Table layout, and Table Row layout. You also can use a combination of layouts, which means you can nest controls within one another.

Designing the Healthy Recipes Opening User Interface

When the Healthy Recipes app opens, the initial screen as shown in Figure 2-1 displays a TextView control with the text Simple Salsa, an ImageView control with a picture of the finished salsa, and a Button control with the text View Recipe. Notice that the controls are not in a Linear layout, but use a Relative layout so they are placed freely on the screen. Instead of using XML code to change the text of each control, in this chapter you modify a control's properties using the Properties pane. To change the property of a control, select the control first, and then change the appropriate property, such as the text or size, in the Properties pane.

Android Text Properties

The most popular text properties change the displayed text, modify the size of the text, and change the alignment of the text. The **Text property** changes the text written within the control. The **Text size property** can use various units of measurement, as shown in Table 2-1. The preferred unit of measurement is often **sp**, which stands for scaled-independent pixels. The reason for using this unit of measurement is that if a user has set up an Android phone to display a large font size for more clarity and easier visibility, the font in the app will be scaled to meet the user's size preference.

Unit of Measure	Abbreviation	Example
Inches	in	"0.5in"
Millimeters	mm	"20mm"
Pixels	px	"100px"
Density-independent pixels	dp or dip	"100dp" or "100dip"
Scaled-independent pixels	sp	"100sp"

Table 2-1 Measurements used for the Text size property

On the opening screen of the Healthy Recipes app, the TextView control for the title, ImageView control for the salsa picture, and Button controls can all be centered on the screen using a guide, a green dashed vertical line that appears when a control is dragged to the emulator window. The Relative layout allows controls to be placed anywhere, but the green dashed line centers each control perfectly.

GTK

All Palette controls such as TextView and ImageView can use a property called Layout margin top. For example, if you type 50dp to the right of the Layout margin top property, the control is placed 50 pixels from the top of the screen to help you design an exact layout. You can also center using the Layout center horizontal property by changing the setting to true.

To place all three centered controls on the form using a Relative layout, follow these steps:

1. In the main.xml window, right-click the emulator window, and then click Change Layout on the shortcut menu. In the Change Layout dialog box, click the New Layout Type button, and then click RelativeLayout.

   The Change Layout dialog box opens and the RelativeLayout is selected (Figure 2-8).

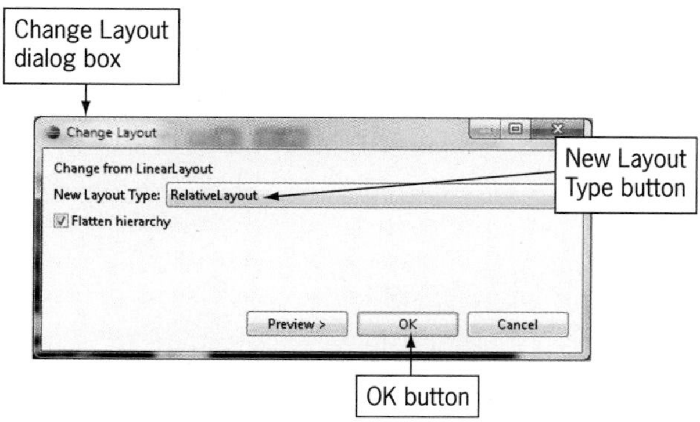

Figure 2-8 Change Layout dialog box

2. Click the OK button. In the Form Widgets Palette, select the Form Widget named TextView. Drag the TextView control to the emulator window and drop it below the Healthy Recipes title. To center the TextView control, drag the control to the center of the window until a green dashed vertical line identifying the window's center is displayed. To open the Properties pane, right-click the emulator window, point to Show In on the shortcut menu, and then click Properties. With the TextView control selected, scroll down the Properties pane, and then click the Text property.

   The TextView object is placed in the emulator window, the Properties pane is opened, and the Text property is selected (Figure 2-9).

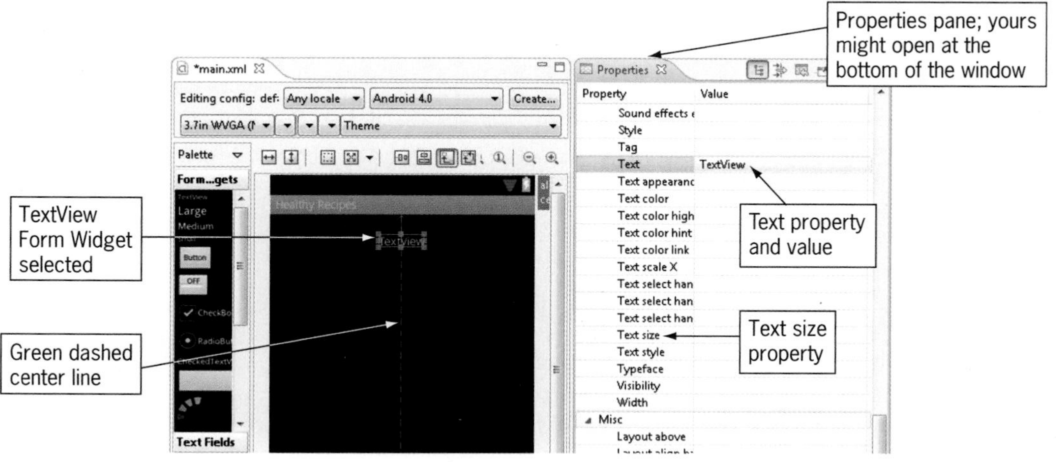

Figure 2-9 Text property in the Properties pane

3. Change the Text property to **Simple Salsa**. In the Properties pane, scroll to the Text size property, type **40sp** to represent the scaled-independent pixel size, and then press Enter.

   The TextView object has the Text property of Simple Salsa and the Text size is 40sp (Figure 2-10).

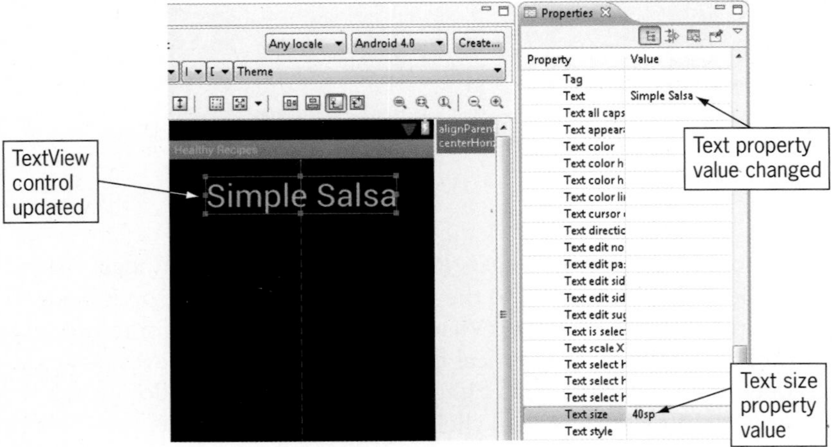

Figure 2-10 Updated Text property

GTK
The top free Android apps are Google Maps, YouTube, Facebook, Pandora, and Netflix, in that order.

GTK
Throughout the book, note that Windows computers have an Enter key, but Mac computers use the Return key.

Adding a File to the Resources Folder

In the Healthy Recipes application, an image of salsa is displayed in an ImageView control. Before you can insert the ImageView control in the emulator window, you must place the appropriate picture file in the resources folder. In the Package Explorer in the left pane of the Eclipse program window, the res (resource) folder contains three subfolders whose names start with *drawable*. The graphics used by the application can be stored in these folders. Android supports three types of graphic formats: .png (preferred), .jpg (acceptable), and .gif (discouraged). Android creates a Drawable resource for any of these files when you save them in the res/drawable folder. The three drawable folders are identified with the following dpi (dots per inch) densities shown in Table 2-2.

Name	Description
hdpi	Resources for high-density screens
mdpi	Resources for medium-density screens
ldpi	Resources for low-density screens

Table 2-2 Drawable folders

Place the salsa image in the res/drawable-hdpi folder to be used by the ImageView control, which links to the resource image. You should already have the student files for this text that your instructor gave you or that you downloaded from the Web page for this book (*www.cengage.com*). To place a copy of the salsa image from the USB drive into the res/drawable-hdpi folder, follow these steps:

1. If necessary, copy the student files to your USB drive. Open the USB folder containing the student files. In the Package Explorer pane, expand the drawable-hdpi folder. A file named ic_launcher.png (the Android logo) is typically contained within this folder already. To add the salsa.png file to the drawable-hdpi resource folder, drag the salsa.png file to the drawable-hdpi folder until a plus sign pointer appears. Release the mouse button.

   The File Operation dialog box opens (Figure 2-11).

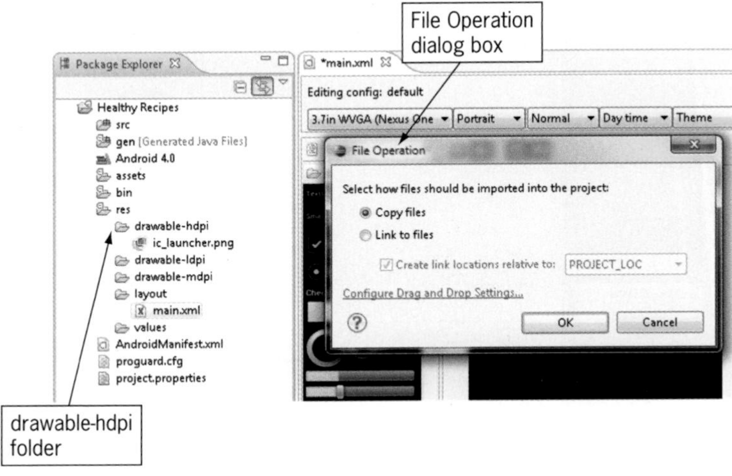

Figure 2-11 File Operation dialog box

2. If necessary, click the Copy files option button, and then click the OK button.

   A copy of the salsa.png file appears in the drawable-hdpi folder.

GTK

High-density graphics have 240 dots per inch, medium-density graphics have 160 dots per inch, and low-density graphics have 120 dots per inch.

Adding an ImageView Control

After an image is placed in a drawable resource folder, you can place an ImageView control in the emulator window. An **ImageView control** can display an icon or a graphic such as a picture file or shape on the Android screen. To add an ImageView control from the Images & Media category of the Palette, follow these steps:

1. Close the Properties pane to create more room to work. Click the Images & Media category in the Palette on the Graphical Layout tab. Drag an ImageView control (the first control in this category) to the emulator window. Drag the control to the center until a green dashed vertical center line appears. Release the mouse button.

   The ImageView control is centered and the Resource Chooser dialog box opens (Figure 2-12).

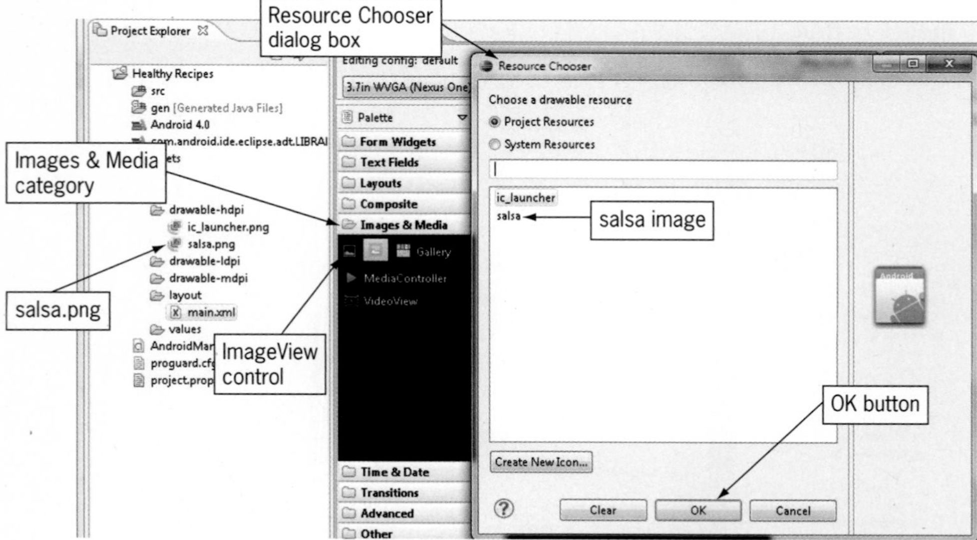

Figure 2-12 Resource Chooser dialog box

2. Click salsa in the Resource Chooser dialog box, and then click the OK button.

   The salsa image is displayed in the emulator window.

IN THE TRENCHES

If you have an image that you want to use in your Android app, but the file type is not .png, open the image in Microsoft Paint or a similar type of program. You can convert the file type by saving the image as a .png file.

Adding a Button Control

A Button control is a commonly used object in a graphical user interface. For example, you probably are familiar with the OK button used in many applications. Generally, when the program is running, buttons are used to cause an event to occur. The Android SDK includes three types of button controls: Button, ToggleButton, and ImageButton. The Button control is provided in the Form Widgets category in the Palette. In the Healthy Recipes app, the user taps a Button control to display the salsa recipe on a second screen. To name the Button control, you use the Id property. For example, use btnRecipe as the Id property for the Button control in the Healthy Recipes app. The prefix btn represents a button in the code. If you intend to use a control in the Java code, it is best to name that control using the Id property. To add a Button control from the Form Widgets category of the Palette, follow these steps:

1. Click the Form Widgets category in the Palette. Drag the Button control to the emulator window below the ImageView control until a green dashed vertical center line appears. Release the mouse button. To open the Properties pane, right-click the emulator window, point to Show In on the shortcut menu, and then select Properties. Click the Button control, and then scroll the Properties pane to the Id property, which is set to @+id/button1 by default. Change the Id property to **@+id/btnRecipe** to provide a unique name for the Button control. Scroll down to the Text property. Change the text to **View Recipe**. Change the Text size property to **30sp** and press Enter.

   The Button control is named btnRecipe and displays the text View Recipe, which has the text size of 30sp (Figure 2-13).

Figure 2-13 Button control

Planning a Program

As you learn the skills necessary to design an Android user interface, you are ready to learn about the program development life cycle. The program development life cycle is a set of phases and steps that developers follow to design, create, and maintain an Android program. Following are the phases of the program development life cycle:

1. *Gather and analyze the program requirements*—The developer must obtain the information that identifies the program requirements and then document these requirements.

2. *Design the user interface*—After the developer understands the program requirements, the next step is to design the user interface. The user interface provides the framework for the processing that occurs within the program.

3. *Design the program processing objects*—An Android app consists of one or more processing objects that perform the tasks required in the program. The developer must determine what processing objects are required, and then determine the requirements of each object.

4. *Code the program*—After the processing object has been designed, the object must be implemented in program code. Program code consists of the instructions written using XML and Java code that ultimately can be executed.

5. *Test the program*—As the program is being coded, and after the coding is completed, the developer should test the program code to ensure it is executing properly.

Creating Activities

The Healthy Recipes application displays two screens, as shown in Figures 2-1 and 2-2. The system requirement for this app is for the user to select a recipe name and then tap the button to display the recipe details. Screens in the Android environment are defined in layout files. Figure 2-13 shows the completed main.xml design. Next, a second screen named recipe.xml must be created and designed. Each of the two screens is considered an Activity. An **Activity**, one of the core components of an Android application, is the point at which the application makes contact with your users. For example, an Activity might create a menu of Web sites, request a street address to display a map, or even show an exhibit of photographs from an art museum. An Activity is an important component of the life cycle of an Android app. In the chapter project, each screen is an Activity where you capture and present information to the user. You can construct Activities by using XML layout files and a Java class.

Creating an XML Layout File

All XML layout files must be placed in the res/layout directory of the Android project so that the Android packaging tool can find the layout files. To create a second XML layout file to construct the second Activity, follow these steps:

1. Close the Properties pane. In the Package Explorer, right-click the layout folder. On the shortcut menu, point to New and then click Other. In the New dialog box, click Android XML Layout File, and then click Next. In the New Android Layout XML File dialog box, type **recipe.xml** in the File text box to name the layout file. In the Root Element list, select RelativeLayout.

   The XML file is named and the layout is set to RelativeLayout (Figure 2-14).

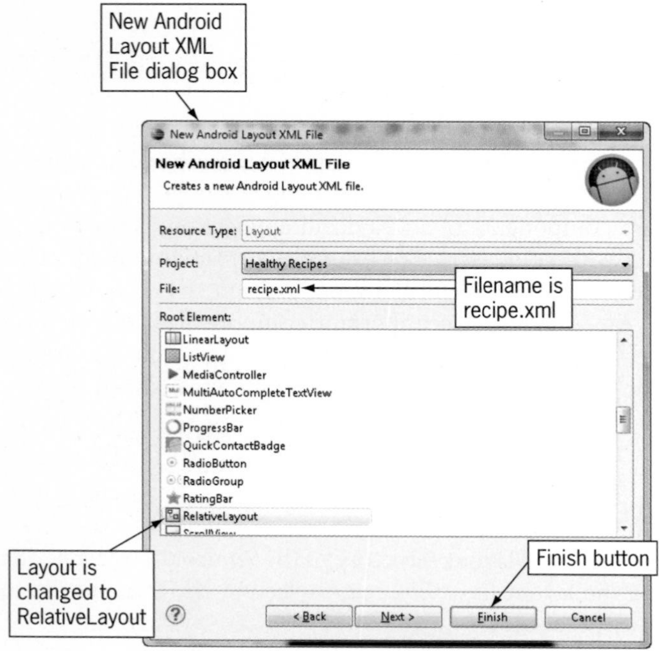

Figure 2-14 Naming the XML file

2. Click the Finish button. Using the techniques taught earlier in the chapter, create the second user interface, recipe.xml, as shown in Figure 2-15.

   The second user interface, recipe.xml, is designed (Figure 2-15).

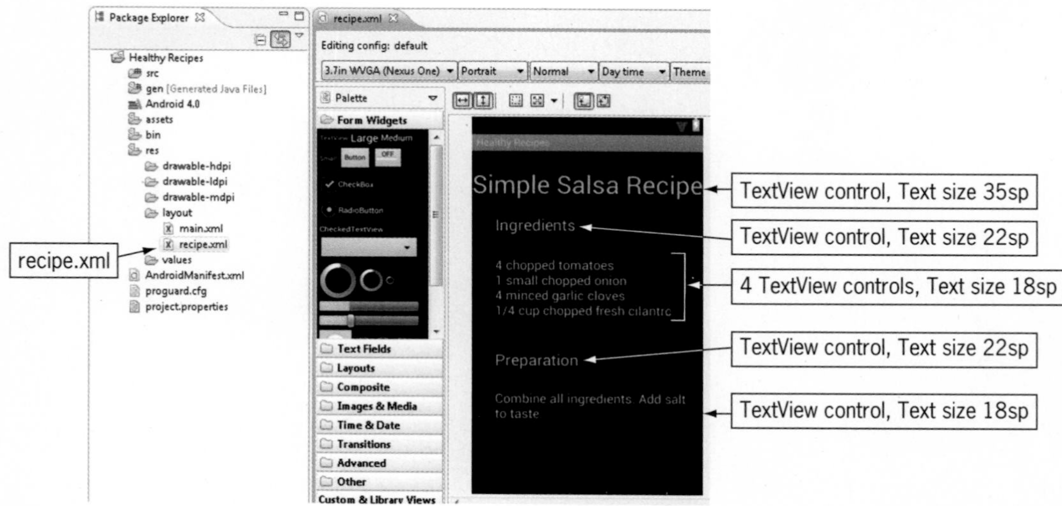

Figure 2-15 User interface for recipe.xml

GTK

You can use comments to document your code. Comments are ignored by the Java compiler. When you want to make a one-line comment, type "//" and follow the two forward slashes with your comment. For example:

// This is a single-line comment

Another way to comment is to use block comments. For example:

/* This is a
block comment
*/

Adding a Class File

In the src folder in the Package Explorer is the Main.java file. This file contains the Main class that opens the main.xml screen, which you designed for the app's user interface. In object-oriented terminology, a class describes a group of objects that establishes an introduction to each object's properties. A **class** is simply a blueprint or a template for creating objects by defining its properties. An **object** is a specific, concrete instance of a class. When you create an object, you instantiate it. When you **instantiate**, you create an instance of the object by defining one particular variation of the object within a class, giving it a name, and locating it in the memory of the computer. Each class needs its own copy of an object. Later in this chapter, Java code is added to the Main class to recognize the action of tapping the Button control to open the recipe screen. Recall that each screen represents an Activity. In addition, each Activity must have a matching Java class file. The recipe.xml file that was designed as shown in Figure 2-15 must have a corresponding Java class file. It is a Java standard to begin a class name with an uppercase letter, include no spaces, and emphasize each new word with an initial uppercase letter. To add a second Java class to the application, follow these steps:

1. In the Package Explorer, expand the src folder and the net.androidbootcamp.healthyrecipes package to view the Main.java existing class. To create a second class, right-click the net.androidbootcamp.healthyrecipes folder, point to New on the shortcut menu, and then click Class.

   The New Java Class dialog box opens (Figure 2-16).

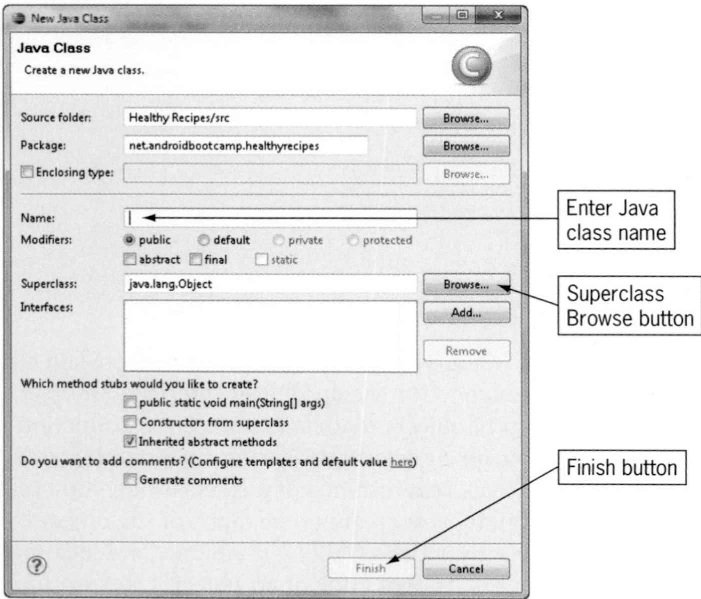

Figure 2-16 New Java Class dialog box

2. Type **Recipe** in the Name text box to create a second class for the recipe Activity. Click the Superclass Browse button. Type **Activity** in the Choose a type text box. As you type, matching items are displayed. Click Activity – android.app and then click the OK button to extend the Activity class.

   A new class named Recipe is created with the Superclass set to android.app.Activity (Figure 2-17).

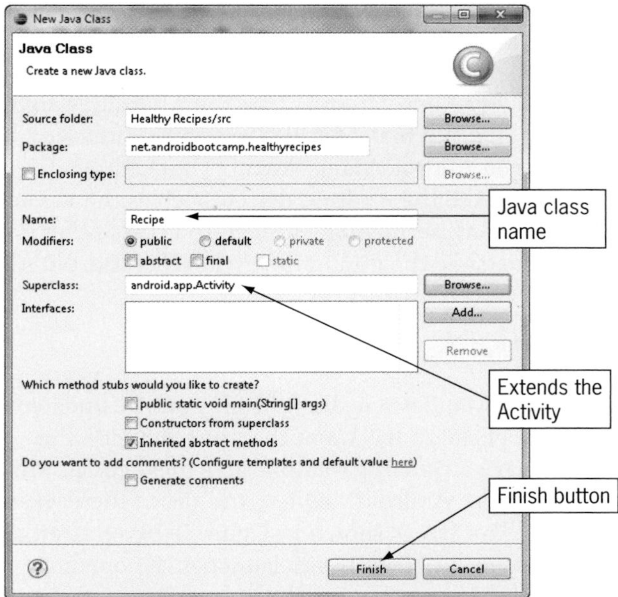

Figure 2-17 Creating the Recipe class

3. Click the Finish button to finish creating the Recipe class. Display line numbers in the code window by clicking Window on the menu bar and then clicking Preferences. In the Preferences dialog box, click General in the left pane, click Editors, and then click Text Editors. Click the Show line numbers check box to select it, and then click the OK button.

   If you are using a Mac, click Eclipse on the menu bar, and then click Preferences to open the Preferences dialog box. Double-click General, double-click Editors, and then click Text Editors.

   The Recipe.java class is created and line numbers are displayed (Figure 2-18).

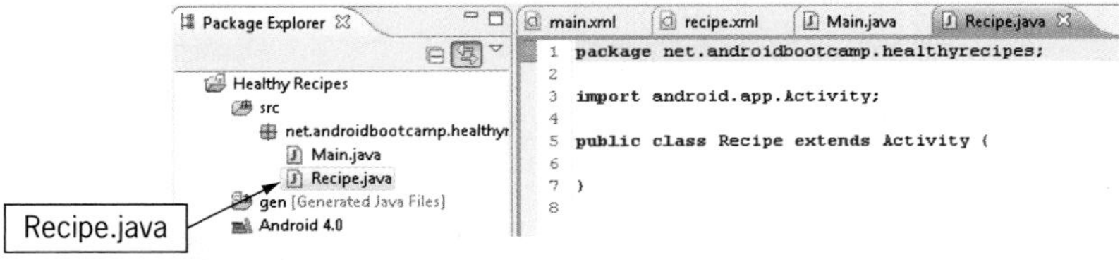

Figure 2-18 New Recipe class in the Healthy Recipes project

GTK

Using an uppercase letter to begin a Java class name and starting each new word with an uppercase letter is known as Pascal case.

The Android Manifest File

An Android project is made up of far more than the XML layout files that create the user interface. The other important components of any Android project are the Android Manifest file and the Java code in the Java classes. The **Android Manifest** file is necessary in every Android application and must have the filename AndroidManifest.xml. The Android Manifest file provides all the essential information to the Android device, such as the name of your Java application, a listing of each Activity, any permissions needed to access other Android functions such as the use of the Internet, and the minimum level of the Android API.

Adding an Activity to the Android Manifest

Eclipse automatically creates the initial Android Manifest file, but this file must be updated to include every Activity in the app. When an application has more than one Activity, the Android Manifest file must have an **intent** to navigate among multiple activities. To see which Activities an application contains, double-click the AndroidManifest.xml file in the Package Explorer, and then click the AndroidManifest.xml tab as shown in Figure 2-19. Notice that Line 14 calls an Activity named .Main. The intent in Lines 16–19 launches the opening screen.

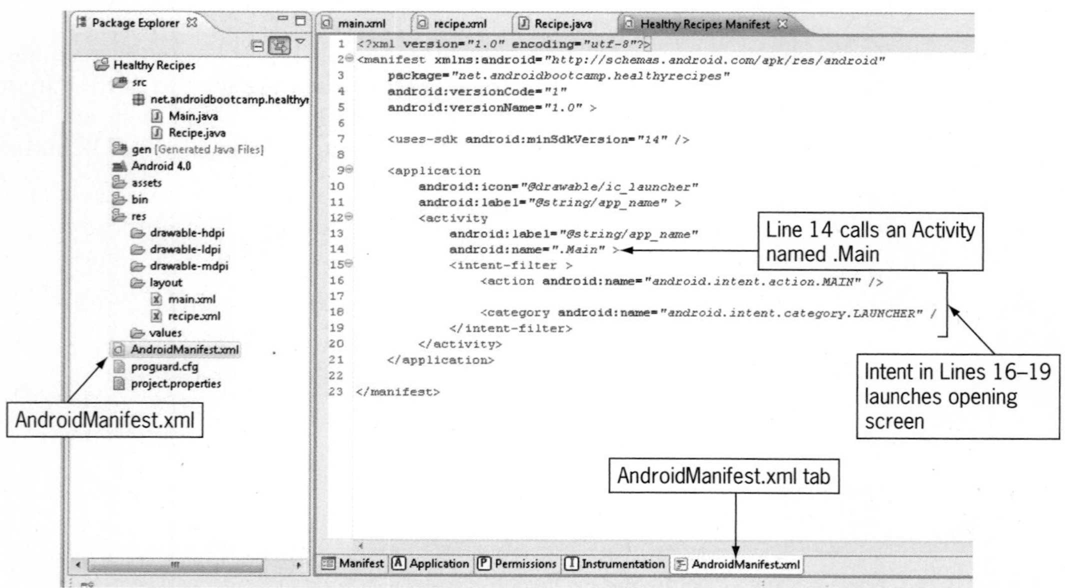

Figure 2-19 Displaying the Activities in an application

The AndroidManifest.xml file must contain an entry for each Activity. To add the second Activity to the Android Manifest file, follow these steps:

1. In the Package Explorer, double-click the AndroidManifest.xml file. To add the Recipe class to the Android Manifest, click the Application tab at the bottom of the Healthy Recipes Manifest page. Scroll down to display the Application Nodes section.

   The AndroidManifest.xml file is opened to the Application tab (Figure 2-20).

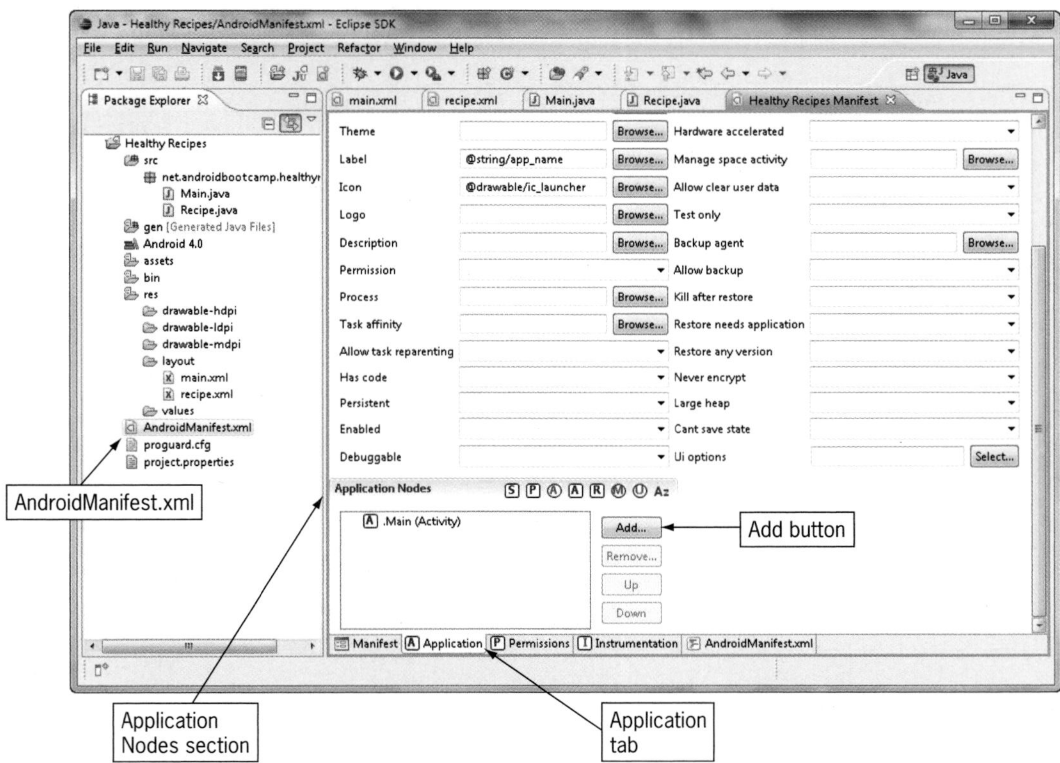

Figure 2-20 Application tab displayed

2. In the Application Nodes section, click the Add button. Select Activity in the Create a new element at the top level, in Application dialog box.

   The Create a new element at the top level, in Application dialog box opens and Activity is selected (Figure 2-21).

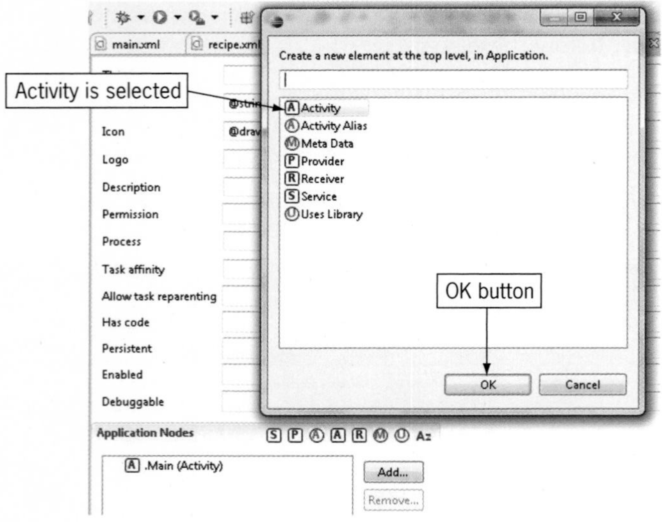

Figure 2-21 Creating an element

3. Click the OK button. The Attributes for Activity section opens in the Application tab. In the Name text box, type the class name preceded by a period (**.Recipe**) to add the Recipe Activity to the AndroidManifest.xml file.

   The class .Recipe is entered in the Name text box of the Attributes for Activity section (Figure 2-22).

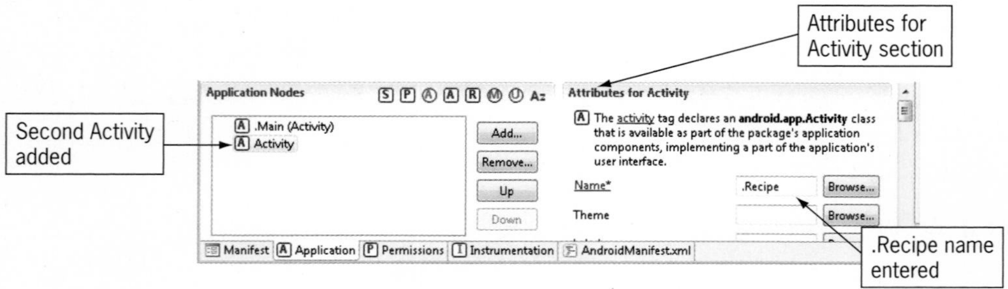

Figure 2-22 Adding the Recipe Activity

4. To view the Main and Recipe Activities in the code, click the AndroidManifest.xml tab at the bottom of the window.

   The AndroidManifest.xml code includes the .Recipe Activity in Line 21 (Figure 2-23).

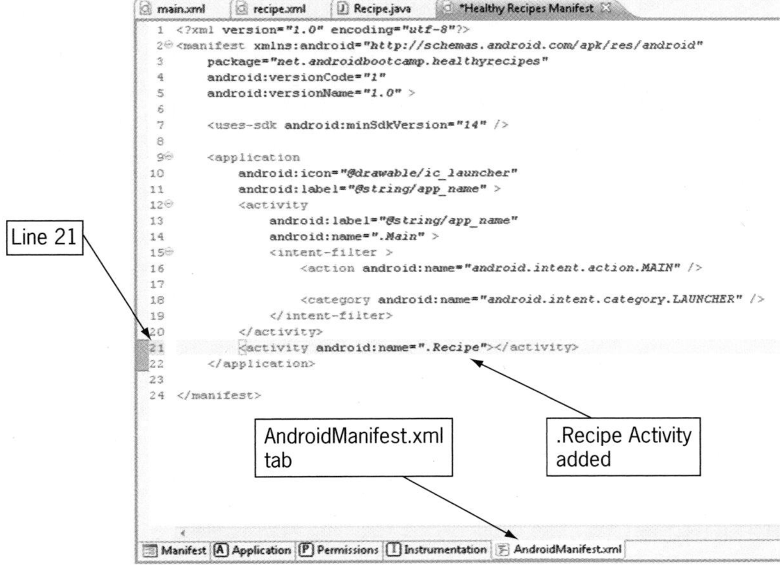

Figure 2-23 AndroidManifest.xml code

Coding the Java Activity

When the user taps an application icon on his or her Android phone or tablet, the Main.java code is read by the phone processor. The entry point of the Activity class is the onCreate( ) event handler, which is called a method. A **method** is a set of Java statements that can be included inside a Java class. The onCreate method is where you initialize the Activity. Imagine a large stack of papers on your desk. The paper on top of the stack is what you are reading right now. The Android also has a stack of Activities. The onCreate method places this new Activity on top of the stack.

Coding an onCreate Method

In the chapter project, the first Activity displayed in the title screen layout designed in main.xml is the currently running Activity. When the user presses the View Recipe button, the main.xml screen closes and a new Activity that displays the actual recipe (recipe.xml) is placed on top of the stack and becomes the running Activity. The syntax for the onCreate method is:

Code Syntax

```
public void onCreate(Bundle savedInstanceState) {
    super.onCreate(savedInstanceState);

}
```

Notice that the syntax of a method begins and ends with a curly brace.

Inside this onCreate method, the first user interface must be opened. Activities have no clue which user interface should be displayed on the screen. For a particular user interface to open on the screen, code must be added inside the onCreate method to place that specific activity on top of the stack. The Java code necessary to display the content of a specific screen is called **setContentView**.

Code Syntax

```
setContentView(R.layout.main);
```

In the code syntax, R.layout.main represents the user interface of main.xml layout, which displays the opening title, salsa image, and View Recipe button. The R represents the term Resource as the layout folder resides in the res folder.

Displaying the User Interface

The Main.java file was created automatically by Eclipse and already contains the onCreate method and setContentView(R.layout.main) code, as shown in Lines 10 and 11 in Figure 2-24. Line 10 starts the Activity and Line 11 displays the main.xml layout when the application begins.

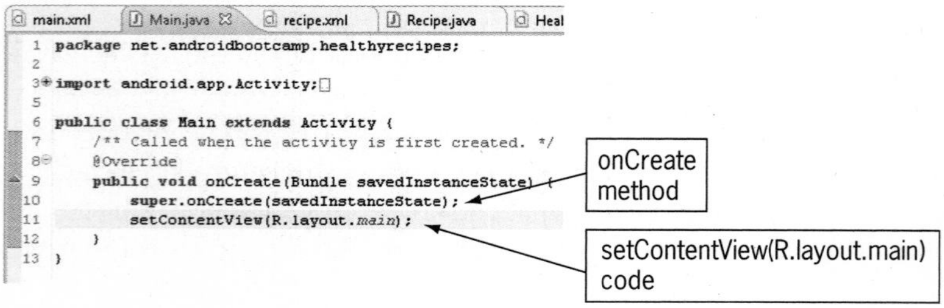

main.xml | Main.java | recipe.xml | Recipe.java | Heal

```
1 package net.androidbootcamp.healthyrecipes;
2
3 import android.app.Activity;
5
6 public class Main extends Activity {
7     /** Called when the activity is first created. */
8     @Override
9     public void onCreate(Bundle savedInstanceState) {
10        super.onCreate(savedInstanceState);
11        setContentView(R.layout.main);
12    }
13 }
```

onCreate method

setContentView(R.layout.main) code

Figure 2-24 Main.java code

To display the second screen (recipe.xml), the onCreate method is necessary to place the second Activity on top of the Activity stack. Next, the setContentView command displays the recipe.xml layout. To add the onCreate and setContentView code to the Recipe.java file, follow these steps:

1. Close the Healthy Recipes Manifest tab, and then click the Yes button to save your changes. Click the Recipe.java tab to display its code. Notice that the Recipe file extends the Activity, as indicated in Line 5 of the code. Click Line 6 to move the insertion point between the two curly braces that open and close the method. Press Tab to indent the line, type **oncreate**, and then press Ctrl+spacebar (simultaneously). When you press Ctrl+spacebar, Eclipse displays an auto-complete listing with all the

possibilities that are valid at that point in the code. A yellow Help window may also appear to the left.

The onCreate method is entered in the Recipe class. A list of possible onCreate methods is displayed after pressing Ctrl+spacebar (Figure 2-25).

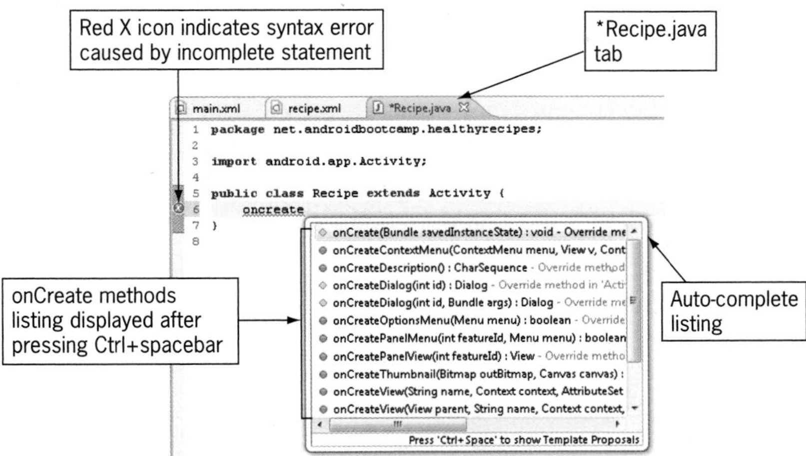

Figure 2-25 onCreate methods

2. Double-click the first onCreate method in the auto-complete listing to generate the method structure.

   The onCreate method is generated in the Recipe class (Figure 2-26).

main.xml | recipe.xml | *Recipe.java

```
1  package net.androidbootcamp.healthyrecipes;
2
3  import android.app.Activity;
4  import android.os.Bundle;
5
6  public class Recipe extends Activity {
7      @Override
8      protected void onCreate(Bundle savedInstanceState) {
9          // TODO Auto-generated method stub
10         super.onCreate(savedInstanceState);
11     }
12 }
13
```

onCreate method added

Figure 2-26 Inserting the onCreate method

3. Click at the end of Line 10 and then press the Enter key to insert a blank line. Type **setContentView(R.** to display an auto-complete listing. Double-click layout. Type a period. Another auto-complete listing requests the XML layout file you intend to display. Double-click recipe : int. Type **)** (a right closing parenthesis) if one does not

appear automatically. Type a semicolon after the parenthesis to complete the statement.

The setContentView command is entered to display the recipe.xml file (Figure 2-27).

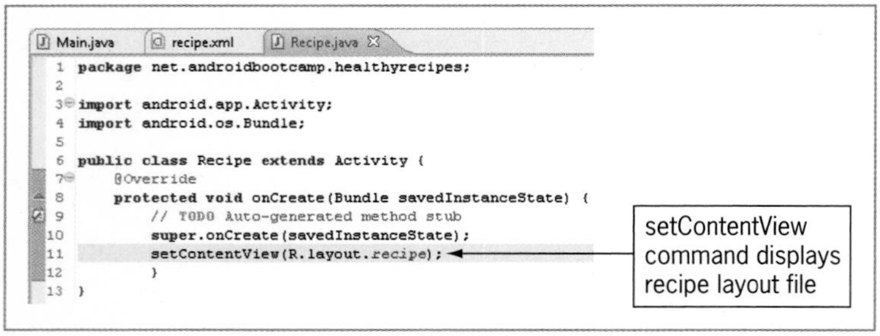

Main.java | recipe.xml | Recipe.java

```
package net.androidbootcamp.healthyrecipes;

import android.app.Activity;
import android.os.Bundle;

public class Recipe extends Activity {
    @Override
    protected void onCreate(Bundle savedInstanceState) {
        // TODO Auto-generated method stub
        super.onCreate(savedInstanceState);
        setContentView(R.layout.recipe);
        }
}
```

setContentView command displays recipe layout file

Figure 2-27 Code for displaying the recipe layout file

Creating a Button Event Handler

Android phones and tablets have touchscreens that create endless possibilities for user interaction, allowing the user to tap, swipe, and pinch in or out to change the size of the screen. As you program with this event-driven language, users typically see an interface containing controls, buttons, menus, and other graphical elements. After displaying the interface, the program waits until the user touches the device. When the user reacts, the app initiates an event, which executes code in an **event handler**, which is a part of the program coded to respond to the specific event. In the Healthy Recipes app, users have only one interaction—they can tap the Button control to start an event that displays the salsa recipe. When the user taps the Button control, code for an event listener is necessary to begin the event that displays the recipe.xml file on the Android screen. This tap event is actually known as a click event in Java code. In the Healthy Recipes application, the Main.java code must first contain the following sections:

- Class property to hold a reference to the Button object
- OnClickListener( ) method to await the button click action
- onClick( ) method to respond to the click event

The Healthy Recipes application opens with a Button control on the screen. To use that button, a reference is required in the Main.java file. To reference a Button control, use the following syntax to create a Button property:

Code Syntax

```
Button b=(Button)findViewById(R.id.btnRecipe);
```

The syntax for the Button property includes the findViewById( ) method, which is used by any Android Activity. This method finds a layout view created in the XML files that you created when designing the user interface. The variable b in the code contains the reference to the Button control. After the code is entered to reference the Button control, you can press Ctrl+spacebar to import the Button type as an Android widget. When you **import** the Button type as an Android widget, you make the classes from the Android Button package available throughout the application. An import statement is automatically placed at the top of the Java code. An **import statement** is a way of making more Java functions available to your specific program. Java can perform almost endless actions, and not every program needs to do everything. So, to limit the size of the code, Java has its classes divided into packages that can be imported at the top of your code.

After the Button property is referenced in Main.java, an OnClickListener( ) method is necessary to detect when the user taps an onscreen button. Event listeners wait for user interaction, which is when the user taps the button to view the recipe in the case of the chapter project. When an OnClickListener is placed in the code window, Java creates an onClick auto-generated stub. A **stub** is a piece of code that actually serves as a placeholder to declare itself, and it has just enough code to link to the rest of the program. The syntax needed for an OnClickListener method that listens for the Button control is shown in the following Code Syntax:

Code Syntax

```
        b.setOnClickListener(new OnClickListener() {

          public void onClick(View v) {
          // TODO Auto-generated method stub

          }
    });
```

The last step to code is to call the startActivity( ) method, which opens the second Activity displaying the recipe.xml user interface. The startActivity( ) method creates an intent to start another Activity such as to start the recipe Activity class. The intent needs two parts known as parameters: a context and the name of the Activity that is being opened. A context in Android coding means that any time you request that program to launch another Activity, a context is sent to the Android system to show which initiating Activity class is making the request. The context of the chapter project is Main.this, which references the Main.java class. The following syntax line launches the Recipe Java class:

Code Syntax

```
startActivity(new Intent(Main.this, Recipe.class));
```

Coding a Button Event Handler

When the main.xml layout is initially launched by the Main.java class, it is necessary to code how the Button control interacts with the user. When this View Recipe button is tapped, the Main.java class must contain code to launch the Recipe.xml layout (Activity) and to begin the second Java class called Recipe.java. To initialize the Button control and code the Button handler to launch the second Activity class, follow these steps:

1. In the Package Explorer, double-click Main.java to open its code window. Click to the right of the setContentView(R.layout.main); line. Press the Enter key. To initialize and reference the Button control with the Id name of btnRecipe, type **Button b = (Button) findViewById(R.id.btnRecipe);**

   After the code is entered to reference the Button control, point to the red curly line below the first Button command and select Import 'Button' (android widget). Click the Save All button on the Standard toolbar to save your work.

   If you are using a Mac, error indicators in the code are red dashed lines.

   The Button control named btnRecipe is referenced in Main.java. In this case, the onCreate method is created for you in Line 11. A curly line appears below the b variable to indicate that this local variable has not been used in the code yet (Figure 2-28).

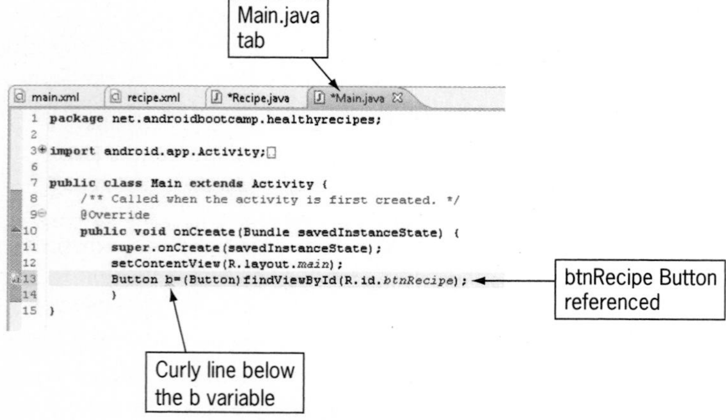

Figure 2-28 Main.java code

2. Press the Enter key. To code the button listener that awaits user interaction, type **b.seton** and then wait for a code listing to open. Double-click the first setOnClickListener to select it.

   In the parentheses, type **new on** and press Ctrl+spacebar to display an auto-complete listing. Double-click the first choice, which lists an OnClickListener with an

Anonymous Inner Type event handler. Point to the red curly line below OnClickListener. Select Import 'OnClickListener' (android.View.view).

Type **;** (semicolon) after the closing parenthesis to complete the auto-generated stub.

An OnClickListener auto-generated stub appears in the code (Figure 2-29).

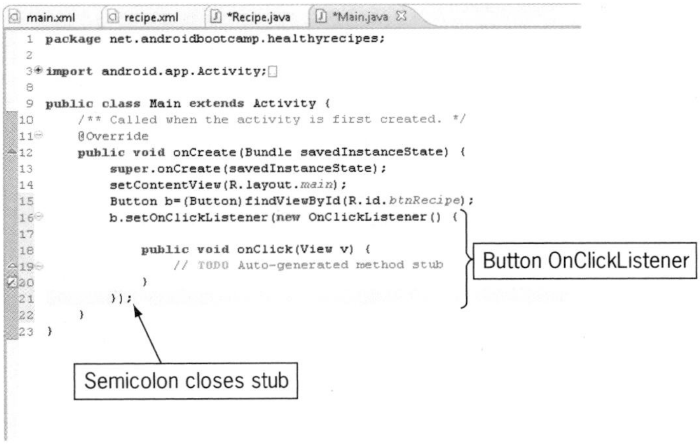

main.xml | recipe.xml | *Recipe.java | *Main.java

```
package net.androidbootcamp.healthyrecipes;

import android.app.Activity;

public class Main extends Activity {
    /** Called when the activity is first created. */
    @Override
    public void onCreate(Bundle savedInstanceState) {
        super.onCreate(savedInstanceState);
        setContentView(R.layout.main);
        Button b=(Button)findViewById(R.id.btnRecipe);
        b.setOnClickListener(new OnClickListener() {

            public void onClick(View v) {
                // TODO Auto-generated method stub
            }
        });
    }
}
```

Button OnClickListener

Semicolon closes stub

Figure 2-29 Inserting the Button OnClickListener stub

3. To launch the Recipe.java class when the Button control is clicked, click inside the public void onClick(View v) braces on the line after the "TODO" comment. Type **startactivity** and press Ctrl+spacebar. Select the first option, startActivity(Intent intent): void – Activity.

   In the parentheses, change the intent text by typing **new int** and then pressing Ctrl+spacebar. In the auto-complete listing, select Intent(Context packageContext, Class<?> cls).

   In the next set of parentheses, change packageContext to **Main.this** and change cls to **Recipe.class**. Place a semicolon at the end of the line after the parenthesis. Click the Save All button on the toolbar.

   The startActivity code launches the intent to open Recipe.class (Figure 2-30).

```
main.xml  recipe.xml  *Recipe.java  *Main.java

package net.androidbootcamp.healthyrecipes;

import android.app.Activity;

public class Main extends Activity {
    /** Called when the activity is first created. */
    @Override
    public void onCreate(Bundle savedInstanceState) {
        super.onCreate(savedInstanceState);
        setContentView(R.layout.main);
        Button b=(Button)findViewById(R.id.btnRecipe);
        b.setOnClickListener(new OnClickListener() {

            public void onClick(View v) {
                // TODO Auto-generated method stub
                startActivity(new Intent(Main.this, Recipe.class));
            }
        });
    }
}
```

startActivity code

Figure 2-30 Complete code

GTK

In Step 3, the packageContext is replaced with Main because it is the name of the Activity. The term *this* refers to the present Activity.

IN THE TRENCHES

In years past, a software developer would have to wait many months for his or her software to be published and placed in stores for sale. In today's mobile market, app stores have become the de facto app delivery channel by reducing time-to-shelf and time-to-payment and by providing developers with unprecedented reach to consumers.

Correcting Errors in Code

Using the built-in auto-complete listing to assist you when entering code considerably reduces the likelihood of coding errors. Nevertheless, because you could create one or more errors when entering code, you should understand what to do when a coding error occurs. One possible error you could commit would be to forget a semicolon at the end of a statement. In Figure 2-31, when the application is run, a dialog box opens stating your project contains error(s), please fix them before running your application. A red curly line identifies the error location. When you point to the red curly line, Java suggests the possible correction to the syntax error in the code. Also notice that Line 15 has an error icon (a red X) at the beginning of the line to identify the location of the error. After a semicolon is placed at the end of the line, the application is run again and the program functions properly.

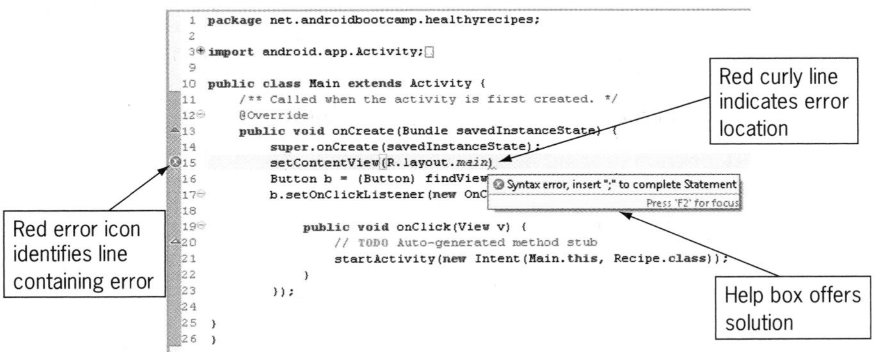

Figure 2-31 Syntax error

Saving and Running the Application

Each time an Android application is tested in the emulator, the programming design and code are automatically saved. If you start your project and need to save it before completion, click the Save All button on the toolbar or click File on the menu bar and then select Save All. As shown in Chapter 1, click Run on the menu bar, and then select Run to save and test the application in the emulator. A dialog box opens the first time the application is executed that requests how you would like to run the application. Select Android Application and click the OK button. When the emulated Android main screen appears, unlock the emulator. The application opens in the emulator window, where you can click the View Recipe button to view the salsa recipe.

Wrap It Up—Chapter Summary

This chapter described the steps to create the graphical user interface for the Healthy Recipes program. As you can see, many of the steps required are somewhat repetitive in the design; that is, the same technique is used repeatedly to accomplish similar tasks. When you master these techniques, together with the principles of user interface design, you will be able to design user interfaces for a variety of different programs.

- Linear layouts arrange screen components in a vertical column or horizontal row. Relative layouts arrange screen components freely on the screen.
- Popular text properties for controls include the Text property, which specifies the text displayed in the control, and the Text size property, which specifies the size of the text.

- To display graphics such as pictures and icons in an Android app, you use an ImageView control. Before you can place an ImageView control in the emulator window, you must place a graphics file in the resources folder.
- An Activity is the point at which the application makes contact with your users and is one of the core components of the Android application. The chapter project has two Activities, one for each screen.
- Each screen represents an Activity and each Activity must have a matching Java class file. To create a Java class file, you can extend the built-in Activity class.
- Every Android application has an Android Manifest file (named AndroidManifest.xml), which provides essential information to the Android device, such as the name of your Java application and a listing of each Activity. Eclipse automatically creates the initial Android Manifest file, but this file must be updated to include every Activity in the app.
- When an application has more than one Activity, the Android Manifest file must have an intent so the application can navigate among multiple Activities.
- A method is a set of Java statements that can be included inside a Java class. The onCreate method is where you initialize an Activity. You use the setContentView command to display the content of a specific screen.
- When the user taps a Button control in an Android app, the code for an event listener, or click event, begins the event associated with the Button control. Event listeners such as the OnClickListener method wait for user interaction before executing the remaining code.
- In an Android app that contains more than one Activity, or screen, you use the startActivity( ) method to create an intent to start another Activity. The intent should contain two parameters: a context and the name of the Activity being opened. A context shows which initiating Activity class is making the request.
- When you run an Android application, a dialog box opens if your project contains any errors. Look for red error icons and red curly lines, which identify the location of the errors. Point to a red curly line to have Java suggest a correction to a syntax error in the code.

Key Terms

Activity—An Android component that represents a single screen with a user interface.

Android Manifest—A file with the filename AndroidManifest.xml that is required in every Android application. This file provides essential information to the Android device, such as the name of your Java application and a listing of each Activity.

class—A group of objects that establishes an introduction to each object's properties.

event handler—A part of a program coded to respond to the specific event.

ImageView control—A control that displays an icon or a graphic from a picture file.

import—To make the classes from a particular Android package available throughout the application.

import statement—A statement that makes more Java functions available to a program.

instantiate—To create an object of a specific class.

intent—Code in the Android Manifest file that allows an Android application with more than one Activity to navigate among Activities.

Linear layout—A layout that arranges components in a vertical column or horizontal row.

method—A set of Java statements that can be included inside a Java class.

object—A specific, concrete instance of a class.

Relative layout—A layout that arranges components in relation to each other.

setContentView—The Java code necessary to display the content of a specific screen.

sp—A unit of measurement that stands for scaled-independent pixels.

stub—A piece of code that serves as a placeholder to declare itself, containing just enough code to link to the rest of the program.

Text property—A property that changes the text written within a control.

Text size property—A property that sets the size of text in a control.

Developer FAQs

1. If you were creating an app in many different languages, would you have to write the entire program from scratch for each language?
2. What part of the program in question 1 would stay the same? What part of the program would be different?
3. In which subfolder in the Package Explorer are the XML files stored?
4. Which three controls were used in the chapter project?
5. What is the difference between Linear layout and Relative layout?
6. Is the default layout for an Android screen Linear or Relative?
7. Which measurement is most preferred for text size? Why?
8. What does px stand for?
9. What does sp stand for?
10. What does dpi stand for?

11. Which picture file types are accepted for an ImageView control?
12. Which picture file type is preferred?
13. In the Palette in the layout folder, in which category is the ImageView control found?
14. Which three properties were changed in the chapter project for the Button control?
15. What is the property that defines the name of a Button control?
16. Write one line of code that would launch a second class named Rental from the present Main class.
17. Write one line of code that declares a Button control with the variable bt that references a button in the XML layout with the Id property of btnReserve.
18. Write one line of code that opens the XML layout named medical.
19. Which two keys are pressed to auto-complete a line of Java code?
20. What symbol is placed at the end of most lines of Java code?

Beyond the Book

Using the Internet, search the Web for the following answers to further your Android knowledge.

1. Linear and Relative layouts are not the only types of Android layouts. Name three other types of layouts and write a paragraph describing each type.
2. Why are .png files the preferred type of image resource for the Android device? Write a paragraph that gives at least three reasons.
3. How much does an average Android app developer profit from his or her apps? Research this topic and write 150–200 words on your findings.
4. Research the most expensive Android apps currently available. Name three expensive apps, their price, and the purpose of each.

Case Programming Projects

Complete one or more of the following case programming projects. Use the same steps and techniques taught within the chapter. Submit the program you create to your instructor. The level of difficulty is indicated for each case programming project.

Easiest: ★

Intermediate: ★ ★

Challenging: ★ ★ ★

Case Project 2–1: Rental Property App ★

Requirements Document

Application title: Rental Property App

Purpose: In an apartment finder app, an apartment is selected and an address and other information are displayed.

Algorithms:

1. The opening screen displays the name of an apartment, an image, and a Button control (Figure 2-32).
2. When the user selects this apartment, an address and a cost range are displayed in a second screen (Figure 2-33).

Note: The apartment image is provided with your student files.

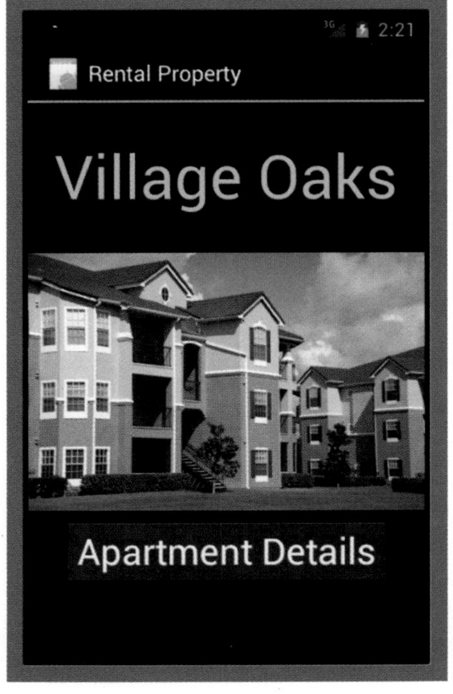

iStockphoto.com/Marje Cannon

Figure 2-32

Figure 2-33

Case Project 2–2: Star Constellation App ★

Requirements Document

Application title:	Star Constellation App
Purpose:	In a star constellation app, the name of a constellation is selected and the constellation image is displayed with information.
Algorithms:	1. The opening screen displays the name of a constellation, a translation name, and a Button control (Figure 2-34). 2. When the user selects this constellation, an image displaying the sky chart, position, month range, and declination is shown (Figure 2-35).
Note:	The pegasus image is provided with your student files.

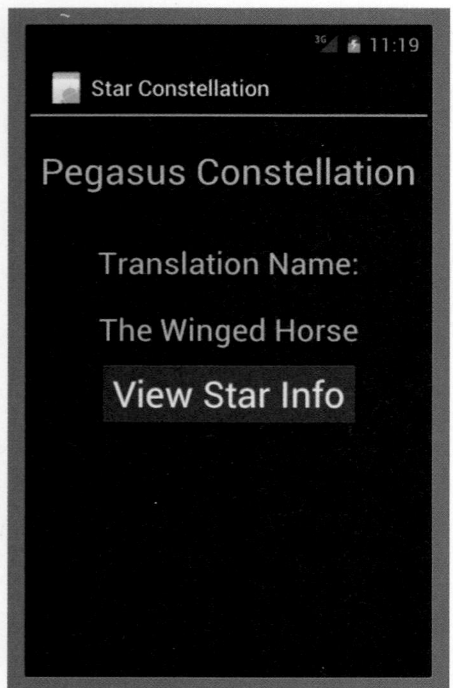

Figure 2-34

iStockphoto.com/Clifford Mueller

Figure 2-35

Case Project 2–3: Your School App ★ ★

Requirements Document

Application title: Your School App

Purpose: This large app contains every school in your country. Create two screens for your school for the app. In a school app, the name of a school is selected and the school address and logo are displayed.

Algorithms:

1. The opening screen displays the name of your school, a picture of your school, and a Button control. Create your own layout.
2. The second screen displays the name of your school, a picture of your logo, the school address, and the phone number. Create your own layout.

Case Project 2–4: Hostel App for Travel ★ ★

Requirements Document

Application title: Hostel App for Travel

Purpose: This large app contains every hostel (small youth hotel) in Italy. Create two screens for the hostel app. In the hostel app, the name of a hostel is selected and the hostel room image is displayed with detailed information.

Algorithms:

1. The opening screen displays the name of the Italian hostel, an exterior image of the hostel, and a Button control. Create your own layout.
2. The second screen displays the name of the hostel, a picture of the interior room, the street address, the Web address, and the rate. Create your own layout.

Case Project 2–5: Your Contacts App – Address Book ★ ★ ★

Requirements Document

Application title: Your Contacts App – Address Book

Purpose: This large app contains every business contact in an address book. Create two screens for contacts for the app. In the contacts app, you can select a particular contact and that person's info is displayed with his or her picture.

Algorithms:

1. The opening screen displays two names of contacts with the last name starting with the letter *J*. Each contact has a separate Button control below the name. Create your own layout.
2. The second screen displays the name, address, phone number, and picture of the contact. Create your own layout.

Conditions: Three Java classes and three XML layouts are needed.

Case Project 2–6: Latest News App ★ ★ ★

Requirements Document

Application title: The Latest Pulse

Purpose: This large app called The Latest Pulse contains the latest news. Create two screens for two news stories for the app. In the news app, you can select a particular news story title and an image and a paragraph about the news story is displayed.

Algorithms:

1. The opening screen displays two news story titles that you can create based on the news stories during this week. Each news story has a separate Button control below the name and displays a small image. Create your own layout.
2. The second screen displays the name of the story and a paragraph detailing the news. Create your own layout.

Conditions: Three Java classes and three XML layouts are needed.

CHAPTER 3

Engage! Android User Input, Variables, and Operations

Unless otherwise noted in the chapter, all screenshots are provided courtesy of Eclipse.

In this chapter, you learn to:

- Use an Android theme
- Add a theme to the Android Manifest file
- Develop the user interface using Text Fields
- State the role of different Text Fields
- Display a hint using the Hint property
- Develop the user interface using a Spinner control
- Add text to the String table
- Add a prompt to a Spinner control
- Declare variables to hold data
- Code the GetText( ) method
- Understand arithmetic operations
- Convert numeric data
- Format numeric data
- Code the SetText( ) method
- Run the completed app in the emulator

In the Healthy Recipes app developed in Chapter 2, when the user clicked the button in the user interface, events were triggered, but the user did not enter data. In many applications, users enter data and then the program uses the data in its processing. Engaging the user by requesting input customizes the user experience each time the application is executed. When processing data entered by a user, a common requirement is to perform arithmetic operations on the data in order to generate useful output information. Arithmetic operations include adding, subtracting, multiplying, and dividing numeric data.

To illustrate the use of user data input and arithmetic operations, the application in this chapter allows the user to enter the number of concert tickets to be purchased from a concert Android app. The application then calculates the total cost to purchase the concert tickets. The user interface for the app named Concert Tickets is shown in Figure 3-1 with the company name Ticket Vault displayed at the top of the screen.

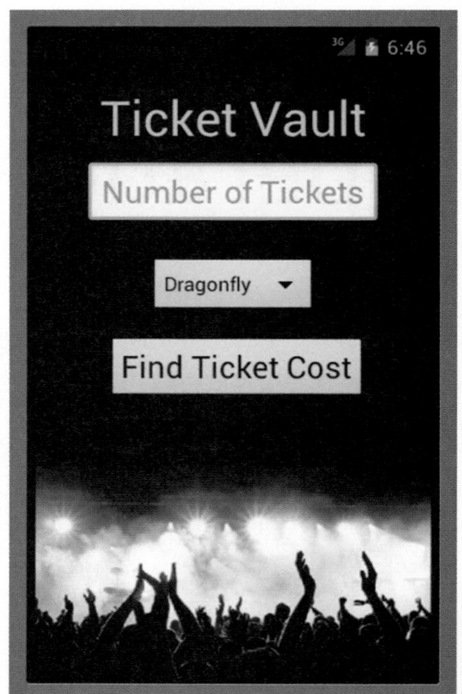

Figure 3-1 Concert Tickets Android app

In Figure 3-2, the user entered 4 as the number of tickets purchased. When the user clicked the Find Ticket Cost button, the program multiplied 4 times the concert ticket cost ($59.99) and then displayed the result as the total cost of the concert tickets, as shown in Figure 3-2. To create this application, the developer must understand how to perform the following processes, among others:

1. Apply a theme to the design of the Android screen.
2. Define a Text Field for data entry. For this app, a number is expected for the quantity of tickets. Using a specific Text Field for positive integers, an incorrect value cannot be entered.

3. Define a Spinner control to allow users to select the performance group.
4. Convert data so it can be used for arithmetic operations.
5. Perform arithmetic operations with the data the user enters.
6. Display formatted results.

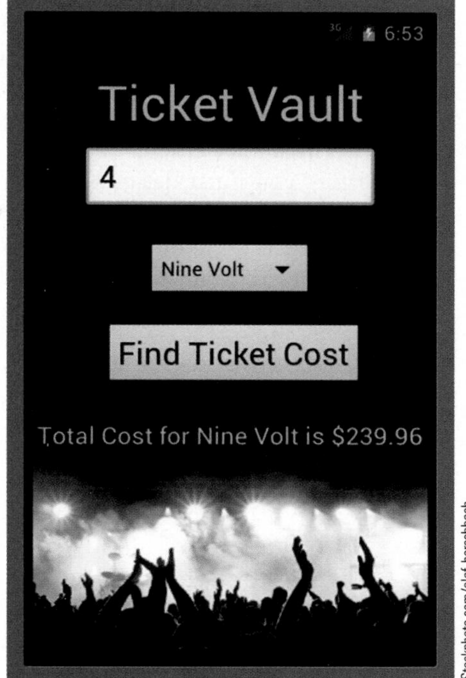

Figure 3-2 Four tickets purchased for a concert

Android Themes

To prevent each Android app from looking too similar, the Android SDK includes multiple themes that provide individual flair to each application. A **theme** is a style applied to an Activity or an entire application. Some themes change the background wallpaper of the Activity, while others hide the title bar or display an action bar. Some themes display a background depending on the size of the mobile device. Themes can be previewed in the emulator window displayed in main.xml. The default theme shows the title bar (often gray) with a black background, as shown in Figure 3-3. Figure 3-4 displays a glowing holographic border with a light translucent background and no title bar. The light and transparent themes are sheer and allow you to see the initial home screen through the background. Figure 3-5 displays the default black background with the default Android icon and an action bar.

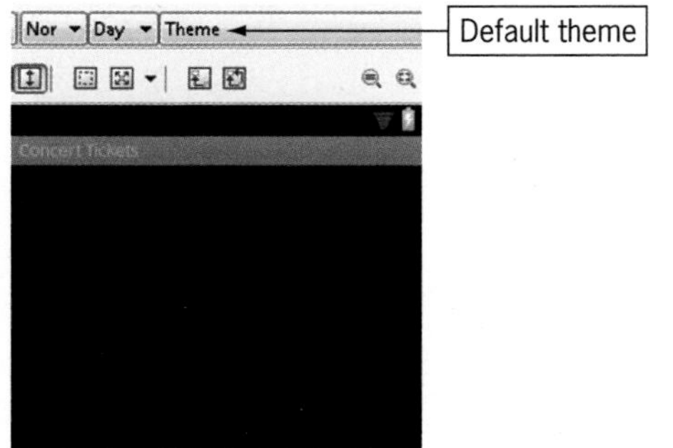

Figure 3-3 Default theme

Figure 3-4 Holographic theme

Previewing a Theme

By changing the theme in the emulator window in the main.xml file, you can preview what the new theme looks like, but to permanently change it in the application, you must define the themes in the Android Manifest for each Activity. You can code a predefined system theme or a customized theme of your own design. The Concert Tickets chapter project uses the predefined system theme named Theme.Black.NoTitleBar. To initiate the Concert Tickets application and preview the Theme.Black.NoTitleBar theme, follow these steps:

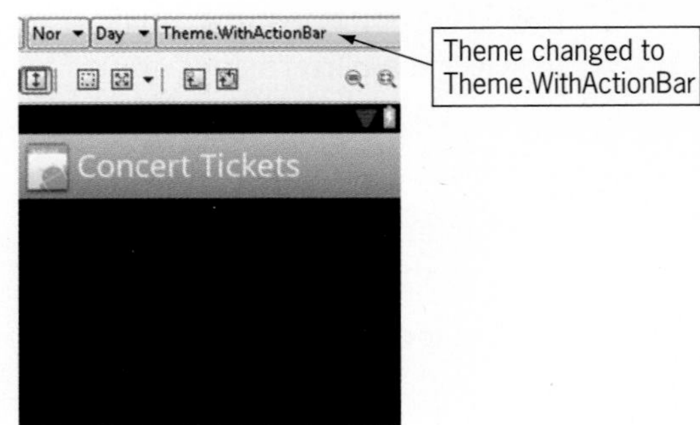

Figure 3-5 Action bar theme

1. Open the Eclipse program. Click the New button on the Standard toolbar. Expand the Android folder, if necessary, and select Android Project. Click the Next button. In the New Android Project dialog box, enter the Project Name **Concert Tickets**. To save the project on your USB drive, click to remove the check mark from the Use default location check box. Type **E:\Workspace** (if necessary, enter a different drive letter that identifies the USB drive). Click Next. For the Build Target, select Android 4.0, if necessary. Click Next. Type the Package Name **net.androidbootcamp.concerttickets**. Enter **Main** in the Create Activity text box.

   The new Android Concert Tickets project has an application name, a package name, and a Main Activity (Figure 3-6).

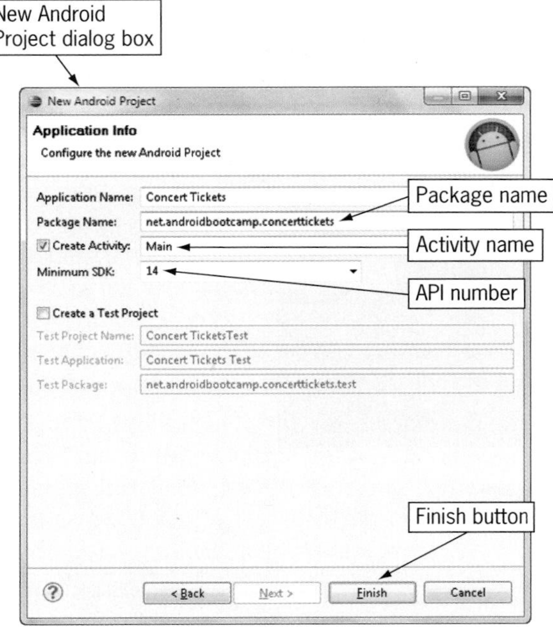

Figure 3-6 Setting up the Concert Tickets project

2. Click the Finish button. Expand the Concert Tickets project in the Package Explorer. Expand the res folder to display its subfolders. Expand the layout subfolder. Double-click the main.xml file. Click the Hello World, Main! TextView widget (displayed by default). Press the Delete key. On the main.xml tab, right-click the emulator window, and then click Change Layout on the shortcut menu. In the Change Layout dialog box, click the New Layout Type button, and then click RelativeLayout. Click the OK button.

   The main.xml tab is displayed in the project window on the right and the Hello World TextView widget is deleted (Figure 3-7).

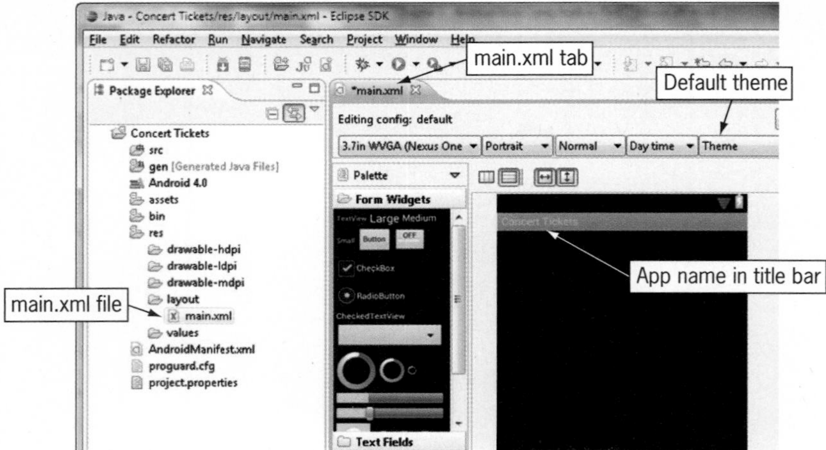

Figure 3-7 main.xml for the Concert Tickets project

3. Click the Theme button to display the list of built-in themes. Select Theme.Black.NoTitleBar.

   The theme is changed to Theme.Black.NoTitleBar. The title bar in the emulator is removed (Figure 3-8).

Figure 3-8 New theme applied

Coding a Theme in the Android Manifest File

At this point, the theme is only displayed in the main.xml graphical layout, but to actually display the theme in the application, code must be inserted in the AndroidManifest.xml file, as shown in the following example:

Code Syntax

```
android:theme="@android:style/Theme.Black.NoTitleBar"
```

Enter the theme code in the Activity section of the Android Manifest file. The code syntax shown above displays the default theme without a title bar. To code the theme within the AndroidManifest.xml file, follow these steps:

1. In the Package Explorer, double-click the AndroidManifest.xml file. Click the AndroidManifest.xml tab at the bottom of the window.

   The AndroidManifest.xml code is displayed (Figure 3-9).

Figure 3-9 Android Manifest file for the Concert Tickets project

2. Inside the activity code, click at the end of the code that states android: name=".Main" (Line 13). Press the Enter key to insert a new blank line. Type **android:theme="@android:style/Theme.Black.NoTitleBar"**.

   The Android theme is coded within the Activity in the Android Manifest file (Figure 3-10).

main.xml | *Concert Tickets Manifest

```
1  <?xml version="1.0" encoding="utf-8"?>
2  <manifest xmlns:android="http://schemas.android.com/apk/res/androi
3      package="net.androidbootcamp.concerttickets"
4      android:versionCode="1"
5      android:versionName="1.0" >
6
7      <uses-sdk android:minSdkVersion="14" />
8
9      <application
10         android:icon="@drawable/ic_launcher"
11         android:label="@string/app_name" >
12
13         <activity
14             android:name=".Main"
15             android:theme="@android:style/Theme.Black.NoTitleBar"
16             android:label="@string/app_name" >
17             <intent-filter >
```

Theme added in Line 14

Figure 3-10 Adding the theme to the Android Manifest file

3. Close the Concert Tickets Manifest tab and save your work.

Simplifying User Input

On the Android phone, users can enter text in multiple ways that include entering input through an onscreen soft keyboard, an attached flip button hard keyboard, and even voice-to-text capabilities on most phone models. The onscreen keyboard is called a **soft keyboard**, which is positioned at the bottom of the screen over the application window. Touch input can vary from tapping the screen to using gestures. Gestures are multitouch interactions such as pressing two fingers to pan, rotate, or zoom. The primary design challenge for mobile Web applications is how do you simplify user experiences for an application that appears on screens measuring from a few inches square to much larger tablets? You need to use legible fonts, simplify input, and optimize each device's capabilities to maximize the user experience. Certain Android Form Widgets such as those in the Text Fields category allow specific data types for user input, which simplifies data entry. For example, a numeric Text Field only allows numbers to be entered from the onscreen keyboard, limiting accidental user input, such as by touching the wrong location on a small touchscreen.

IN THE TRENCHES

A decade ago, nearly every mobile phone offered an alphanumeric keypad as part of the device. Today a touchscreen full QWERTY keyboard is available to allow users to enter information, engage in social networking, surf the Internet, and view multimedia.

Android Text Fields

In the Concert Tickets application shown in Figure 3-1, the user enters the quantity of tickets that he or she intends to purchase to attend the concert event. The most common type of mobile input is text entered from the soft keyboard or the attached keyboard. User keyboard input can be requested with the Text Fields in the Eclipse Palette (Figure 3-11). With Text Fields, the input can be received on the mobile device with an onscreen keyboard or the user can elect to use the physical keyboard if the device provides one to enter input.

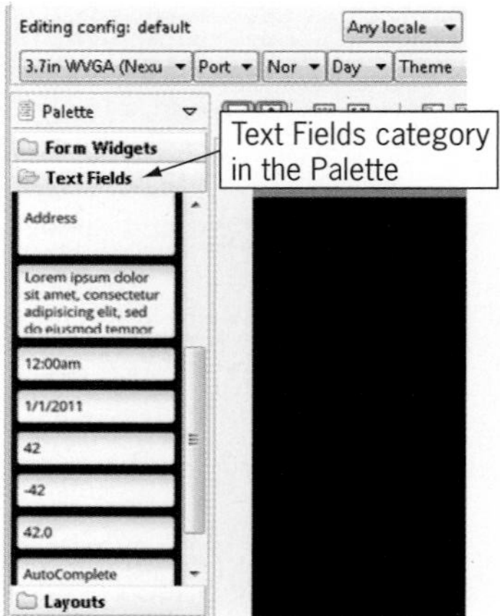

Figure 3-11 Text Fields category

A mobile application's Text Field controls can request different input types, such as free-form plain text; numbers; a person's name, password, e-mail address, and phone number; a date; and multiline text. You need to select the correct Text Field for the specific type of data you are requesting. As shown in Figure 3-12, each Text Field control allows you to enter a specific data type from the keyboard. For example, if you select the Phone Number Text Field, Android deactivates the letters on the keyboard because letters are not part of a phone number.

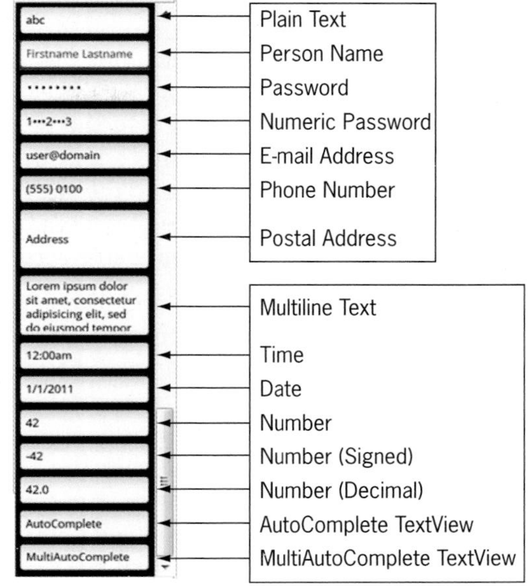

Figure 3-12 Types of Text Field controls

GTK

The AutoComplete TextView control can suggest the completion of a word after the user begins typing the first few letters. For example, if the input control is requesting the name of a city where the user wants to book a hotel, you could suggest the completed name from a coded listing of city names that match the prefix entered by the user.

In the chapter project, the Concert Tickets application requests the number of concert tickets. This quantity is an integer value because you cannot purchase part of a ticket. By selecting the Number Text Field, only positive integers can be entered from the keyboard. Letters and symbols from the keyboard are not accepted, which saves you time as the developer because you do not have to write lengthy data validation code. When the app opens in the emulator and you click the Number Text Field control, the soft keyboard opens, as shown in Figure 3-13.

Figure 3-13 Onscreen keyboard

IN THE TRENCHES

An application with appealing graphical design is preferred over applications that are textual in nature. Good graphic design communicates simplicity and engages the user.

Adding a Text Field

In the Concert Tickets application, a single screen opens when the application runs, requesting the number of concert tickets desired in a Number Text Field. To name a Text Field, use the Id property in the Properties pane to enter a name that begins with the prefix txt, which represents a text field in the code. The Id property of any widget is used in the Java code to refer to the widget. A descriptive variable name such as txtTickets can turn an unreadable piece of code into one that is well documented and easy to debug. To begin the design of the emulator screen and to add a Text Field, follow these steps:

1. With main.xml open and displaying the emulator screen, click the Form Widgets category in the Palette. Select the form widget named TextView. Drag and drop the TextView control onto the top part of the emulator user interface. To center the TextView control, drag the control to the center of the screen until a green dashed vertical line identifying the screen's center is displayed. To open the Properties pane, right-click the emulator window, point to Show In on the shortcut menu, and then select Properties. To view the properties of the TextView control, click the TextView control that you placed on the emulator. Scroll the Properties pane, and then click the Text property. Change the Text property to **Ticket Vault**. In the Properties pane, scroll to the Text size property, type **40sp**, and then press the Enter key.

   A TextView control is added to the emulator to represent the company name with the text Ticket Vault and size of 40sp (Figure 3-14).

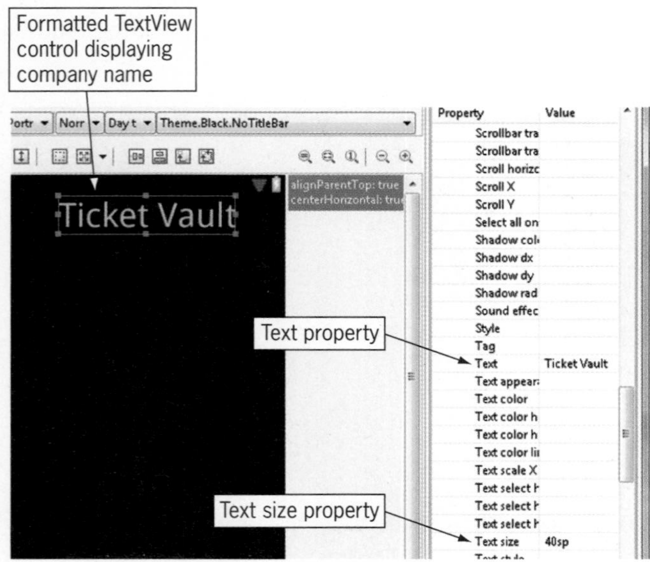

Figure 3-14 TextView control added and formatted

2. Click the Text Fields category in the Palette. Scroll down to the Number (example shows a 42) Text Field. Drag and drop the Number Text Field control onto the emulator's user interface below the Ticket Vault text. Drag the control to the center of the screen until a green dashed vertical line identifying the screen's center is displayed. Change the Id property of the Text Field to **@+id/txtTickets**. Set the Text size property to **25sp**.

   A Number Text Field control named txtTickets with the size of 25sp is added to the emulator to allow the user to enter the number of tickets (Figure 3-15).

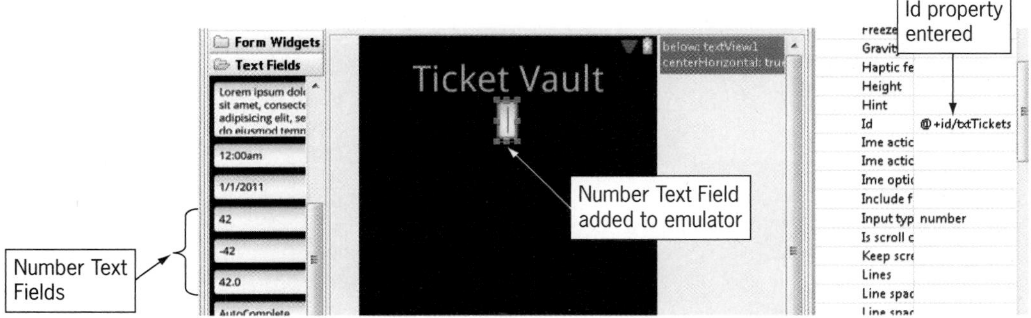

Figure 3-15 Number Text Field control

GTK

You might need to click controls in the emulator to select them before assigning properties.

IN THE TRENCHES

Iris, a popular Android app, provides a voice-recognition system for user input. Siri is a similar voice-recognition system on the iOS platform. "Iris," which is the reverse of "Siri," stands for "Intelligent Rival Imitator of Siri."

Setting the Hint Property for the Text Field

When the Concert Tickets program is executed, the user needs guidelines about the input expected in the Text Field control. These guidelines can be included in the Hint property of the Text Field control. A **hint** is a short description of a field that is visible as light-colored text (also called a watermark) inside a Text Field control. When the user clicks the control, the hint is removed and the user is free to type the requested input. The purpose of the hint in Figure 3-16

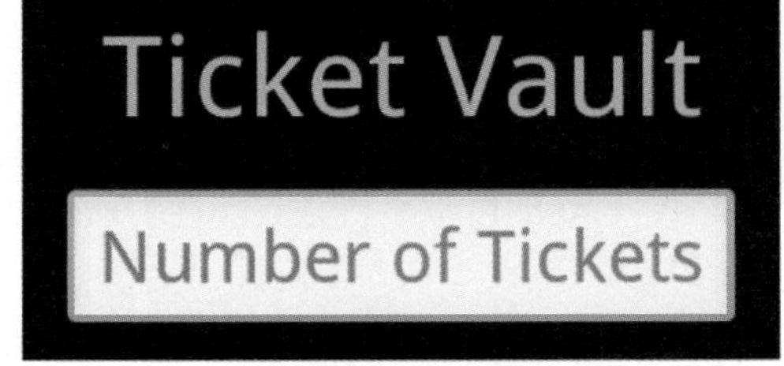

Figure 3-16 Hint in a Text Field control

is to request what is expected in this field, without the user having to select and delete default text.

To set the Hint property for the Text Field control, follow this step:

1. With the txtTickets Text Field control selected on the emulator screen, click the Hint property in the Properties pane and type **Number of Tickets**. Press the Enter key.

   A watermark hint indicates that the number of tickets is needed as input in the Text Field control (Figure 3-17).

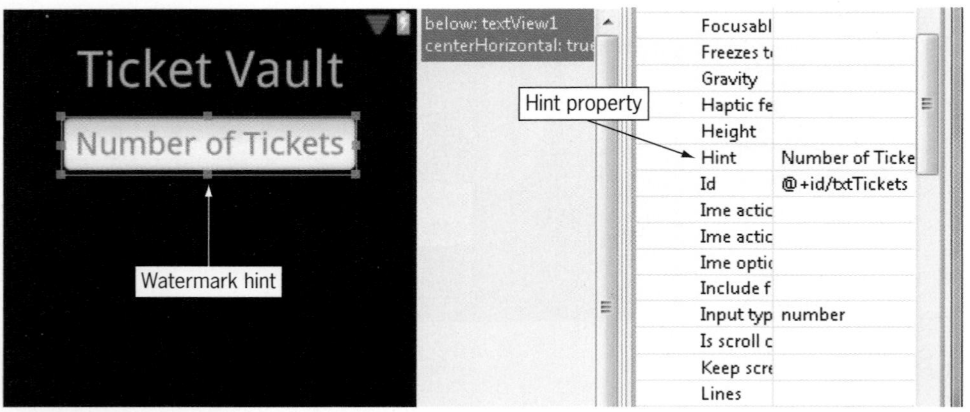

Figure 3-17 Hint added to Text Field control

Coding the EditText Class for the Text Field

To handle the input that the user enters into the numeric Text Field control in the chapter project, you use the EditText class, which extracts the text and converts it for use in the Java code. The extracted text must be assigned to a variable. A **variable** is used in a Java program to contain data that changes during the execution of the program. In the chapter project, a variable named tickets holds the text entered in the Text Field for the number of tickets. The following code syntax declares (or initializes) the variable named tickets, which contains the extracted EditText class text from the user's input. Notice the code syntax begins with the word **final**, indicating that tickets is a final variable. A final variable can only be initialized once and any attempt to reassign the value results in a compile error when the application is executed.

Code Syntax

```
final EditText tickets=(EditText) findViewById(R.id.txtTickets);
```

Recall that if you want to refer to a control in the Java code, you need to name the control when you add it to the interface using the Id property. For example, the Text Field control was assigned the id txtTickets. Now you can access the control in the code using the findViewById( ) method. In the parentheses, the R refers to resources available to the app, such as a layout control, the id indicates that the resource is identified by the Id property, and txtTickets is the assigned id.

Next, the txtTickets Text Field control should be assigned to the variable named tickets. To collect the ticket input from the user, code the EditText class for the Text Field by following these steps:

1. Close the Properties pane. In the Package Explorer, expand src and net.androidbootcamp.concerttickets, and then double-click Main.java to open the code window. Click to the right of the line setContentView(R.layout.*main*);. Press the Enter key to insert a blank line. To initialize and reference the EditText class with the Id name of txtTickets, type **final EditText tickets=(EditText) findViewById(R.id.txtTickets);**. Point to the red curly line under EditText and select Import 'EditText' (android widget) on the pop-up menu.

   The EditText class extracts the value from the user's input for the number of tickets and assigns the value to the variable named tickets (Figure 3-18).

main.xml | Main.java

```
package net.androidbootcamp.concerttickets;

import android.app.Activity;

public class Main extends Activity {
    /** Called when the activity is first created. */

    @Override
    public void onCreate(Bundle savedInstanceState) {
        super.onCreate(savedInstanceState);
        setContentView(R.layout.main);
        final EditText tickets =(EditText) findViewById(R.id.txtTickets);
    }
}
```

EditText code assigns input value in the txtTickets control to a variable named tickets

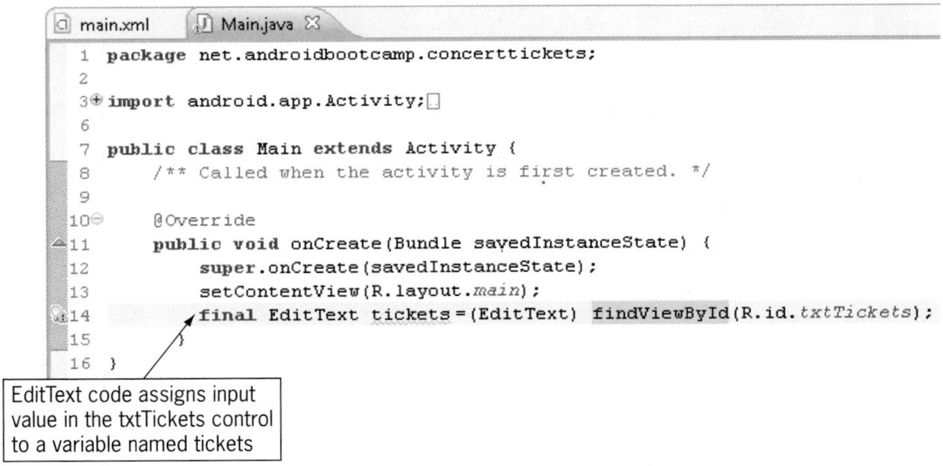

Figure 3-18 Coding the EditText class for the Text Field

2. Close the Main.java tab and save your work.

Android Spinner Control

After the user enters the number of tickets, the next step is to select which concert to attend. Three musical groups are performing next month: Dragonfly, Nine Volt, and Red Road. Due to possible user error on a small mobile keyboard, it is much easier for a user to use a Spinner control instead of actually typing in the group names. A **Spinner control** is a widget similar to a drop-down list for selecting a single item from a fixed listing, as shown in Figure 3-19. The Spinner control displays a prompt with a list of strings called **items** in a pop-up window without taking up multiple lines on the initial display. A **string** is a series of alphanumeric characters that can include spaces.

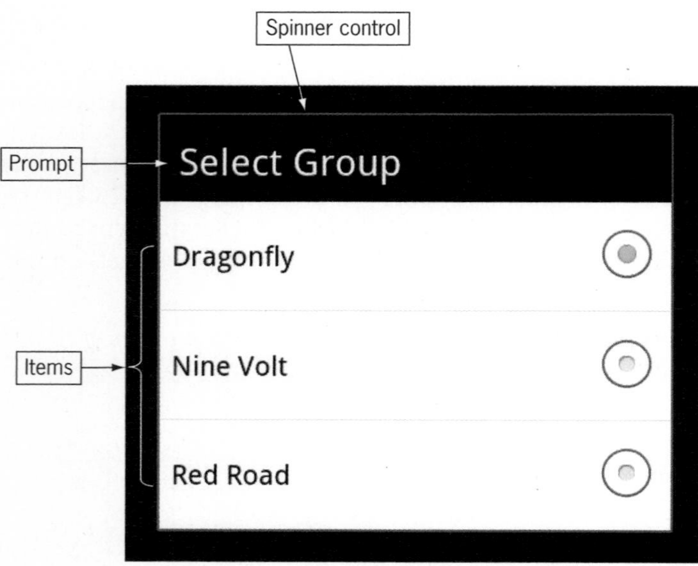

Figure 3-19 Spinner control and items

Using the String table

The string items that are displayed in the Spinner control cannot be typed directly in the Properties pane, but instead are created in a values string array in the res/values folder. A file named **strings.xml** is a default file that is part of every Android application and contains commonly used strings for an application. The String Array is part of the String table, which is best to use for text displayed in the application because it can easily be changed without changing code. Android loads text resources from the project's String table. The String table can also be used for localization. **Localization** is the use of the String table to change text based on the user's preferred language. For example, Android can select text in Spanish from the String table, based on the current device configuration and locale. The developer can add multiple translations in the String table.

In the Concert Tickets app, a String Array for the Spinner control is necessary to hold the three concert group names as individual string resources in the strings.xml resource file. The strings.xml file already has two default string variables named hello and app_name. The string resources file provides an easy way to update commonly used strings throughout your project, instead of searching through code and properties to alter string names within the application. For example, each month the concert planners can simply change the text in the strings.xml file to reflect their new concert events. A **prompt**, which can be used to display instructions at the top of the Spinner control, can also be stored in strings.xml. To add a String Array for the three musical groups and to add a prompt to display in the Spinner control, follow these steps:

1. Expand the values folder in the Package Explorer. Double-click strings.xml. Click the Add button in the Android Resources strings.xml tab.

   A dialog box opens to create a new element at the top level, in Resources (Figure 3-20).

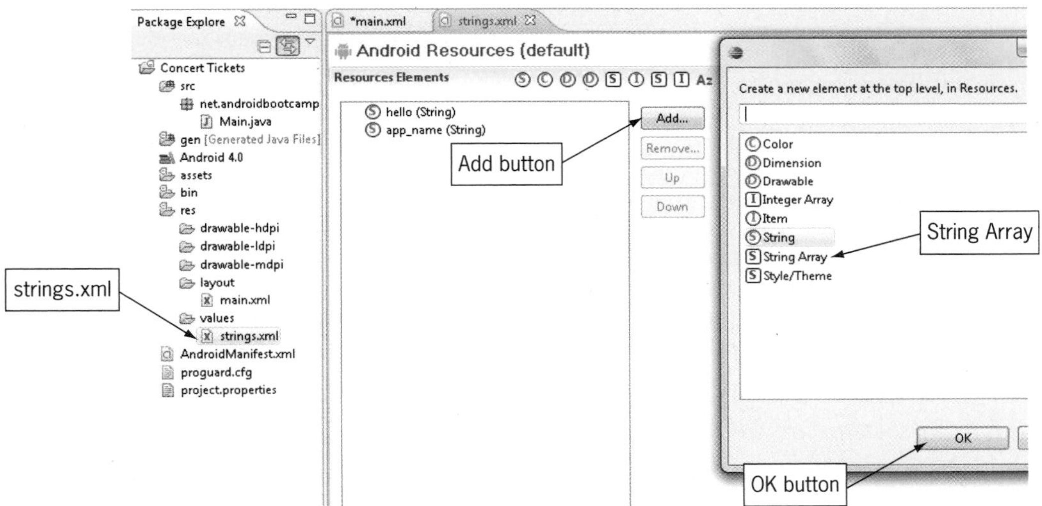

Figure 3-20 Adding a string resource

2. In the dialog box, select String Array and then click the OK button. Type **Groups** in the Name text box to name the String Array.

   The String Array is named Groups (Figure 3-21).

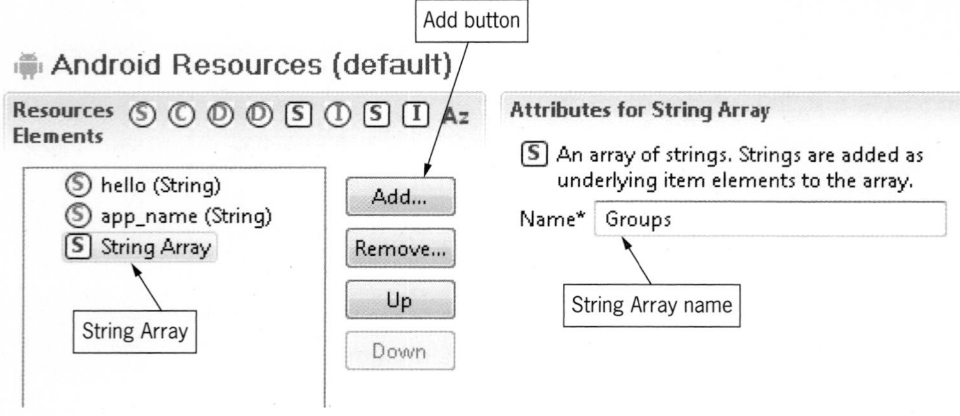

Figure 3-21 Naming the String Array

3. Click the Add button. Select Item, and then click the OK button. In the Value box, type **Dragonfly** as the name of the first item, and then click the Add button. Select Item, and then click the OK button. In the Value box, type **Nine Volt** as the name of the second item. Click the Add button again. Select Item, and then click the OK button. In the Value box, type **Red Road** as the name of the last item.

   Three items are added to the String Array named Groups (Figure 3-22).

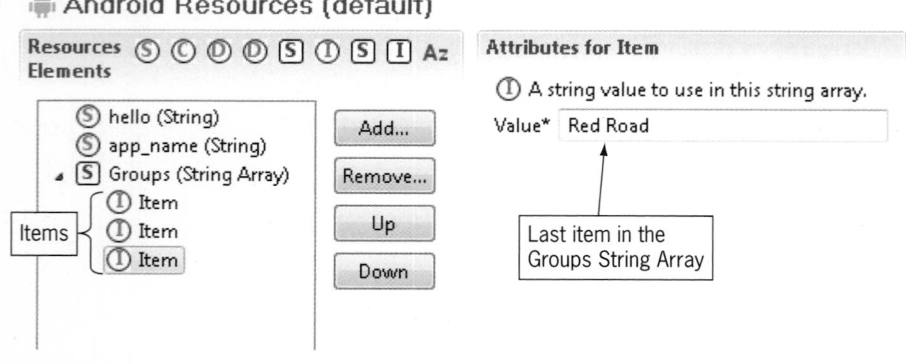

Figure 3-22 Adding items to the Groups String Array

4. To add a prompt represented as a String at the top of the Spinner, click the Add button. At the top of the dialog box, select the Create a new element at the top level, in Resources option button to create a new element at the top level, in Resources. Select String, and then click the OK button. In the Name box, type **Title**. In the Value box, type **Select Group**.

A String named Title is added to strings.xml that contains the text Select Group for the Spinner prompt (Figure 3-23).

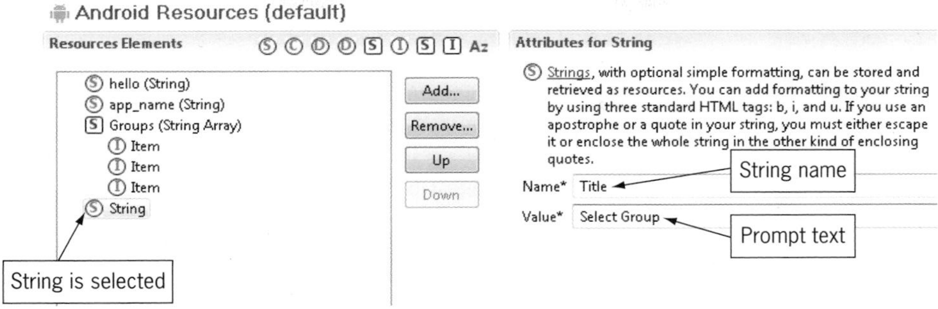

Figure 3-23 Adding a prompt

5. Close the strings.xml tab and save your work.

GTK

If your main.xml emulator window fails to update, try saving your project to update it. You can also refresh your Android project by clicking Project on the menu bar and then clicking Clean.

Adding a Spinner Control with String Array Entries

After entering the items in an array, the Spinner property called **Entries** connects the String Array to the Spinner control for display in the application. The Spinner control is located in the Form Widgets category. The following steps add the Spinner control to the Android application:

1. With the main.xml tab open, click the Form Widgets category in the Palette. Drag and drop the Spinner control below the Text Field and center it horizontally. Change the Id property of the Spinner control to **@+id/txtGroup**.

   The Spinner control is added to the emulator window and named txtGroup (Figure 3-24).

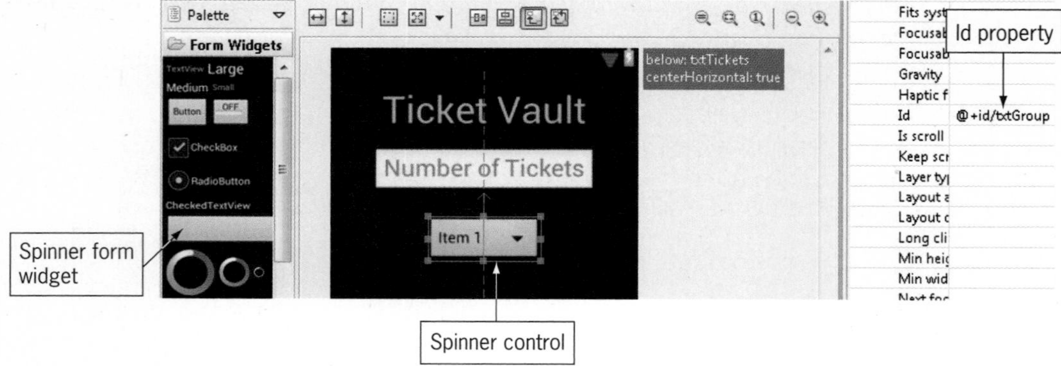

Figure 3-24 Spinner control

2. Click File on the menu bar and then click Save All to update all resources. In the Properties pane, click the Prompt property, and then click the ellipsis (...) button. In the Reference Chooser dialog box, click the expand arrow for String. Select Title and click the OK button. To display the String Array, click to the right of the Entries property. Click the ellipsis button. In the Reference Chooser dialog box, click the expand arrow for Array. Select Groups and click the OK button.

   The Prompt property connects to the resource named @string/Title. The Entries property connects to the resources of the String Array @array/Groups. The actual groups are displayed when the app is executed in the emulator (Figure 3-25).

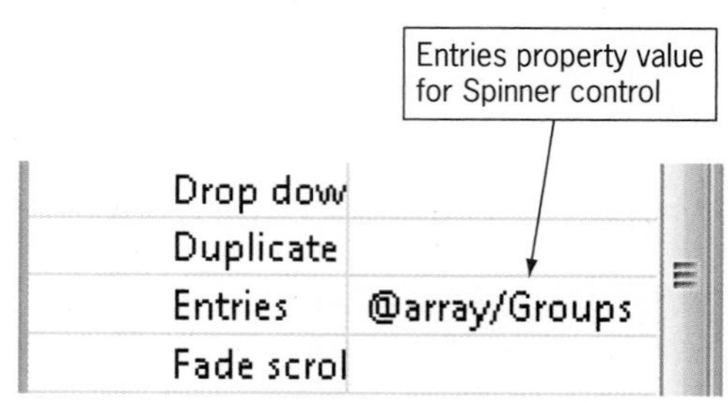

Figure 3-25 Entries property for the Spinner control

Coding the Spinner Control

The user's selection of the concert group must be assigned to a variable and stored in the computer's memory. For this application, the selection made from the Spinner control (txtGroup) is assigned to a variable named group using the following code:

Code Syntax

```
final Spinner group = (Spinner) findViewById(R.id.txtGroup);
```

To collect the input from the user's group selection, code the Spinner control by following these steps:

1. Close the Properties pane. In the Package Explorer, double-click Main.java. After the EditText line, press the Enter key to create a new line. To initialize and reference the Spinner control with the Id name of txtGroup, type **final Spinner group = (Spinner) findViewById(R.id.txtGroup);**. Point to the red curly line under Spinner and select Import 'Spinner' (android widget) on the pop-up menu.

   The Spinner control assigns the value from the user's input to the variable named group. Notice variables that have not been used in the program have a curly underline. This underline is removed when a value is assigned later in the program (Figure 3-26).

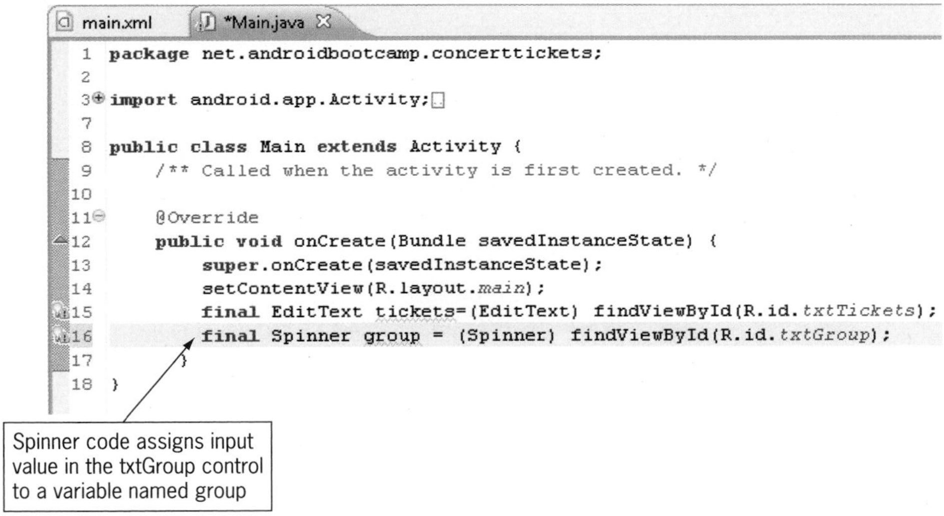

main.xml | *Main.java

```
package net.androidbootcamp.concerttickets;

import android.app.Activity;

public class Main extends Activity {
    /** Called when the activity is first created. */

    @Override
    public void onCreate(Bundle savedInstanceState) {
        super.onCreate(savedInstanceState);
        setContentView(R.layout.main);
        final EditText tickets=(EditText) findViewById(R.id.txtTickets);
        final Spinner group = (Spinner) findViewById(R.id.txtGroup);
    }
}
```

Spinner code assigns input value in the txtGroup control to a variable named group

Figure 3-26 Coding the Spinner control

2. Close the Main.java tab and save your work.

Adding the Button, TextView, and ImageView Controls

After the user inputs the number of tickets and the concert group name, the user taps the Find Ticket Cost button to calculate the cost in a Button event. After the total cost is calculated by multiplying the number of tickets by the cost of each ticket ($59.99), the name of the group and total cost of the tickets are displayed in a TextView control. The TextView control is assigned to the variable named result using the following code:

Code Syntax

```
final TextView result = ((TextView) findViewById (R.id.txtResult));
```

You need an image file named concert.png, provided with your student files, to display in an ImageView control for the Concert Tickets app. You should already have the student files for this text that your instructor gave you or that you downloaded from the Web page for this book (*www.cengagebrain.com*). To add the Button, TextView, and ImageView controls to the emulator window, follow these steps:

1. In the main.xml tab, drag the Button control from the Form Widgets category in the Palette to the emulator and center it below the Spinner control. Release the mouse button. Open the Properties pane, click the new Button control, and then change its Id property to **@+id/btnCost**. Scroll to the Text property, and then change the text to **Find Ticket Cost**. Change the Text size property to **25sp**. Save your work.

   The Button control named btnCost displays the text Find Ticket Cost and the size is changed to 25sp (Figure 3-27).

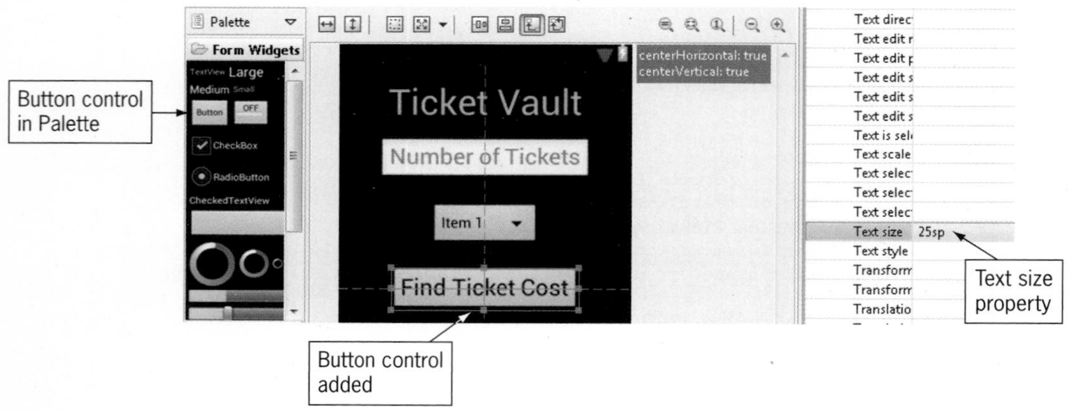

Figure 3-27 Adding a Button control

2. To code the button, open the Main.java file from the Package Explorer. Click to the right of the code line that assigned the Spinner control to the variable named group. Press the Enter key. To initialize the Button control with the Id name of btnCost, type **Button cost = (Button) findViewById(R.id.btnCost);**. Point to Button and import the Button type as an Android widget. Press the Enter key. To code the button listener that awaits user interaction, type **cost.setOn** and wait as a code listing opens. Double-click the first setOnClickListener displayed in the auto-complete listing. Inside the parentheses, type **new on** and press Ctrl+spacebar to display an auto-complete listing. Double-click the first choice, which lists an OnClickListener with an Anonymous Inner Type event handler. Point to OnClickListener and import 'OnClickListener' (android.view.View). Place a semicolon at the end of the auto-generated stub closing brace and parenthesis.

   The Button control is initialized and an OnClickListener auto-generated stub appears in the code window (Figure 3-28).

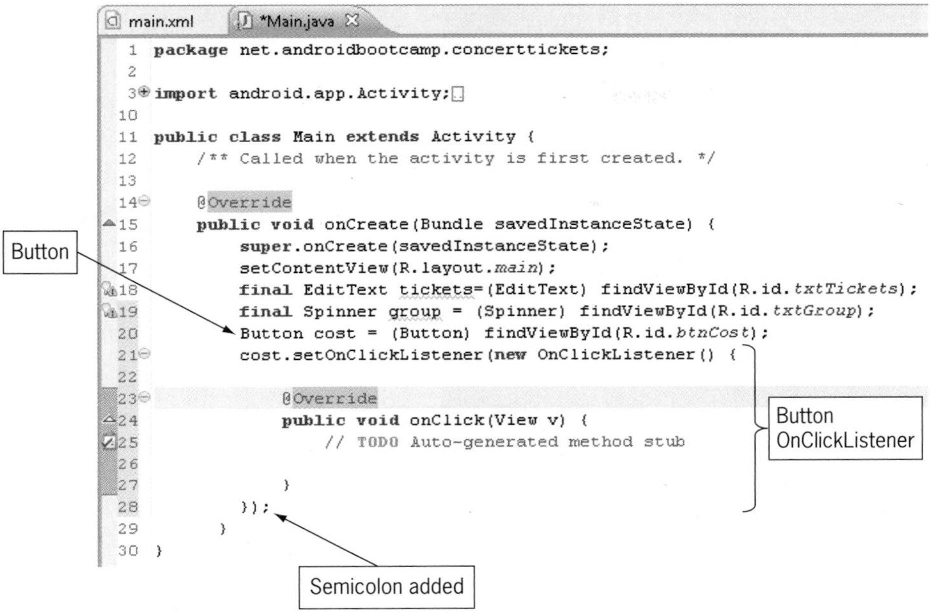

main.xml *Main.java

```
package net.androidbootcamp.concerttickets;

import android.app.Activity;

public class Main extends Activity {
    /** Called when the activity is first created. */

    @Override
    public void onCreate(Bundle savedInstanceState) {
        super.onCreate(savedInstanceState);
        setContentView(R.layout.main);
        final EditText tickets=(EditText) findViewById(R.id.txtTickets);
        final Spinner group = (Spinner) findViewById(R.id.txtGroup);
        Button cost = (Button) findViewById(R.id.btnCost);
        cost.setOnClickListener(new OnClickListener() {

            @Override
            public void onClick(View v) {
                // TODO Auto-generated method stub

            }
        });
    }
}
```

Button

Button OnClickListener

Semicolon added

Figure 3-28 Coding the button

3. To add a TextView control to display the final cost of the tickets, click the main.xml tab. From the Form Widgets category in the Palette, drag the TextView control to the emulator and center it below the Button control. Release the mouse button. In the Properties pane, change the Id property of the TextView control to **@+id/txtResult**. Change the Text size property to **20sp**. Click to the right of the Text property and delete the text.

   The txtResult TextView control is added to the emulator window (Figure 3-29).

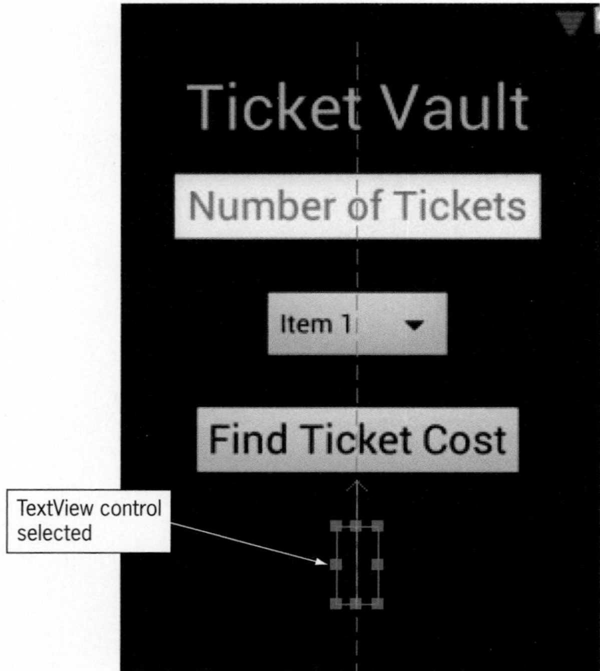

Figure 3-29 Adding a TextView control to display results

4. To code the TextView control, save your work and then click the Main.java tab. After the line of code referring to the Button cost, type **final TextView result = ((TextView) findViewById (R.id.txtResult));**. Import the 'TextView' (android.widget).

   The TextView control txtResult is assigned to the variable named result (Figure 3-30).

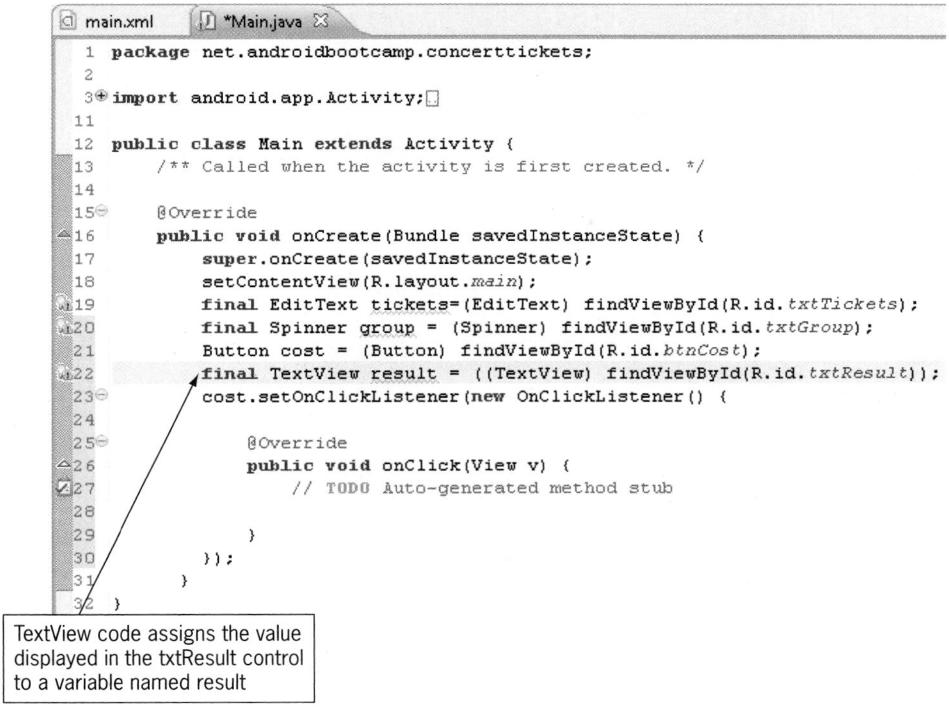

main.xml *Main.java

```
package net.androidbootcamp.concerttickets;

import android.app.Activity;

public class Main extends Activity {
    /** Called when the activity is first created. */

    @Override
    public void onCreate(Bundle savedInstanceState) {
        super.onCreate(savedInstanceState);
        setContentView(R.layout.main);
        final EditText tickets=(EditText) findViewById(R.id.txtTickets);
        final Spinner group = (Spinner) findViewById(R.id.txtGroup);
        Button cost = (Button) findViewById(R.id.btnCost);
        final TextView result = ((TextView) findViewById(R.id.txtResult));
        cost.setOnClickListener(new OnClickListener() {

            @Override
            public void onClick(View v) {
                // TODO Auto-generated method stub

            }
        });
    }
}
```

TextView code assigns the value displayed in the txtResult control to a variable named result

Figure 3-30 Assigning the TextView control to a variable

5. To add the ImageView control, first copy the student files to your USB drive (if necessary). Open the USB folder containing the student files. In the Package Explorer, expand the drawable-hdpi folder. Drag the concert.png file to the drawable-hdpi folder until a plus sign pointer appears. Release the mouse button. Click the OK button in the File Operation dialog box. In the main.xml tab, click the Images & Media category in the Palette. Drag the ImageView control to the emulator and center it below the TextView control at the bottom of the emulator window. Click concert in the Resource Chooser dialog box, and then click the OK button. With the image selected, click to the right of the Layout margin bottom property in the Properties pane and type **0dp**. Click a blank area on the emulator to deselect the image.

   The concert image is displayed at the bottom of the emulator window (Figure 3-31).

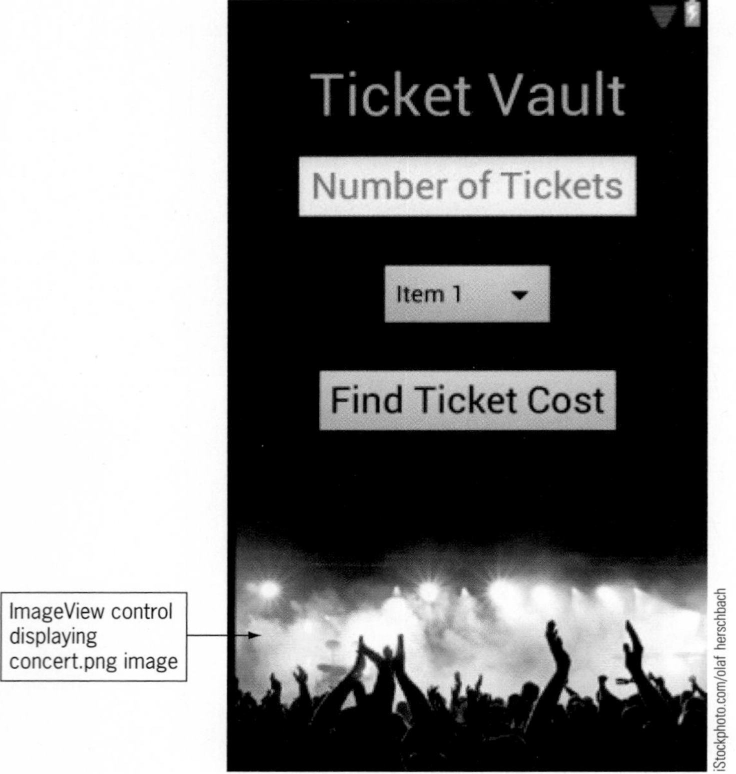

Figure 3-31 Adding an ImageView control

GTK

Variable names are case sensitive and should be mixed case (camel case) when they include more than one word, as in costPerItem. Java variables cannot start with a number or special symbol. Subsequent characters in the variable name may be letters, digits, dollar signs, or underscore characters.

Declaring Variables

As you have seen, the user can enter data in the program through the use of a Text Field control. In the Concert Tickets app, a mathematical equation multiplying the number of tickets and the cost of the tickets is calculated to find the total cost. When writing programs, it is convenient to use variables instead of the actual data such as the cost of a ticket ($59.99). Two steps are necessary in order to use a variable:

1. Declare the variable.
2. Assign a value to the variable.

The declared type of a value determines which operations are allowed. At the core of Java code are eight built-in primitive (simple) types of data.

Primitive Data Types

Java requires all variables to have a data type. Table 3-1 displays the primitive data types that are supported across all computer platforms, including the Android SDK.

Type	Meaning	Range	Default Value
byte	Often used with arrays	–128 to 127	0
short	Often used with arrays	–32,768 to 32,767	0
int	Most commonly used number value	–2,147,483,648 to 2,147,483,647	0
long	Used for numbers that exceed int	–9,223,372,036,854,775,808 to 9,223,372,036,854,775,807	0
float	A single precision 32-bit floating-point number	+/–3.40282347^38	0
double	Most common for decimal values	+/–1.79769313486231570^308	0
char	Single character	Characters	0
boolean	Used for conditional statement	True or false	False

Table 3-1 Primitive data types in Java

In the Concert Tickets program, the tickets cost $59.99 each. This cost is best declared as a double data type, which is appropriate for decimal values. The variable costPerTicket both declares the variable and assigns a value, as shown in the following code syntax. The requested quantity of tickets is assigned to a variable named numberOfTickets, which represents an integer. To multiply two values, the values must be stored in one of the numeric data types. When the total cost of the tickets is computed, the value is assigned to a variable named totalCost, also a double data type, as shown in the following code:

Code Syntax

```
double costPerTicket=59.99;
int numberOfTickets;
double totalCost;
```

String Data Type

In addition to the primitive data types, Java has another data type for working with strings of text. The String type is a class and not a primitive data type. Most strings that you use in the Java language are an object of type String. A string can be a character, word, or phrase. If you assign a phrase to a String variable, place the phrase between double quotation marks. In the Concert Tickets app, after the user selects a musical group from the Spinner control, that group is assigned to a String type variable named groupChoice, as shown in the following code:

Code Syntax

```
String groupChoice;
```

GTK

When defining variables, good programming practice dictates that the variable names you use should reflect the actual values to be placed in the variable. That way, anyone reading the program code can easily understand the use of the variable.

Declaring the Variables

Variables in an Android application are typically declared at the beginning of an Activity. A variable must first be declared before the variable can be used in the application. To initialize, or declare, the variables, follow this step:

1. In Main.java, below the comment /** Called when the activity is first created */, insert the following four lines of code to initialize the variables in this Activity:

   double costPerTicket=59.99;

   int numberOfTickets;

   double totalCost;

   String groupChoice;

   The variables are declared at the beginning of the Activity (Figure 3-32).

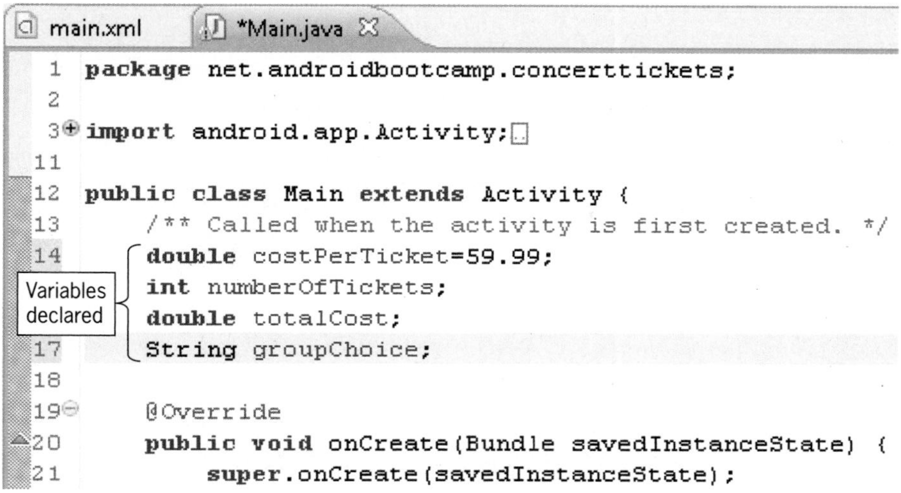

main.xml *Main.java

```
package net.androidbootcamp.concerttickets;

import android.app.Activity;

public class Main extends Activity {
    /** Called when the activity is first created. */
    double costPerTicket=59.99;
    int numberOfTickets;
    double totalCost;
    String groupChoice;

    @Override
    public void onCreate(Bundle savedInstanceState) {
        super.onCreate(savedInstanceState);
```

Variables declared

Figure 3-32 Declaring variables for the Activity

GetText( ) Method

At this point in the application development, all the controls have been assigned variables to hold their values. The next step is to convert the values in the assigned variables to the correct data type for calculation purposes. After the user enters the number of tickets and the concert group name, the Find Ticket Cost button is clicked. Inside the OnClickListener code for the button control, the text stored in the EditText control named tickets can be read with the **GetText( )** method. By default, the text in the EditText control is read as a String type. A String type cannot be used in a mathematical function. To convert a string into a numerical data type, a **Parse** class is needed to convert strings to a number data type. Table 3-2 displays the Parse types that convert a string to a common numerical data type.

Numerical Data Type	Parse Types
Integer	Integer.parseInt( )
Float	Float.parseFloat( )
Double	Double.parseDouble( )
Long	Long.parseLong( )

Table 3-2 Parse type conversions

To extract the string of text typed into the EditText control and convert the string representing the number of tickets to an integer data type, the following syntax is necessary:

Code Syntax

```
numberOfTickets = Integer.parseInt(tickets.getText().toString());
```

To code the GetText( ) method and convert the value in the tickets variable into an integer data type named numberOfTickets, follow this step:

1. In Main.java, inside the OnClickListener onClick method stub, type **numberOfTickets = Integer.parseInt(tickets.getText().toString());**.

   The GetText( ) method extracts the text from tickets, converts the string to an integer, and assigns the value to numberOfTickets (Figure 3-33).

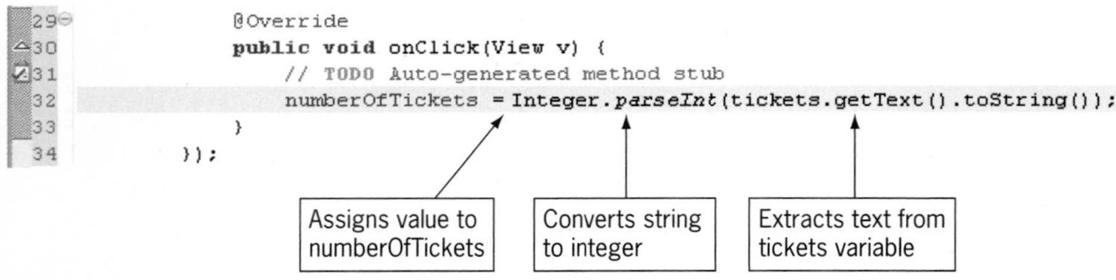
@Override
public void onClick(View v) {
// TODO Auto-generated method stub
numberOfTickets = Integer.parseInt(tickets.getText().toString());
}
});
Assigns value to numberOfTickets
Converts string to integer
Extracts text from tickets variable

Figure 3-33 Converting a string to an integer

Working with Mathematical Operations

The ability to perform arithmetic operations on numeric data is fundamental to many applications. Many programs require arithmetic operations to add, subtract, multiply, and divide numeric data. For example, in the Concert Tickets app in this chapter, the cost of each ticket must be multiplied by the number of tickets in order to calculate the total cost of the concert tickets.

Arithmetic Operators

Table 3-3 shows a listing of the Java arithmetic operators, along with their use and an example of an arithmetic expression showing their use.

Arithmetic Operator	Use	Assignment Statement
+	Addition	value = itemPrice + itemTax;
–	Subtraction	score = previousScore – 2;
*	Multiplication	totalCost = costPerTicket * numberOfTickets;
/	Division	average = totalGrade / 5.0;
%	Remainder	leftover = widgetAmount % 3; If widgetAmount = 11 the remainder = 2
++	Increment (adds 1)	golfScore ++
--	Decrement (subtracts 1)	points --

Table 3-3 Java arithmetic operators

When multiple operations are included in a single assignment statement, the sequence of performing the calculations is determined by the rules shown in Table 3-4, which is called the order of operations.

Order of Operations Highest to Lowest Precedence	Description
( )	Parentheses
++ --	Left to right
* / %	Left to right
+ –	Left to right

Table 3-4 Order of operations

For example, the result of 2 + 3 * 4 is 14 because the multiplication is of higher precedence than the addition operation.

Formatting Numbers

After the total ticket cost is computed, the result is displayed in currency format, which includes a dollar sign and commas if needed in larger values, and rounds off to two places past the decimal point. Java includes a class called **DecimalFormat** that provides patterns for formatting numbers for output on the Android device. For example, the pattern "$###,###.##" establishes that a number begins with a dollar sign character, displays a comma if the number has more than three digits, and rounds off to the nearest penny. If the pattern "###.#%" is used, the number is multiplied by 100 and rounded to the first digit past the decimal. To establish a currency decimal format for the result of the ticket cost, the following code syntax is assigned to currency and later applied to the variable totalCost to display a currency value:

Code Syntax

```
DecimalFormat currency = new DecimalFormat("$###,###.##");
```


To code the calculation computing the cost of the tickets and to create a currency decimal format, follow this step:

1. In Main.java, after the last line entered, insert a new line, type **totalCost = costPerTicket * numberOfTickets;** and then press Enter. To establish a currency format, type **DecimalFormat currency = new DecimalFormat("$###,###.##");**. Import the 'DecimalFormat' (java.text) class.

   The equation computes the total cost of the tickets and DecimalFormat creates a currency format that is used when the total cost is displayed (Figure 3-34).

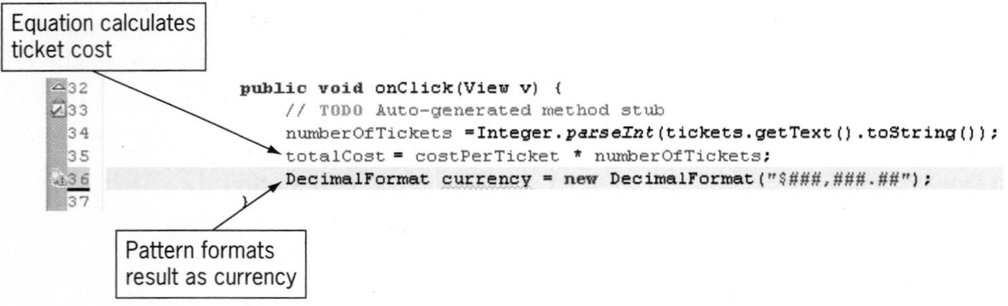

Equation calculates ticket cost
public void onClick(View v) {
// TODO Auto-generated method stub
numberOfTickets =Integer.parseInt(tickets.getText().toString());
totalCost = costPerTicket * numberOfTickets;
DecimalFormat currency = new DecimalFormat("$###,###.##");
}
Pattern formats result as currency

Figure 3-34 Calculating and formatting the ticket cost

Displaying Android Output

In Java, computing the results does not mean displaying the results. To display the results that include the name of the group and the final cost of the tickets, first the name of the group must be assigned to a String variable.

GetSelectedItem( ) Method

To obtain the text name of the concert group that was selected by the user in the Spinner control, you use a method named GetSelectedItem( ). The **GetSelectedItem( )** method returns the text label of the currently selected Spinner item. For example, if the user selects Nine Volt, the GetSelectedItem( ) method assigns this group to a String variable named groupChoice that was declared at the beginning of the Activity, as shown in the following code:

Code Syntax

```
groupChoice = group.getSelectedItem().toString();
```

GTK

A method named GetSelectedIndex( ) can be used with a Spinner control to determine if the user selected the first, second, or subsequent choice. For example, if GetSelectedIndex( ) is equal to the integer 0, the user selected the first choice.

SetText( ) Method

Earlier in the Android project, the method GetText( ) extracted the text from the Text Field control. In an opposite manner, the method SetText( ) displays text in a TextView control. SetText( ) accepts a string of data for display. To join variable names and text, you can concatenate the string text with a plus sign (+). In the following example, the variable completeSentence is assigned *Android is the best phone platform.* This sentence is displayed in a TextView object named result.

Example:

```
String mobile = "Android";
String completeSentence = mobile + " is the best phone platform";
result.setText(completeSentence);
```

The syntax for the SetText( ) method is shown in the following code. In this example, the result is displayed in the result TextView control and includes the string that uses the concatenating operator, the plus sign connecting variables to the string text.

Code Syntax

```
result.setText("Total Cost for " + groupChoice + " is " +
currency.format(totalCost));
```

The currency.format portion of the code displays the variable totalCost with a dollar sign and rounds off to the nearest penny. The output for result is displayed in Figure 3-2: Total Cost for Nine Volt is $239.96. To code the GetSelectedItem( ) method and the SetText( ) method, follow these steps to complete the application:

1. In Main.java after the last line of code entered, insert a new line and type **groupChoice = group.getSelectedItem().toString();** to assign the concert group to the String variable groupChoice. On the next line, type **result.setText("Total Cost for " + groupChoice + " is " + currency.format(totalCost));** to display the output.

   The getSelectedItem( ) method identifies the selected group and setText( ) displays the selected group with the total cost of the tickets (Figure 3-35).

main.xml Main.java

```
package net.androidbootcamp.concerttickets;

import java.text.DecimalFormat;

public class Main extends Activity {
    /** Called when the activity is first created. */
    double costPerTicket=59.99;
    int numberOfTickets;
    double totalCost;
    String groupChoice;

    @Override
    public void onCreate(Bundle savedInstanceState) {
        super.onCreate(savedInstanceState);
        setContentView(R.layout.main);
        final EditText tickets =(EditText) findViewById(R.id.txtTickets);
        final Spinner group = (Spinner) findViewById(R.id.txtGroup);

        Button cost = (Button) findViewById(R.id.btnCost);
        final TextView result = ((TextView) findViewById (R.id.txtResult));
        cost.setOnClickListener(new OnClickListener() {

            @Override
            public void onClick(View v) {
                // TODO Auto-generated method stub
                numberOfTickets = Integer.parseInt(tickets.getText().toString());
                totalCost= costPerTicket * numberOfTickets;
                DecimalFormat currency = new DecimalFormat("$###,###.##");
                groupChoice = group.getSelectedItem().toString();
                result.setText("Total Cost for " + groupChoice + " is " + currency.format(totalCost));
            }
        });
    }
}
```

Figure 3-35 Completed code

2. To view the finished application, click Run on the menu bar, and select Run to save and test the application in the emulator. A dialog box opens the first time the application is executed to request how to run the application. Select Android Application and click the OK button. Save all the files in the next dialog box and unlock the emulator. When the application opens in the emulator, enter the number of tickets and select a group from the Spinner control. To view the results, click the Find Ticket Cost button.

   The Concert Tickets Android app is executed (Figures 3-1 and 3-2).

Wrap It Up—Chapter Summary

In this chapter, you have learned to declare variables and write arithmetic operations. New controls such as the Text Field to enter text and the Spinner control to select from multiple items were used in the chapter project. GetText( ) and SetText( ) methods were used to extract and display data, respectively. An Android theme was also applied to the application.

- You can assign a theme to an Activity or entire application to define its appearance and style and to prevent each Android app you develop from looking too similar.
- Preview a theme by clicking the Theme button in the emulator window and then selecting a theme. To permanently change the theme in the application, define the theme in the Android Manifest file for each Activity.
- Use Text Fields to request input from users, who can enter characters using an onscreen keyboard or a physical keyboard. You need to select the correct type of Text Field control for the type of data you are requesting.
- To provide guidelines so users enter the correct data in a Text Field control, use the control's Hint property to display light-colored text describing what to enter. The user clicks the control to remove the hint and type the requested input.
- To handle the input that users enter into a Text Field control, you use the EditText class, which extracts the text and converts it for use in the Java code. The extracted text must be assigned to a variable, which holds data that changes during the execution of the program. To extract the string of text entered in an EditText control, use the GetText( ) method. To display the extracted text in a TextView control, use the SetText( ) method.
- The strings.xml file is part of every Android application by default and contains strings used in the application, such as text displayed in a Spinner control. You can edit a string in strings.xml to update the text wherever it is used in the application. In strings.xml, you can also include prompt text that provides instructions in a Spinner control. In the Java code, use the GetSelectedItem( ) method to return the text of the selected Spinner item.
- To use a variable, you must first declare the variable and then assign a value to it. The declared type of a value determines which mathematical operations are allowed. Variables in an Android application are typically declared at the beginning of an Activity.
- After assigning variables to hold the values entered in controls, you often need to convert the values in the assigned variables to the correct data type so the values can be used in calculations. To use string data in a mathematical function, you use the Parse class to convert the string into a numerical data type.

Key Terms

DecimalFormat—A class that provides patterns for formatting numbers in program output.

Entries—A Spinner property that connects a string array to the Spinner control for display.

final—A type of variable that can only be initialized once; any attempt to reassign the value results in a compile error when the application is executed.

GetSelectedItem( )—A method that returns the text of the selected Spinner item.

GetText( )—A method that reads text stored in an EditText control.

hint—A short description of a field that appears as light text in a Text Field control.

item—In a Spinner control, a string of text that appears in a list for user selection.

localization—The use of the String table to change text based on the user's preferred language.

Parse—A class that converts a string into a number data type.

prompt—Text that displays instructions at the top of the Spinner control.

soft keyboard—An onscreen keyboard positioned over the lower part of an application's window.

Spinner control—A widget similar to a drop-down list for selecting a single item from a fixed listing.

string—A series of alphanumeric characters that can include spaces.

strings.xml—A default file that is part of every Android application and holds commonly used strings in an application.

theme—A style applied to an Activity or an entire application.

variable—A name used in a Java program to contain data that changes during the execution of the program.

Developer FAQs

1. What is an Android theme?
2. Which theme was used in the chapter project?
3. In an app, suppose you want to use the theme named Theme.Translucent. What code is needed in the AndroidManifest.xml file to support this theme?
4. What is a soft keyboard? Be sure to include its location in your answer.
5. Which five controls were used in the chapter project?
6. Which Text Field control is best for entering an amount that contains a paycheck amount?
7. Which property of the Spinner control adds text at the top of the control such as instructions?
8. What is the name of the file that holds commonly used phrases (arrays) of text in an application?
9. What is a single string of information called in a string array?
10. Which property do you assign to the string array that you create for a Spinner?
11. Write the following variable in camel case: NUMBEROFCOMPUTERJOBS.

12. Write a declaration statement for each of the following variables using the variable type and variable name that would be best for each value. Assign values if directed.
    a. The population of the state of Alaska
    b. Your weekly pay using the most common type for this type number
    c. The smallest data type you can use for your age
    d. Assign the first initial of your first name
    e. Assign the present minimum wage using the most common type for this type of number
    f. Assign the name of the city in which you live
    g. The answer to a true/false question
13. Name two numeric data types that can contain a decimal point.
14. What is the solution to each of the following arithmetic expressions?
    a. 3 + 4 * 2 + 6
    b. 16 / 2 * 4 - 3
    c. 40 - (6 + 2) / 2
    d. 3 + 68 % 9
15. Write a GetText( ) statement that converts a variable named deficit to a double data type and assigns the value to the variable named financeDeficit.
16. Assign the text of the user's choice of a Spinner control named collegeName to the variable named topCollege.
17. If a variable named amount is assigned to the value 47199.266, what would these statements display in the variable called price?

```
DecimalFormat money = new DecimalFormat("$###,###.##");
price.setText("Salary = " + money.format(amount));
```

18. Write a line of Java code that assigns the variable jellyBeans to a decimal format with six digits and a comma if needed, but no dollar sign or decimal places.
19. Write a line of Java code to use concatenation to join the phrase "Welcome to the ", versionNumber (an int variable), and the phrase "th version" to the variable combineStatement.
20. Write a line of Java code that assigns a number to the variable numberChoice, which indicates the user's selection. If the user selects the first group, the number 0 is assigned; if the user selects the second group, the number 1 is assigned; and if the user selects the third group, the number 2 is assigned with the same variables used in the chapter project.

Beyond the Book

Using the Internet, search the Web for the answers to the following questions to further your Android knowledge.

1. Name 10 themes used in your Android SDK not mentioned in this chapter.
2. Search the Internet for three real Android apps that sell any type of tickets. Name five features of each of the three apps.
3. A good Android developer always keeps up with the present market. Open the page *https://market.android.com*. Find this week's featured tablet apps and write about the top five. Write a paragraph on the purpose and cost of each for a total of five paragraphs.
4. Open the search engine Bing.com and then click the News tab. Search for an article about Androids with this week's date. Insert the URL link at the top of a new document. Write a 150–200–word summary of the article in your own words.

Case Programming Projects

Complete one or more of the following case programming projects. Use the same steps and techniques taught within the chapter. Submit the program you create to your instructor. The level of difficulty is indicated for each case programming project.

Easiest: ★

Intermediate: ★★

Challenging: ★★★

Case Project 3–1: Study Abroad App ★

Requirements Document

Application title: Study Abroad App

Purpose: Your school is offering a summer study abroad program. A simple app determines how many tickets are needed for a group and lets a user select the location lets a user study abroad. The app displays the location and the total price for the group's airfare.

Algorithms:

1. The app displays a title; an image; and a Text Field, Spinner, and Button control (Figure 3-36). The three cities in the Spinner control include Rome, Dublin, and Tokyo. Each round trip plane fare is $1,288.00 per person.
2. When the user clicks the Button control, the location and the cost of the group airfare are displayed for the flight in a TextView control (Figure 3-37).

Conditions: Use a theme, Spinner prompt, string array, and Hint property.

Figure 3-36

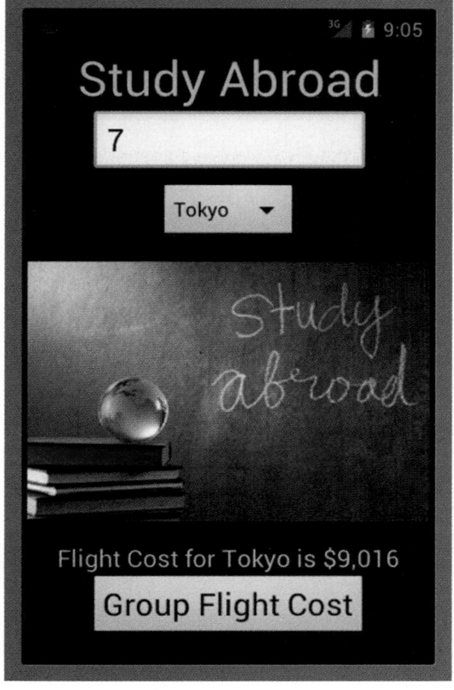

Figure 3-37

Case Project 3–2: Tuition App ★

Requirements Document

Application title: Tuition App

Purpose: A college tuition app allows a student to compute the tuition for a semester.

Algorithms:

1. The college tuition app has two Text Fields: One requests the cost of each credit, and the other requests the number of credits a student intends to take during the semester. A Spinner control allows the student to select one of the three possible semesters: Fall, Spring, and Summer. The app also displays a title, an image, and a Button control (Figure 3-38).
2. After the user clicks the Button control, the selected semester and the total cost of tuition with an added student technology fee of $125.00 are displayed in a TextView control (Figure 3-39).

Conditions: Use a theme, a title, an image, a Spinner prompt, a string array, and a Hint property.

Figure 3-38

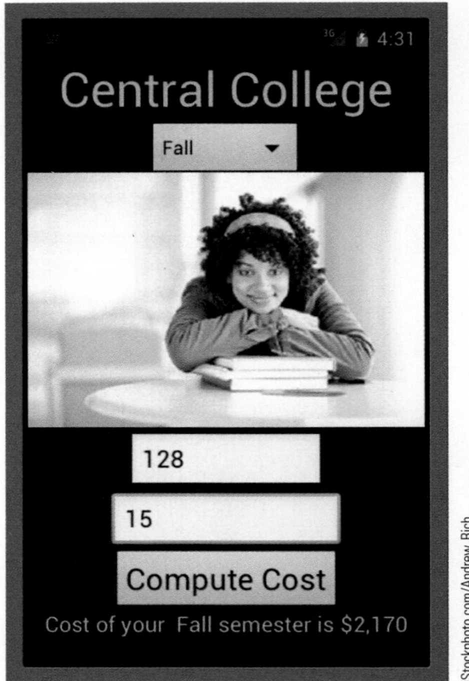

Figure 3-39

Case Project 3–3: New York City Cab Fare App ★★

Requirements Document

Application title: NYC Cab Fare App

Purpose: Create an app that estimates the cost for cab fare in New York City. The app calculates the cost of the trip and requests a reservation for a smart car, traditional sedan, or minivan.

Algorithms:

1. The app requests the distance in miles for the cab ride and your preference for the requested cab: a smart car, traditional sedan, or minivan. The cab company has an initial rate of $3.00. The mileage rate of $3.25 per mile is charged.
2. The app displays the name of a cab company, a picture of a logo, and the results of the requested type of cab with the cost of the fare. Create your own layout.

Conditions: Use a theme, Spinner prompt, string array, and Hint property. Decimal mileage is possible.

Case Project 3–4: Paint Calculator App ★★

Requirements Document

Application title: Paint Calculator App

Purpose: The paint calculator app is needed in the paint section of a large home store to calculate the number of gallons needed to paint a room. The amount of paint in gallons is displayed.

Algorithms:

1. The app displays a title; an image; two Text Fields; and a Spinner, Button, and TextView control. The Spinner control allows five colors of paint to be selected. The room's height in feet and the distance in feet around the room are entered.
2. The color and the exact number of gallons in decimal form are displayed.

Conditions: A gallon is needed for every 250 square feet for a single coat of paint. Display the result rounded to two decimal places. Select five names for paint for the Spinner control. Use a theme, Spinner prompt, string array, and Hint property.

Case Project 3–5: Split the Bill App ★★★

Requirements Document

Application title: Split the Bill App

Purpose: You are out with friends at a nice restaurant and the bill comes! This app splits the bill, including the tip, among the members of your party.

Algorithms:

1. A welcome screen displays the title, image, and button that takes the user to a second screen. The input/output screen requests the restaurant bill and the number of people in your group. The Spinner control asks about the quality of service: Excellent, Average, or Poor.
2. Calculate an 18% tip and divide the restaurant bill with the tip included among the members of your party. Display the service and the individual share of the bill.

Conditions: Use a theme, Spinner prompt, string array, and Hint property.

Case Project 3–6: Piggy Bank Children's App ★★★

Requirements Document

Application title: Piggy Bank Children's App

Purpose: A piggy bank app allows children to enter the number of quarters, dimes, nickels, and pennies that they have. The child can select whether to save the money or spend it. Calculate the amount of money and display the amount that the child is saving or spending. Create two screens: a welcome screen and an input/output screen.

Algorithms:

1. A welcome screen displays the title, image, and button that takes the user to a second screen. The input/output screen requests the number of quarters, dimes, nickels, and pennies. A Spinner control should indicate whether the children are saving or spending their coins. Create your own layout.
2. The results display how much the child is saving or spending.

Conditions: Use a theme, Spinner prompt, string array, and Hint property.

CHAPTER 4

Explore! Icons and Decision-Making Controls

In this chapter, you learn to:

- Create an Android project with a custom icon
- Change the text color in controls using hexadecimal colors
- Align controls using the Change Gravity tool
- Determine layout with the Change Margins tool
- Place a RadioGroup and RadioButtons in Android applications
- Write code for a RadioGroup control
- Make decisions using an If statement
- Make decisions using an If Else statement
- Make decisions using logical operators
- Display an Android toast notification
- Test the isChecked property
- Make decisions using nested If statements

Developers can code Android applications to make decisions based on the input of users or other conditions that occur. Decision making is one of the fundamental activities of a computer application. In this chapter, you learn to write decision-making statements in Java, which allows you to test conditions and perform different operations depending on the results of that test. You can test for a condition being true or false and change the flow of what happens in a program based on the user's input.

The sample program in this chapter is designed to run on an Android phone or tablet device at a hospital. The Medical Calculator application provides nurses a mobile way to convert the weight of a patient from pounds to kilograms and kilograms to pounds. Most medication amounts are prescribed based on the weight of the patient. Most hospital scales display weight in pounds, but the prescribed medication is often based on the weight of a patient in kilograms. For safety reasons, the exact weight of the patient must be correctly converted between pounds and kilograms. The nurse enters the weight of the patient and selects a radio button, as shown in Figure 4-1, to determine whether pounds are being converted to kilograms or kilograms are being converted to pounds. The mobile application then computes the converted weight based on the conversion formulas: The conversion formulas are: kilograms = pounds * 2.2 and pounds = kilograms / 2.2. To validate that correct weights are entered, if the value is greater than 500 for the conversion from pounds to kilograms or greater than 225 for the conversion from kilograms to pounds, the user is asked for a valid entry. If the user enters a number out of the acceptable range, a warning called a toast message appears on the screen. When the app is running, a nurse enters 225 for the value of the weight of the patient and selects the Convert Pounds to Kilograms radio button shown in Figure 4-1. After tapping the Convert Weight button, the application displays 102.3 kilograms (rounded off to the nearest tenth place) in a red font, as shown in Figure 4-2. By using a mobile device, the nurse can capture patient information such as weight directly at the point of care anywhere and anytime and reduce errors made by delaying entry on a traditional computer in another location.

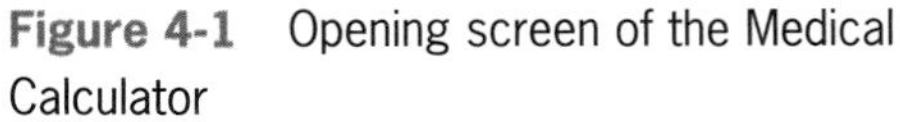

iStockphoto.com/O'Luk

Figure 4-1 Opening screen of the Medical Calculator

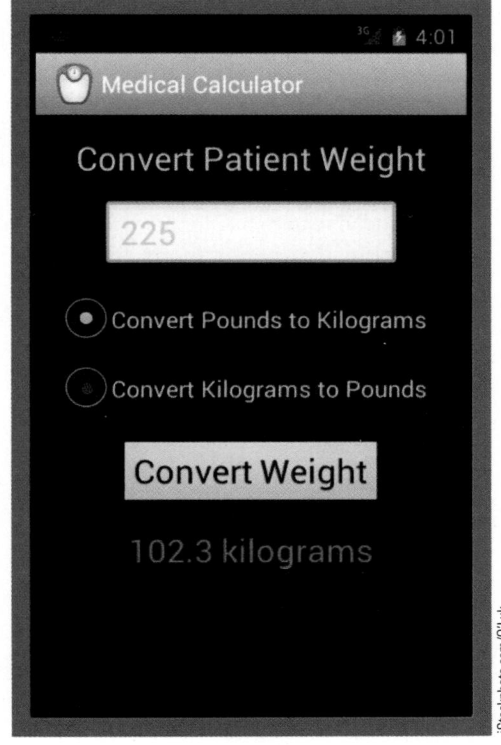

iStockphoto.com/O'Luk

Figure 4-2 Results screen of the Medical Calculator

To create this application, the developer must understand how to perform the following processes:

1. Create a customized launcher icon.
2. Define a TextField for the data entry of the weight of the patient.
3. Define a RadioGroup to select pounds to kilograms or kilograms to pounds.
4. Display a Toast message for data validation.
5. Convert data so it can be used for arithmetic operations.
6. Perform arithmetic operations on data the user enters.
7. Display formatted results.

IN THE TRENCHES

Medical phone apps are changing the entire patient point-of-care system. Apps now used in hospitals include mobile patient records, drug prescription references, medical journals, surgical checklists, dosage calculators, radiology imagery, and disease pathology.

The Launcher Icon

By default, Android places a standard Android icon, as shown in Figure 4-3, as the graphic to represent your application on the device's home screen and in the Launcher window. To view the opening icon called the **launcher icon** on the home screen, click the application listing icon at the bottom of the emulator when an application begins to execute, as shown in Figure 4-3. Instead of a default icon, each app published to the Android Market should have a custom graphic representing the contents of your application. Launcher icons form the first impression of your app on prospective users in the Android Market. With so many apps available, a high-quality launcher icon can influence users to purchase your Android app.

Figure 4-3 Android home screen and launcher icons

As you design a launcher icon, consider that an icon can establish brand identity. A unique image logo and program name can communicate your brand to potential customers. In the Medical Calculator app, the scale icon shown in Figure 4-4 clearly communicates that this icon launches a program about weight. A simple image with a clear visual cue like the scale has a memorable impact. It also helps users find the app in the Android Market. The Android Market suggests icons should be simple and bold in design. For example, for a paint graphics program, an icon shaped like a thin art paintbrush may be hard to distinguish from a pencil image, but a large cartoonlike paintbrush can convey its purpose easily.

The Android Market also specifies the size and format of all launcher icons for uniformity. Launcher icons should be saved in the .png file format. Based on your target device, Table 4-1 specifies the size of a finished launcher icon. You can use programs such as Microsoft Paint, Mac Paintbrush, and Adobe Photoshop to resize the icon to the correct number of pixels. In the chapter project, the icon dimension is 72 × 72 pixels for the high-density screen used by the application. If you are creating an application that can be deployed on any Android device, you can use the same name for the icon, but resize it four times and place each image in the appropriate res/drawable folder.

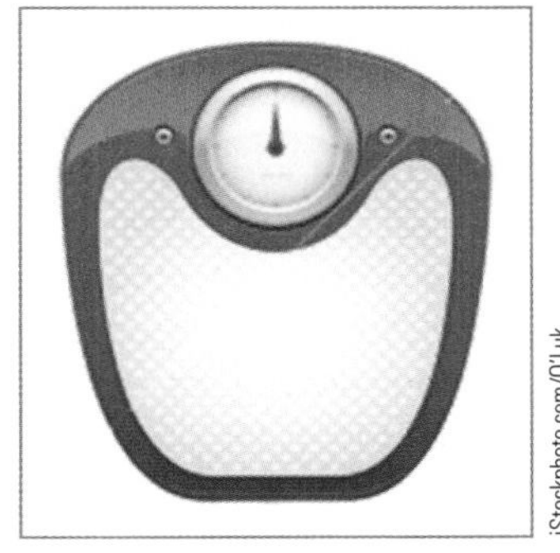

iStockphoto.com/O'Luk

Figure 4-4 Launcher icon for the Medical Calculator app

Resolution	**Dots per Inch (dpi)**	**Size (px)**
ldpi (low-density screen)	120	36 × 36
mdpi (medium-density screen)	160	48 × 48
hdpi (high-density screen)	240	72 × 72
xhdpi (extra high-density screen)*	320	96 × 96

* Used by some tablets

Table 4-1 Launcher icon sizes

GTK

When you publish an app to the Android Market, you must provide a 512 × 512 pixel, high-resolution application icon in the developer console as you upload your program. This icon is displayed in the Android Market to provide a description of the app and does not replace your launcher icon.

The Android Market recommends a naming convention for launcher icons. Typically, the prefix ic_launcher is used to name launcher icons for Android apps. In the case of the Medical Calculator app, the launcher icon is named ic_launcher_weight.png.

GTK

Vector-based graphics are best to use for icon design because the images can be scaled without the loss of detail and are easily resized.

Customizing a Launcher Icon

To display a custom launcher icon instead of the default icon on the home screen, first the custom icon image must be placed in the res\drawable folder. In addition, the Android Manifest file must be updated to include the new filename of the image file. The application code within the Android Manifest file for the chapter project should be changed to android: icon = "ic_launcher_weight.png". To perform the following steps, you need an image file named ic_launcher_weight.png, provided with your student files, to use as the custom launcher icon for the Medical Calculator app. You should already have the student files for this text that your instructor gave you or that you downloaded from the Web page for this book (*www.cengagebrain.com*). To begin the chapter project and add a customized launcher icon, follow these steps:

1. Open the Eclipse program. Click the New button on the Standard toolbar. Expand the Android folder, if necessary, and select Android Project. Click the Next button. In the New Android Project dialog box, enter the Project name **Medical Calculator**. To save the project on your USB drive, click to remove the check mark from the Use default location check box. Type **E:\Workspace** (if necessary, enter a different drive letter that identifies the USB drive). Click the Next button. For the Build Target, select Android 4.0, if necessary. Click the Next button. Type the Package name **net.androidbootcamp.medicalcalculator**. Enter **Main** in the Create Activity text box. Click the Finish button. Expand the Medical Calculator project in the Package Explorer. Expand the res folder to display its subfolders. Expand the layout subfolder. Right-click main.xml, point to Open With, and then click Android Layout Editor. Click the Hello World, Main! TextView widget, and then press the Delete key. Click the Theme button to display the list of built-in themes, and then select Theme.WithActionBar.

   The New Android Medical Calculator project uses the Theme.WithActionBar theme, and the default icon is displayed in the action bar (Figure 4-5).

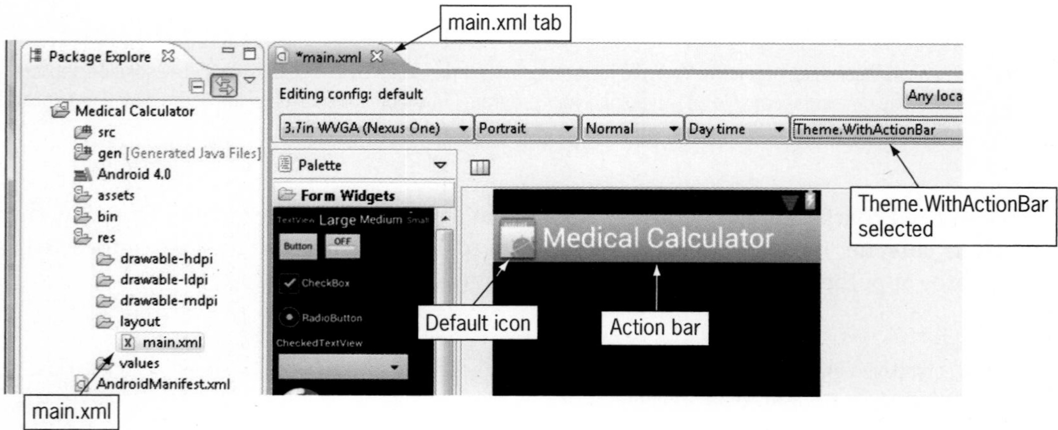

Figure 4-5 Theme with action bar

2. To add the custom launcher icon to the project, copy the student files to your USB drive (if necessary). Open the USB folder containing the student files. In the Package Explorer, expand the drawable-hdpi folder. Drag the ic_launcher_weight.png file to the drawable-hdpi folder until a plus sign pointer appears. Release the mouse button. Click the OK button in the File Operation dialog box. Click the default icon ic_launcher.png file and press the Delete key, and then click the OK button to confirm the deletion.

   The custom launcher icon image is placed in the drawable-hdpi folder. The image in the emulator does not update until the Android Manifest file is changed (Figure 4-6).

Figure 4-6 New launcher icon file

3. To change the code in the Android Manifest file so the application displays the custom icon, double-click the AndroidManifest.xml file in the Package Explorer. Click the AndroidManifest.xml tab at the bottom of the window. Inside the application code, click in the line android:icon="drawable/ic_launcher". Change the filename portion from ic_launcher" to **ic_launcher_weight**".

   The Android launcher icon is coded in the Android Manifest file (Figure 4-7).

main.xml | *Medical Calculator Manifest

```
<?xml version="1.0" encoding="utf-8"?>
<manifest xmlns:android="http://schemas.android.com/apk/res/android"
    package="net.androidbootcamp.medicalcalculator"
    android:versionCode="1"
    android:versionName="1.0" >

    <uses-sdk android:minSdkVersion="14" />

    <application
        android:icon="@drawable/ic_launcher_weight"
        android:label="@string/app_name" >
        <activity
            android:label="@string/app_name"
            android:name=".Main" >
            <intent-filter >
```

Icon name changed

Figure 4-7 Android Manifest code with new launcher icon filename

4. To add the selected theme to the Android Manifest, inside the activity code, click at the end of the line android:label="@string/app_name". Press the Enter key to insert a blank line. Type **android:theme="@android:style/Theme.WithActionBar"**.

   The Android theme is coded in the Android Manifest file (Figure 4-8).

main.xml | Medical Calculator Manifest

```
<?xml version="1.0" encoding="utf-8"?>
<manifest xmlns:android="http://schemas.android.com/apk/res/and
    package="net.androidbootcamp.medicalcalculator"
    android:versionCode="1"
    android:versionName="1.0" >

    <uses-sdk android:minSdkVersion="14" />

    <application
        android:icon="@drawable/ic_launcher_weight"
        android:label="@string/app_name" >
        <activity
            android:label="@string/app_name"
            android:theme="@android:style/Theme.WithActionBar"
            android:name=".Main">
```

New Android theme referenced

Figure 4-8 Android Manifest code with new theme

5. Click the Save All button on the Standard toolbar, and then close the Medical Calculator Manifest tab.

RadioButton and RadioGroup Controls

RadioButton controls are used to select or deselect an option. In the chapter project, the user can select which mathematical conversion is needed. When a RadioButton is placed on the emulator, by default each control is arranged vertically. If you prefer the RadioButton controls to be listed horizontally, you can set the orientation property to horizontal. Each RadioButton control has a label defined by the Text property and a Checked property set to either true or false. RadioButton controls are typically used together in a **RadioGroup**. Checking one radio button unchecks the other radio buttons within the group. In other words, within a RadioGroup control, only one RadioButton control can be selected at a time. When the RadioGroup control on the Palette is placed on the emulator window, three RadioButton controls are included in the group by default. If you need additional RadioButton controls, drag them from the Palette into the group. In the case of the Medical Calculator app, only two radio buttons are needed, so the third radio button is deleted.

To make the user's input as simple as possible, offer a default selection. For example, nurses more often convert weight from pounds to kilograms, so that RadioButton option should be checked initially. The Checked property of this RadioButton control is set to true to provide a default selection.

GTK

Like RadioButton controls, a CheckBox control allows a user to check or uncheck a listing. A user may select any number of check boxes, including zero, one, or several. In other words, each check box is independent of all other check boxes in the list, so checking one box does not uncheck the others. The shape of a radio button is circular and the check box is square.

Changing the Text Color of Android Controls

Thus far, each application in this text used the default color of white for the text color for each Android control. The Android platform uses a color system called hexadecimal color codes to display different colors. A **hexadecimal color code** is a triplet of three colors. Colors are specified first by a pound sign followed by how much red (00 to FF), how much green (00 to FF), and how much blue (00 to FF) are in the final color. For example, the hexadecimal color of #FF0000 is a true red. The TextView and RadioGroup controls displayed in the chapter project have light gray text, which you designate by typing #CCCCCC as the Text color property. To look up these color codes, search for hexadecimal color codes in a search engine or refer to *http://html-color-codes.com*.

Changing the Layout Gravity

The Medical Calculator app displays controls from the Palette with a Linear layout, which is the default setting for layouts on the Android emulator. As you place controls on the emulator, each control snaps to the left edge of the screen by default. You can use a property named Layout gravity to center a control horizontally as well as position it at other places on the screen. When you place a control on the emulator, a toolbar appears above the emulator screen. You can change the gravity using the Properties pane or a button on the toolbar. The **Change Gravity** tool shown in Figure 4-9 changes the linear alignment. Layout gravity is similar to the alignment feature in Microsoft Office that allows a control to snap to the left, center, right, top, or bottom of another object or the screen.

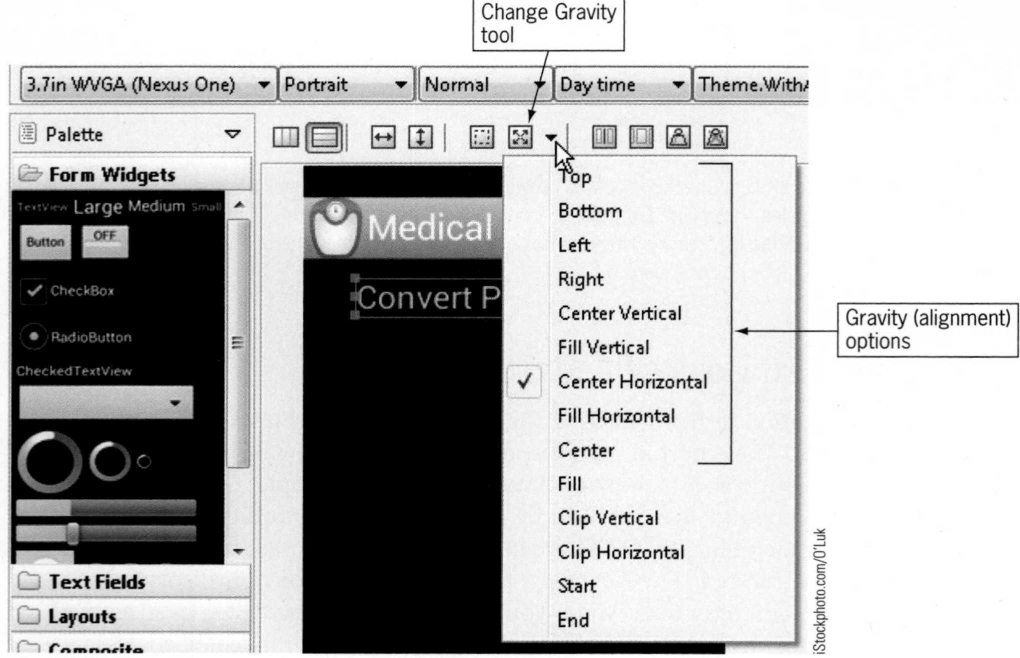

Figure 4-9 Change Gravity tool

Changing the Margins

After placing a control on the user interface, you can change the alignment by adjusting the gravity of the control. For more flexibility in controlling your layout, use **margins** to change the spacing around each object. Each control in the Medical Calculator app can use margins to add a certain amount of blank space measured in density independent pixels (dp) on each of its four sides. Instead of "eyeballing" the controls on the user interface for alignment, the Change Margins tool creates equal spacing around controls. Using the Change Margins tool helps make your user interface more organized and ultimately easier to use. The Change Margins tool is displayed when a control is selected on the user interface. For example, in Figure 4-10 a margin spacing of 15dp (pixels) specifies 15 extra pixels on the top side of the selected TextView control. As you design the user interface, use the same specified margins around each control to provide a symmetrical layout.

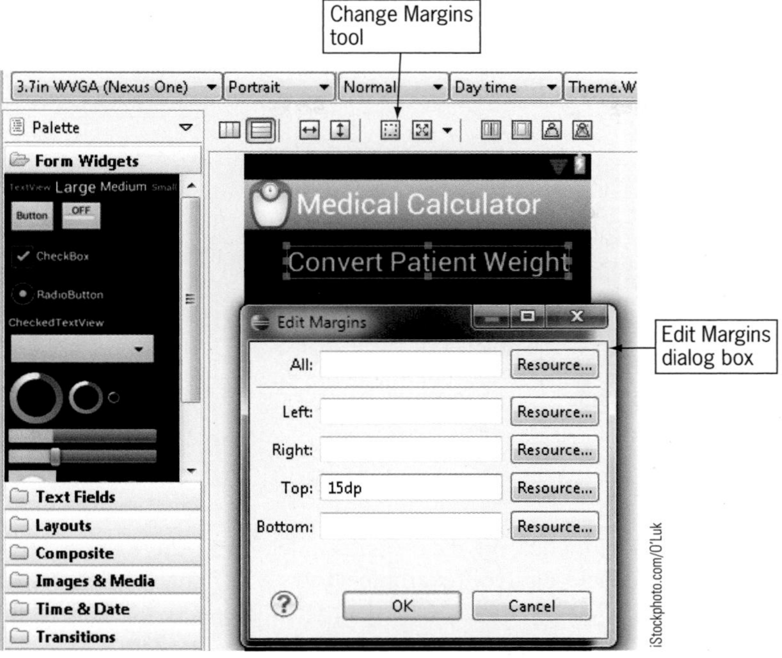

Figure 4-10 Change Margins tool

Adding the RadioButton Group

The Medical Calculator app displays a TextView control, Number Text Field, and RadioGroup control, all centered horizontally. The TextView and RadioGroup controls use the text color of gray. To name a RadioButton control, use the Id property in the Properties pane to enter a name that begins with the prefix rad, which represents a radio button in the code. To begin the design of the Android user interface and to add a RadioGroup to the Medical Calculator app, follow these steps:

1. With the main.xml tab open, click the Form Widgets category in the Palette, if necessary. Select the Form Widget named TextView. Drag and drop the TextView control onto the emulator user interface. Right-click the emulator window, point to Show In, and then select Properties to open the Properties pane, if necessary. Click the TextView control that you placed on the emulator. In the Properties pane, change the Text property to **Convert Patient Weight**. Change the Text size property to **25sp**. Click the Text color property and type **#CCCCCC** to change the text color to a light gray to match the action bar. Click the Change Gravity tool on the toolbar. Select Center Horizontal to center the control. With the control selected, click the Change Margins tool on the toolbar. In the Top text box of the Edit Margins dialog box, type **15dp** and then click the OK button to place 15 pixel spaces above the control.

The TextView control is added to the form with the text, size, text color, gravity, and margins changed (Figure 4-11).

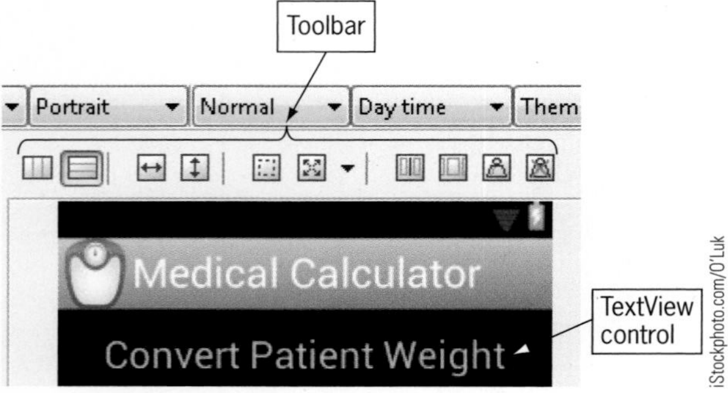

Figure 4-11 TextView control

2. To add the Number Text Field, click the Text Fields category in the Palette. Drag and drop the Number Text Field control (example shows a 42) onto the emulator's user interface below the TextView control. Change the Id property of the Number Text Field to **@+id/txtWeight**. Change the Text size property to **25sp**. Change the Hint property to **Weight of Patient**. Click the Text color property and type **#CCCCCC** as the hexadecimal color code for light gray. Resize the control to fit the hint by dragging a selection handle on the control. Select the control, click the Change Gravity tool, and select Center Horizontal to center the control. Select the control, click the Change Margins tool, and in the Top text box of the Edit Margins dialog box, type **15dp** and then click the OK button to place 15 pixel spaces between the TextView and the Number Text Field control.

   A Number Text Field control is placed on the emulator with the id, text size, text color, hint, gravity, and margins changed (Figure 4-12).

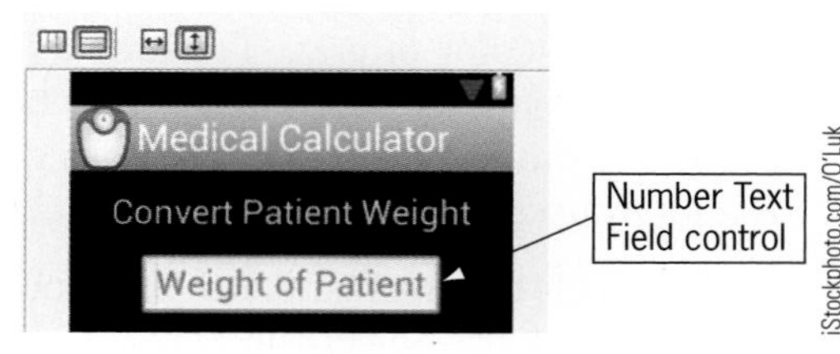

Figure 4-12 Number Text Field control

3. In the Palette, select the Form Widget named RadioGroup. Drag and drop the RadioGroup control onto the user interface below the Number Text Field. Only two radio buttons are needed for this app, so click the third RadioButton control and press the Delete key. Select the first RadioButton control. In the Properties pane, change the Id property of the RadioButton control to **@+id/radLbToKilo**. Change the Text property to **Convert Pounds to Kilograms**. Change the Text size property to **18sp**. Notice the Checked property is preset as true, indicating that the first radio button is the default selection. Click the Change Margins tool to open the Edit

Margins dialog box. In the Left text box, type **12dp** and in the Top text box, type **15dp**. Click the OK button. Select the second RadioButton control. In the Properties pane, change the Id property to **@+id/radKiloToLb**. Change the Text property to **Convert Kilograms to Pounds**. Change the Text size property to **18sp**. Click the Change Margins tool to open the Edit Margins dialog box. In the Left text box, type **12dp** and in the Top text box, type **5dp** to keep the RadioButtons close to one another within the group. Click the OK button.

The RadioGroup object is placed on the emulator with the id, text, color, and margin properties changed (Figure 4-13).

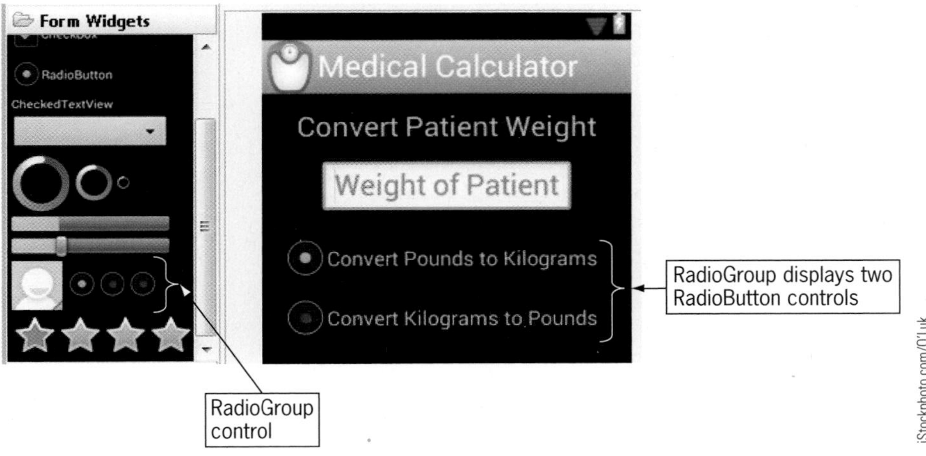

Figure 4-13 RadioGroup control

Coding a RadioButton Control

Each of the RadioButton controls placed on the emulator need to be referenced by using the findViewById Java command. In the following code syntax, lbsToKilo and kiloToLbs reference the two RadioButton controls in the Medical Calculator application:

Code Syntax

```
final RadioButton lbsToKilo = (RadioButton) findViewById(R.id.radLbToKilo);
final RadioButton kiloToLbs = (RadioButton) findViewById(R.id.radKiloToLb);
```

After the RadioButton controls have been referenced, the next priority is to determine which of the two radio buttons the user selected. If the user selected the Convert Pounds to Kilograms radio button, the weight entered is divided by 2.2, but if the user selected the Convert Kilograms to Pounds radio button, the weight is multiplied by 2.2. A variable named conversionRate is assigned the decimal value 2.2. The variables weightEntered and convertedWeight contain the patient weight and converted weight result, respectively.

To create the Java code to declare the variables used in the application and to reference the RadioButton controls, follow these steps:

1. In the Package Explorer, expand src and net.androidbootcamp.medicalcalculator, and then double-click Main.java to open the code window. Click after the comment line: /** Called when the activity is first created. */. Press the Enter key to insert a new blank line. To initialize the conversion rate value of 2.2, type **double conversionRate = 2.2;**. Press the Enter key. To initialize the weightEntered variable, type **double weightEntered;** and press the Enter key. To initialize the variable that will hold the converted weight, type **double convertedWeight;**. Press the Enter key.

   Three variables are declared in the Java code (Figure 4-14).

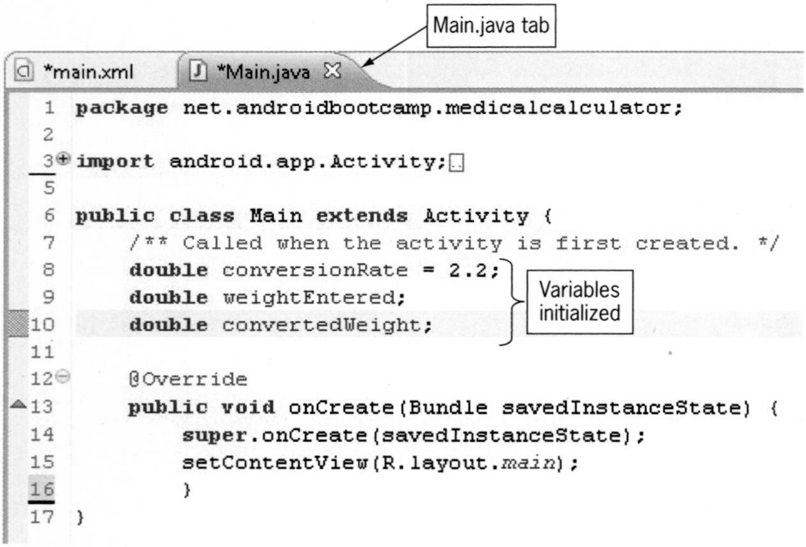

Main.java tab

*main.xml | *Main.java

```
package net.androidbootcamp.medicalcalculator;

import android.app.Activity;

public class Main extends Activity {
    /** Called when the activity is first created. */
    double conversionRate = 2.2;
    double weightEntered;
    double convertedWeight;

    @Override
    public void onCreate(Bundle savedInstanceState) {
        super.onCreate(savedInstanceState);
        setContentView(R.layout.main);
        }
}
```

Variables initialized

Figure 4-14 Variables declared

2. Click at the end of the line setContentView(R.layout.*main*);. Press the Enter key. To initialize and reference the EditText class with the Id name of txtWeight, type **final EditText weight = (EditText) findViewById(R.id.txtWeight);**. Point to the red curly line under EditText and select Import 'EditText' (android widget) on the pop-up menu. Press the Enter key. To initialize and reference the RadioButton class with the Id name of radLbToKilo, type **final RadioButton lbToKilo = (RadioButton) findViewById(R.id.radLbToKilo);**. Point to the red curly line under RadioButton and select Import 'RadioButton' (android widget). Press the Enter key. To initialize and reference the RadioButton class for the second radio button with the Id name of radKiloToLb, type **final RadioButton kiloToLb = (RadioButton) findViewById(R.id.radKiloToLb);**.

The EditText class extracts the value from the user's input for the patient weight and the RadioButton class extracts the checked value from the radio buttons (Figure 4-15).

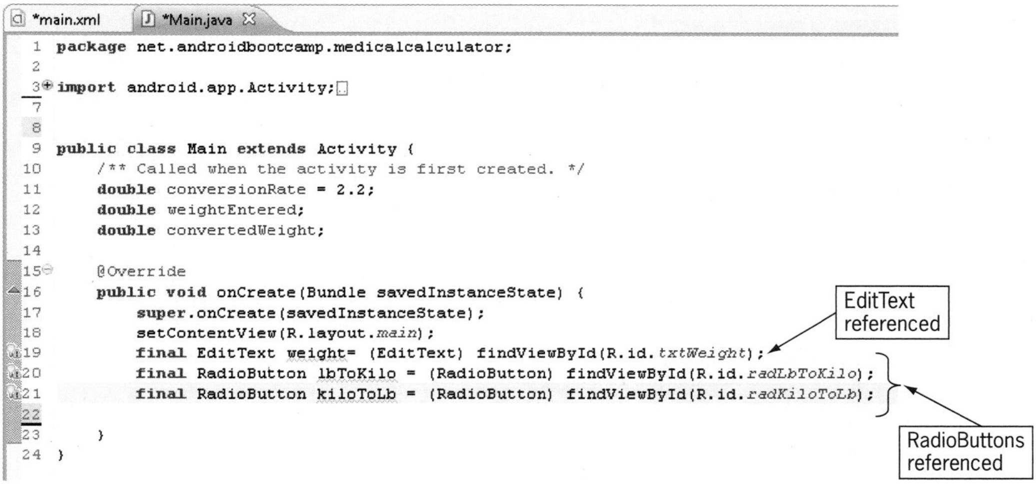

*main.xml | *Main.java

```
package net.androidbootcamp.medicalcalculator;

import android.app.Activity;


public class Main extends Activity {
    /** Called when the activity is first created. */
    double conversionRate = 2.2;
    double weightEntered;
    double convertedWeight;

    @Override
    public void onCreate(Bundle savedInstanceState) {
        super.onCreate(savedInstanceState);
        setContentView(R.layout.main);
        final EditText weight= (EditText) findViewById(R.id.txtWeight);
        final RadioButton lbToKilo = (RadioButton) findViewById(R.id.radLbToKilo);
        final RadioButton kiloToLb = (RadioButton) findViewById(R.id.radKiloToLb);

    }
}
```

EditText referenced

RadioButtons referenced

Figure 4-15 EditText and RadioButtons referenced

3. Save your work.

Completing the User Interface

As you design the Android interface, it is important to have a clean layout and use the entire screen effectively. To complete the user interface by adding a Button and TextView control and code the Button and TextView controls, follow these steps:

1. In the main.xml tab, drag the Button control from the Palette to the emulator below the RadioGroup. In the Properties pane, change the Id property of the Button control to **@+id/btnConvert**. Change the Text property to **Convert Weight**. Change the Text size property to **25sp**. Click the Change Gravity tool on the toolbar, and then click Center Horizontal to center the control. Select the Button control, click the Change Margins tool, and in the Top text box of the Edit Margins dialog box, type **15dp** and then click the OK button to place 15 pixel spaces above the control.

   Drag another TextView control to the emulator below the Button. Change the Id property of the TextView control to **@+id/txtResult**. Change the Text size property to **25sp**. For the Text color property, type **#FF0000** (red). Click the Change Gravity tool on the toolbar, and then click Center Horizontal to center the control. Click the Change Margins tool, and in the Top text box of the Edit Margins dialog box, type **15dp** to place 15 pixels of space above the control, and then click the OK button. Delete the text in the Text property. Click the Save All button on the Standard toolbar.

The Button control named btnConvert displays the text Convert Weight and its id, text, text size, gravity, and margins are changed. The TextView control is placed on the emulator with an empty Text property (Figure 4-16).

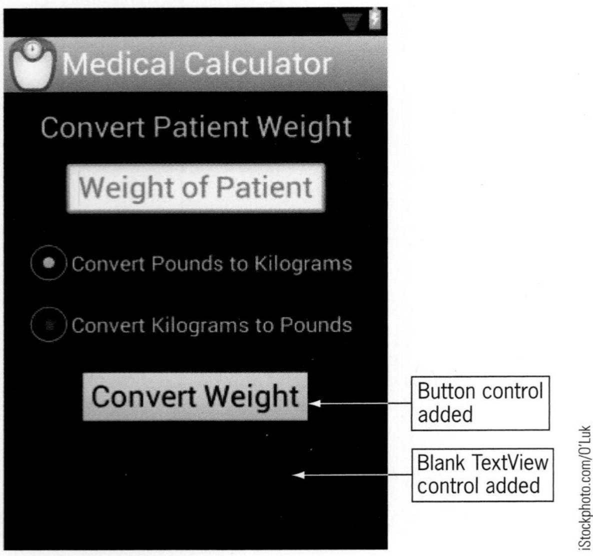

Figure 4-16 Button and blank TextView controls

2. To code the TextView control, click the Main.java tab. After the two lines of code referring to the RadioButton controls, type a new line with the code **final TextView result = (TextView) findViewById(R.id.txtResult);**. Import the 'TextView' (android.widget). Press the Enter key twice to insert two blank lines. To code the button, type **Button convert = (Button) findViewById(R.id.btnConvert);**. Point to Button and import the Button type as an Android widget. Press the Enter key. To code the Button listener, type **convert.setOn** and wait for a code listing to open. Double-click the first setOnClickListener displayed in the auto-complete listing. Inside the parentheses, type **new on** and press Ctrl+spacebar to display the auto-complete listing. Double-click the first choice, which lists an OnClickListener with an Anonymous Inner Type event handler. Point to OnClickListener and select Import 'OnClickListener' (android.view.View). Place a semicolon at the end of the auto-generated stub closing brace and parenthesis.

   The TextView control txtResult is assigned to the variable result and the btnConvert Button control is coded (Figure 4-17).

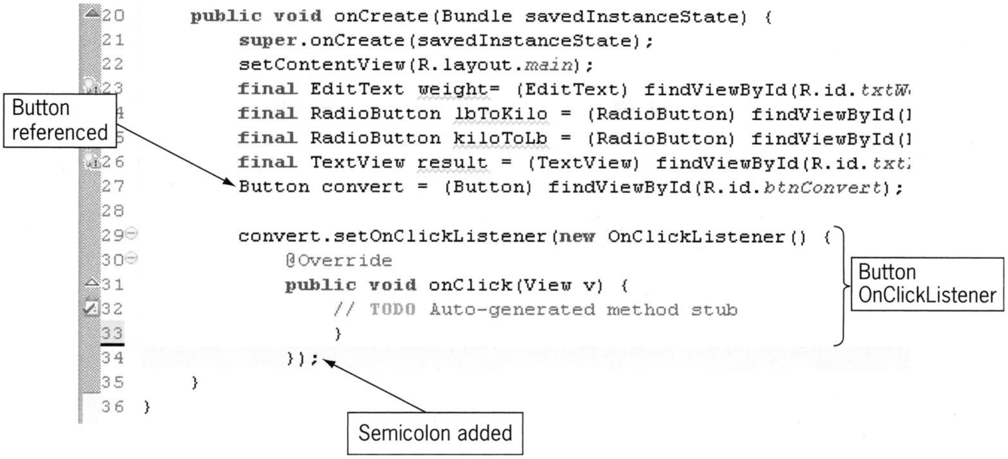

```
    public void onCreate(Bundle savedInstanceState) {
        super.onCreate(savedInstanceState);
        setContentView(R.layout.main);
        final EditText weight= (EditText) findViewById(R.id.txtW
        final RadioButton lbToKilo = (RadioButton) findViewById(
        final RadioButton kiloToLb = (RadioButton) findViewById(
        final TextView result = (TextView) findViewById(R.id.txt
        Button convert = (Button) findViewById(R.id.btnConvert);

        convert.setOnClickListener(new OnClickListener() {
            @Override
            public void onClick(View v) {
                // TODO Auto-generated method stub
                }
            });
    }
}
```

Button referenced

Button OnClickListener

Semicolon added

Figure 4-17 Button and Button OnClickListener

Making Decisions with Conditional Statements

In the Medical Calculator chapter project, which converts the weight entered to either pounds or kilograms, the user selects one of two radio buttons. Then, based on the choice, the application either divides by 2.2 or multiplies by 2.2.

Java uses decision structures to deal with the different conditions that occur based on the values entered into an application. A **decision structure** is a fundamental control structure used in computer programming. A statement that tests the radio button is called a conditional statement and the condition checked is whether the first or second radio button is selected. If the first radio button is selected, the weight is divided by 2.2. When a condition is tested in a Java program, it is either true or false. To execute a conditional statement and the statements that are executed when a condition is true, Java uses the If statement and its variety of formats.

Using an If Statement

In the chapter program, an **If statement** is used to determine which RadioButton control is selected. The simplest form of the If statement is shown in the following code:

Code Syntax

```
if (condition){
   //Statements completed if true
}
```

The statement(s) between the opening and closing braces are executed if the condition is true. If the condition is not true, no statements between the braces are executed, and program execution continues with the statement(s) that follows the closing brace.

Using If Else Statements

In many applications, the logic requires one set of instructions to be executed if a condition is true and another set of instructions to be executed if a condition is false. For example, a program requirement may specify that if a student's test score is 60 or greater, a message stating "You passed the examination" is displayed, but if the test score is less than 60, a message stating "You failed the examination" is displayed.

To execute one set of instructions if a condition is true, and another set of instructions if the condition is false, you can use the **If Else statement**, as shown in the following code:

Code Syntax

```
if (condition){
      //Statements completed if condition is true
  } else {
      //Statements completed if condition is false
  }
```

GTK
Java automatically indents statements to be executed when a condition is true or not true to indicate that the lines of code are within the conditional If structure.

Relational Operators

In the syntax of the condition portion of the If statement, a condition is tested to determine if it is true or false. The conditions that can be tested are:

- Is one value equal to another value?
- Is one value not equal to another value?
- Is one value greater than another value?
- Is one value less than another value?
- Is one value greater than or equal to another value?
- Is one value less than or equal to another value?

To test these conditions, Java provides relational operators that are used within the conditional statement to express the relationship between the numbers being tested. Table 4-2 shows these relational operators.

Relational Operator	Meaning	Example	Resulting Condition
= =	Equal to	6 = = 6	True
! =	Not equal to	4 ! = 7	False
>	Greater than	3 > 2	True
<	Less than	8 < 1	False
>=	Greater than or equal to	5 >= 5	True
<=	Less than or equal to	9 <= 6	False

Table 4-2 Relational operators

In the chapter project, an If Else statement determines if the entered weight is valid. If the nurse is converting pounds to kilograms, the weight entered must be less than or equal to 500 to be considered within a valid range of acceptable entries. If the entered weight is valid, the weight is converted by dividing it by the conversion rate of 2.2, as shown in the following code:

Code Syntax

```
if (weightEntered <=500){
   convertedWeight = weightEntered / conversionRate;
 } else {
     //Statements completed if condition is false
 }
```

GTK

The most common mistake made with an If statement is the use of a single equal sign to compare equality. A single equal sign (=) is used for assigning a value to a variable, not for comparison.

In addition to numbers, strings can also be compared in a conditional statement. A string value comparison compares each character in two strings, starting with the first character in each string. All characters found in strings, including letters, numbers, and special characters, are ranked in a sequence from low to high based on how the characters are coded internally on the computer. The relational operators from Table 4-2 cannot be used with string comparisons. If you are comparing equality, string characters cannot be compared with the "= =" operator. Java strings are compared with the **equals method** of the String class.

If you are comparing whether a string is alphabetically before another string, use the compareTo method to determine the order of strings. Do not use the less-than or greater-than symbols as shown in Table 4-2 to compare string data types. The compareTo method returns a negative integer if the first string precedes the second string. It returns zero if the two strings being compared are equal. It returns a positive integer if the first string follows the second string. Examples of the equals and compareTo methods are shown in Table 4-3 using the following initialized variables:

```
String name1 = "Sara";
String name2 = "Shawna";
String name3 = "Ryan";
```

If Statement	Comparison	Resulting Condition
if (name1.equals(name2))	Strings are not equal	False
if (name1.compareTo(name1) = = 0)	Strings are equal	True
if (name1.compareTo(name3) = = 0)	Strings are not equal	False
if (name1.compareTo(name2) > 0)	The first string precedes the second string; returns a negative number	False
if (name1.compareTo(name3) < 0)	The first string follows the third string; returns a negative number	True
If (name3.compareTo(name2) > 0)	The first string follows the second string; returns a positive number	True

Table 4-3 Examples of the equals and compareTo methods

Logical Operators

An If statement can test more than one condition within a single statement. In many cases, more than one condition must be true or one of several conditions must be true in order for the statements within the braces to be executed. When more than one condition is included in an If statement, the conditions are called a **compound condition**. For example, consider the following business traveling rule: "If the flight costs less than $400.00 and the hotel is less than $120.00 per night, the business trip is approved." In this case, both conditions (flight less than $400.00 and hotel less than $120.00 per night) must be true for the trip to be approved. If either condition is not true, then the business trip is not approved.

To create an If statement that processes the business traveling rule, you must use a logical operator. The most common set of logical operators is listed in Table 4-4.

Logical Operator	Meaning	Example
&&	And—all conditions must be true	if (flight < 400 && hotel < 120)
||	Or—at least one condition must be true	if (stamp < 0.49 || rate = = 2)
!	Not—reverses the meaning of a condition	if (! (grade > 70))

Table 4-4 Common logical operators

Data Validation

In the chapter project, it is important to confirm that the number entered by the user is not a typo or other type of mistake. If a value greater than 500 is entered for the conversion from pounds to kilograms or greater than 225 for the conversion from kilograms to pounds, the user should be notified and asked for a valid entry. To alert the user that an incorrect value was entered, a message called a toast notification (or toast message) can appear on the screen temporarily.

Toast Notification

A **toast notification** communicates messages to the user. These messages pop up as an overlay onto the user's current screen, often displaying a validation warning message. For example, a weather application may display a toast notification if a town is under a tornado warning. An instant messaging app might display a toast notification stating that a text message has been sent. In the chapter project, a toast notification displays a message warning the user that an invalid number was entered. A toast message only fills the amount of space required for the message to be displayed while the user's current activity remains visible and interactive. The notification automatically fades in and out on the screen.

The toast notification code uses a Toast object and the MakeText( ) method with three parameters: the context (displays the activity name), the text message, and the duration of the interval that the toast is displayed (LENGTH_SHORT or LENGTH_LONG). To display the toast notification, a show( ) method displays the Toast object.

Code Syntax

```
Toast toast = Toast.makeText(context, text, duration).show();
```

The toast message is best used for short messages. If the user enters an invalid number into the Medical Calculator, a warning toast notification fades in and then out on the screen. Notice in the following syntax that the text notification message displays *Pounds must be less than 500.*

Code Syntax

```
Toast.makeText(Main.this,"Pounds must be less than 500", Toast.LENGTH_LONG).show();
```

GTK

An ex-Microsoft employee of Google is credited with coining the term *toast*, which is a small notification window that slides upward into view, like toast popping out of a toaster.

Using the isChecked( ) Method of RadioButton Controls

You will recall that the RadioButton controls in the Medical Calculator Android application allow the user to select one conversion option. When the user selects the second radio button, a shaded small circle is displayed in that radio button. When a RadioButton is selected, the Checked property of the second RadioButton control changes from False (unselected) to True (selected). The Java code must check each RadioButton to determine if that RadioButton has been selected by the user. This checked property can be tested in an If statement using the **isChecked( ) method** to determine if the RadioButton object has been selected.

Code Syntax

```
if (lbToKilo.isChecked){
        //Statements completed if condition is true
  } else {
        //Statements completed if condition is false
  }
```

If the user selects the lbToKilo RadioButton control, the statements within the If portion between the braces are completed. If the user selects the kiloToLb RadioButton control, the statements within the Else portion are completed.

Nested If Statements

At times, more than one decision must be made to determine what processing must occur. For example, if one condition is true, a second condition might need to be tested before the correct code is executed. To test a second condition only after determining that a first condition is true (or false), you must place an If statement within another If statement. When you do this, the inner If statement is said to be **nested** within the outer If statement. In the chapter Android app, if the user checks the first radio button to convert pounds to kilograms and if the entered weight is equal to 500 pounds or less, then the weight can be converted. If the weight is above 500 pounds, a toast notification appears with a warning. A second nested If statement evaluates whether the second radio button is checked and if the user entered 225 kilograms or less as part of the final code.

Code Syntax

```
if (lbToKilo.isChecked()){
  if (weightEntered <=500){
     convertedWeight = weightEntered / conversionRate;
   } else {
     Toast.makeText(Main.this,"Pounds must be less than 500", Toast.LENGTH_LONG).show();
   }
}
```

Coding the Button Event

After the user enters the weight and selects the desired RadioButton, the Button control is tapped. The OnClickListener event is triggered and the conversion of the weight entered occurs. Within the onClick method, the weight entered must be converted to double data. A DecimalFormat layout is necessary to format the result to one place past the decimal point ("#.#"). To convert the weight to a double data type and establish the format for the output, follow these steps:

1. On a new line inside the OnClickListener onClick method stub of the Main.java code, type **weightEntered=Double.parseDouble(weight.getText().toString());** to convert the weight entered to a double data type.

   The weight entered by the user is converted to a double data type (Figure 4-18).

Text entered for weight is converted to a double data type

```
convert.setOnClickListener(new OnClickListener() {
    @Override
    public void onClick(View v) {
        // TODO Auto-generated method stub
        weightEntered=Double.parseDouble(weight.getText().toString());
        }
```

Figure 4-18 Weight converted to a double data type

2. Press the Enter key. To create a decimal layout that changes the weight to a decimal rounded to the nearest tenth for use in the result later in the code, type **DecimalFormat tenth = new DecimalFormat("#.#");**. Point to the red curly line below DecimalFormat and select Import 'DecimalFormat' (java.text).

   The DecimalFormat code rounds off to the nearest tenth (Figure 4-19).

```
convert.setOnClickListener(new OnClickListener() {
    @Override
    public void onClick(View v) {
        // TODO Auto-generated method stub
        weightEntered=Double.parseDouble(weight.getText().toString());
        DecimalFormat tenth = new DecimalFormat("#.#");
        }
    });
```

DecimalFormat rounds off to one place past the decimal point

Figure 4-19 Rounding off a number

Coding the Nested If Statements

After the weight entered is converted to a double and a format is set, code is necessary to determine which RadioButton was selected by using the isChecked property. Within each RadioButton If statement, the weight entered is converted to the appropriate weight unit and displayed, only if that weight is within the valid weight ranges (500 pounds or 225 kilograms). If the weight is not within the valid range, a toast notification appears warning the user to enter a value within the acceptable range. To code a nested If statement to display the result, follow these steps:

1. After the DecimalFormat line of code, to determine if the first RadioButton control is selected, type **if(lbToKilo.isChecked()) {** and press the Enter key. Java automatically adds the closing brace.

   An If statement determines if the lbToKilo RadioButton control is checked (Figure 4-20).

```
            public void onClick(View v) {
                // TODO Auto-generated method stub
                weightEntered=Double.parseDouble(weight.getText().toString());
                DecimalFormat tenth = new DecimalFormat("#.#");
                if(lbToKilo.isChecked()){

                }
            }
        });
```

If statement determines if the first RadioButton is checked

Figure 4-20 If statement

2. Within the first If statements, braces create a nested If Else statement that determines if the weight entered for pounds is less than or equal to 500. Type **if (weightEntered <=500) {** and press the Enter key. Java automatically adds the closing brace. After the closing brace, type **else {** and press the Enter key. Java automatically adds the closing brace.

   A nested If Else statement determines if the number of pounds entered is valid (Figure 4-21).

```
            public void onClick(View v) {
                // TODO Auto-generated method stub
                weightEntered=Double.parseDouble(weight.getText
                DecimalFormat tenth = new DecimalFormat("#.#");
                if(lbToKilo.isChecked()){
                    if (weightEntered <=500){

                    }else {

```

Nested If Else statement determines if weight is valid

Figure 4-21 Nested If Else statement

3. After the pounds variable is validated, the weight must be converted. To divide the weight by the conversion rate of 2.2, inside the nested If statement, type **convertedWeight = weightEntered / conversionRate;** and press the Enter key. To display the result of the equation rounded to one place past the decimal point, type **result.setText(tenth.format(convertedWeight) + " kilograms");**.

   The number of pounds is converted to kilograms and displayed in the result TextView control (Figure 4-22).

```
public void onClick(View v) {
    // TODO Auto-generated method stub
    weightEntered=Double.parseDouble(weight.getText().toString());
    DecimalFormat tenth = new DecimalFormat("#.#");
    if(lbToKilo.isChecked()){
        if (weightEntered <=500){
            convertedWeight = weightEntered / conversionRate;
            result.setText(tenth.format(convertedWeight) + " kilograms");
        }else {
```

Equation to convert pounds to kilograms

Displays converted weight

Figure 4-22 Equation for weight conversion and displayed results

4. If the weight is not within the valid range, a toast message requesting that the user enter a valid weight is displayed briefly. Click the line after the Else statement and type **Toast.makeText(Main.this,"Pounds must be less than 500", Toast. LENGTH_LONG).show();** and then point to Toast and select Import 'Toast' (android.widget).

   A toast message displays a reminder to enter a valid weight (Figure 4-23).

```
public void onClick(View v) {
    // TODO Auto-generated method stub
    weightEntered=Double.parseDouble(weight.getText().toString());
    DecimalFormat tenth = new DecimalFormat("#.#");
    if(lbToKilo.isChecked()){
        if (weightEntered <=500){
            convertedWeight = weightEntered / conversionRate;
            result.setText(tenth.format(convertedWeight) + " kilograms");
        }else {
            Toast.makeText(Main.this,"Pounds must be less than 500", Toast.LENGTH_LONG).show();
        }
    }
    }
});
```

Toast message

Figure 4-23 Toast message added to enter a valid weight

5. For when the user selects the Convert the Kilograms to Pounds RadioButton control, type the following lines of code, as shown in Figure 4-24:

```
if(kiloToLb.isChecked()) {
     if (weightEntered <=225) {
         convertedWeight = weightEntered * conversionRate;
         result.setText(tenth.format(convertedWeight) + " pounds");
     }else {
      Toast.makeText(Main.this, "Kilos must be less than 225",
Toast.LENGTH_LONG).show();
              }
              }
```

   The nested If statement is executed if the second RadioButton control is selected (Figure 4-24).

main.xml Main.java

```
package net.androidbootcamp.medicalcalculator;

import java.text.DecimalFormat;[]


public class Main extends Activity {
    /** Called when the activity is first created. */
    double conversionRate = 2.2;
    double weightEntered;
    double convertedWeight;

    @Override
    public void onCreate(Bundle savedInstanceState) {
        super.onCreate(savedInstanceState);
        setContentView(R.layout.main);
        final EditText weight= (EditText) findViewById(R.id.txtWeight);
        final RadioButton lbToKilo = (RadioButton) findViewById(R.id.radLbToKilo);
        final RadioButton kiloToLb = (RadioButton) findViewById(R.id.radKiloToLb);
        final TextView result = (TextView) findViewById(R.id.txtResult);
        Button convert = (Button)findViewById(R.id.btnConvert);

        convert.setOnClickListener(new OnClickListener() {
            @Override
            public void onClick(View v) {
                // TODO Auto-generated method stub
                weightEntered=Double.parseDouble(weight.getText().toString());
                DecimalFormat tenth = new DecimalFormat("#.#");
                if(lbToKilo.isChecked()){
                    if (weightEntered <=500){
                        convertedWeight = weightEntered / conversionRate;
                        result.setText(tenth.format(convertedWeight) + " kilograms");
                    }else {
                        Toast.makeText(Main.this,"Pounds must be less than 500", Toast.LENGTH_LONG).show();
                    }
                }
                if(kiloToLb.isChecked()){
                    if (weightEntered <=225){
                       convertedWeight = weightEntered * conversionRate;
                       result.setText(tenth.format(convertedWeight) + " pounds");
                    }else {
                        Toast.makeText(Main.this, "Kilos must be less than 225", Toast.LENGTH_LONG).show();
                    }
                  }
                }
          });
    }
}
```

Second nested If statement

Figure 4-24 Completed code

6. To view the finished application, click Run on the menu bar, and then select Run to save and test the application in the emulator. The first time the application is executed, a dialog box opens asking how to run the application. Select Android Application and click the OK button. Save all the files in the next dialog box and unlock the emulator. The application opens in the emulator where you enter a weight and select a radio button. To view the results, click the Convert Weight button.

   The Medical Calculator Android app is executed (see Figures 4-1 and 4-2).

Wrap It Up—Chapter Summary

Beginning with a customized icon, this chapter has completed the steps to create the graphical user interface including a RadioGroup control for the Medical Calculator program. The decision structure including a nested If Else statement determines different outcomes based on user input. If necessary, a toast message reminds the user of the expected input. You have learned to customize feedback and make decisions based on any user's input.

- To display a custom launcher icon instead of the default icon on the home screen of an Android device, copy the custom icon image to the res/drawable folder for the project, and then update the Android Manifest file to include the filename of the image file.
- Include RadioButton controls to allow users to select or deselect an option. Each RadioButton control has a label defined by the Text property and a Checked property set to either true or false. In a RadioGroup control, only one RadioButton control can be selected at a time.
- Android apps use hexadecimal color codes to set the color displayed in controls.
- Use the Layout gravity property to position a control precisely on the screen. You can change this property using the Properties pane or the Change Gravity tool on the toolbar. For more flexibility in controlling your layout, use the Change Margins tool to change the spacing between objects.
- A decision structure includes a conditional statement that checks whether the condition is true or false. To execute a conditional statement and the statements that are executed when a condition is true, Java uses the If statement and its variety of formats, including the If Else statement. An If statement executes one set of instructions if a specified condition is true and takes no action if the condition is not true. An If Else statement executes one set of instructions if a specified condition is true and another set of instructions if the condition is false.
- To test the conditions in a conditional statement such as an If statement, Java provides relational operators that are used within the conditional statement to express the relationship between the numbers being tested. For example, you can use a relational operator to test whether one value is greater than another.
- If more than one condition is tested in a conditional statement, the conditions are called a compound condition. To create an If statement that processes a compound condition, you must use a logical operator such as && (And).
- After including code that validates data, you can code a toast notification (also called a toast message) to display a brief message indicating that an incorrect value was entered.
- To test a second condition only after determining that a first condition is true or false, you nest one If statement within another If statement.

Key Terms

Change Gravity—A tool that changes the linear alignment of a control, so that it is aligned to the left, center, right, top, or bottom of an object or the screen.

compound condition—More than one condition included in an If statement.

decision structure—A fundamental control structure used in computer programming that deals with the different conditions that occur based on the values entered into an application.

equals method—A method of the String class that Java uses to compare strings.

hexadecimal color code—A triplet of three colors using hexadecimal numbers, where colors are specified first by a pound sign followed by how much red (00 to FF), how much green (00 to FF), and how much blue (00 to FF) are in the final color.

If Else statement—A statement that executes one set of instructions if a specified condition is true and another set of instructions if the condition is false.

If statement—A statement that executes one set of instructions if a specified condition is true and takes no action if the condition is not true.

isChecked( ) method—A method that tests a checked property to determine if a RadioButton object has been selected.

launcher icon—An icon that appears on the home screen to represent the application.

margin—Blank space that offsets a control by a certain amount of density independent pixels (dp) on each of its four sides.

nest—To place one statement, such as an If statement, within another statement.

RadioGroup—A group of RadioButton controls; only one RadioButton control can be selected at a time.

toast notification—A message that appears as an overlay on a user's screen, often displaying a validation warning.

Developer FAQs

1. What is the icon found on the Android home screen that opens an app?
2. What is the preferred prefix for a filename and file extension of the icon described in question 1?
3. What is the pixel size for the icon described in question 1 for a high-density pixel image?
4. To display a custom icon, you must perform two steps. First, add the icon image file to the drawable-hdpi folder. What is the second step?
5. Which TextView property is changed to identify the color of the control?

6. Which primary color is represented by the hexadecimal code of #00FF00?
7. What is the name of the tool used to center a TextView control horizontally?
8. Using the Change Margins tool, in which text box would you type 22dp to move a control 22 density pixels down from the upper edge of the emulator?
9. When a RadioGroup control is placed on the emulator, the first RadioButton control is selected by default. Which property is set as true by default?
10. Write an If statement that tests if the value in the variable age is between 18 and 21 years of age, inclusive, with empty braces.
11. Write an If statement that tests if the radio button named *gender* is selected with empty braces.
12. Rewrite the following line of code without a Not logical operator but keeping the same logical processing: if (! (waist <= 36) {
13. Write an If statement to compare if a string variable named *company* is equal to *Verizon* with empty braces.
14. Fix this statement: if (hours < 1 | | > 8) {
15. How many radio buttons can be selected at one time in a RadioGroup control?
16. Write an If statement that compares if wage is equal to 7.25 with empty braces.
17. If you compare two strings and the result is a positive number, what is the order of the two strings?
18. Using a relational operator, write an If statement that evaluates if a variable named *tipPercent* is not equal to .15 with empty braces.
19. Write a warning message that would display the comment "The maximum credits allowed is 18" with a long interval.
20. Write a quick reminder message that would display the comment "File saved" with a short interval.

Beyond the Book

Using the Internet, search the Web for the answers to the following questions to further your Android knowledge.

1. You have developed an application on music downloads. Search using Google Images to locate an appropriate icon and resize the icon using a paint-type program for use as a phone app launcher icon.
2. Search the Android Market site for a popular app that has a Sudoku puzzle. Take a screen shot of one Sudoku puzzle's launcher icon and another screen shot of the larger graphic used for the description of the app.

3. An Android toast message can also be coded to appear at an exact location on the screen. Explain how this works and give an example of the code that would do this.
4. Research the average price of an individual paid app. Write 75–100 words on the average selling prices of Android and iPhone apps.

Case Programming Projects

Complete one or more of the following case programming projects. Use the same steps and techniques taught within the chapter. Submit the program you create to your instructor. The level of difficulty is indicated for each case programming project.

Easiest: ★

Intermediate: ★ ★

Challenging: ★ ★ ★

Case Project 4–1: Temperature Conversion App ★

Requirements Document

Application title:	Temperature Conversion App
Purpose:	The app converts temperatures from Fahrenheit to Celsius or Celsius to Fahrenheit.
Algorithms:	1. The opening screen requests the outside temperature (Figure 4-25). 2. The user selects a radio button labeled Fahrenheit to Celsius or Celsius to Fahrenheit and then selects the Convert Temperature button. 3. The converted temperature is displayed (Figure 4-26).
Conditions:	1. The result is rounded off to the nearest tenth. 2. Formulas: C = (F – 32) * 5 / 9 and F = (C * 9 / 5) + 32 3. Do not enter more than 130 degrees Fahrenheit or 55 degrees Celsius. 4. Use Theme with no title bar.

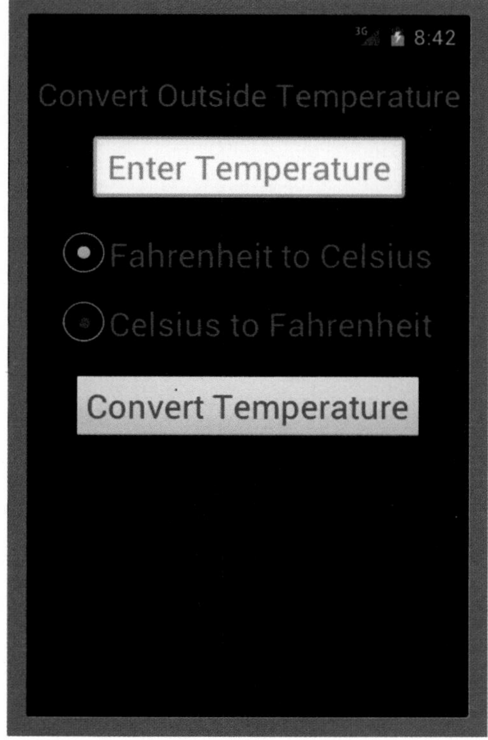

Figure 4-25

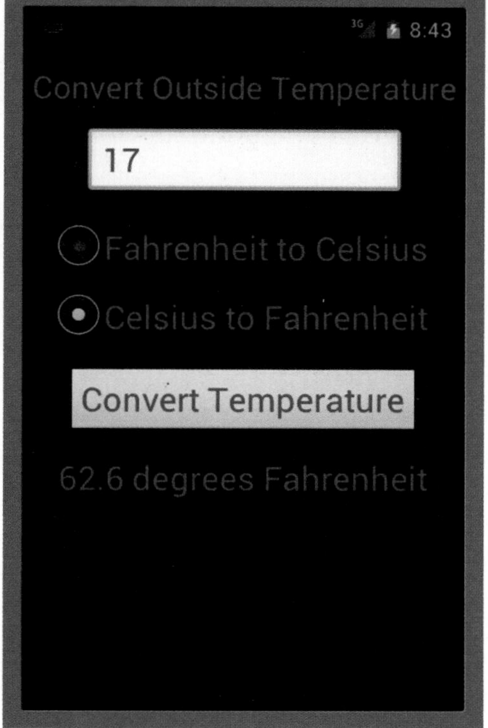

Figure 4-26

Case Project 4–2: Movie Time App ★

Requirements Document

Application title: Movie Time App

Purpose: A Movie Time app charges a monthly fee based on whether you want streaming movies, DVD movies, or combined services (three choices). The app has a customized launcher icon (Figure 4-27).

Algorithms:

1. The opening screen requests the number of months that you would like to subscribe to the movie service (Figure 4-28).
2. The user selects which service: streaming movies for $7.99 per month, DVD movies by mail for $8.99 per month, or a combined service for $15.99 per month.
3. When the Compute Price button is selected, the total price is displayed for the number of months subscribed (Figure 4-29).

Conditions:

1. The app allows you to subscribe for up to 24 months.
2. Use a customized launcher icon (ic_launcher_movie.png).
3. Use a theme with an action bar.

iStockphoto.com/Viktor Chornobay

Figure 4-27

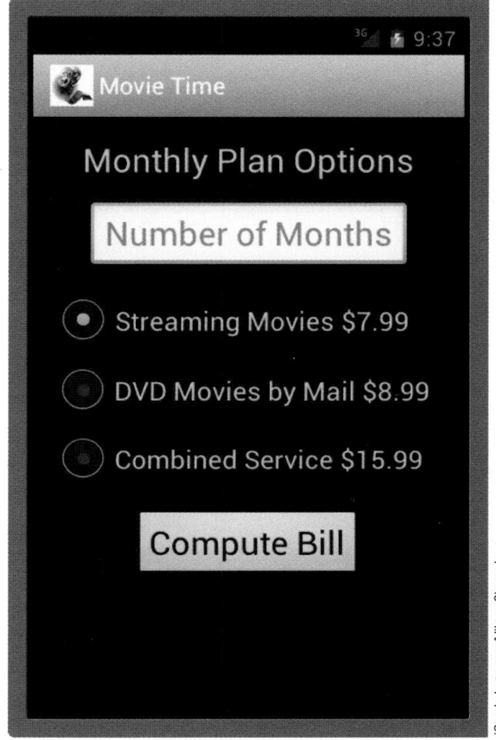

iStockphoto.com/Viktor Chornobay

Figure 4-28

iStockphoto.com/Viktor Chornobay

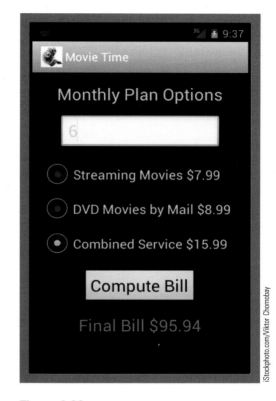

Figure 4-29

Case Project 4–3: Floor Tiling App ★ ★

Requirements Document

Application title:	Floor Tiling App
Purpose:	The tiling app allows you to calculate how many tiles you need to cover a rectangular area.
Algorithms:	1. The opening screen requests the length and the width of a room in whole feet. 2. The user selects whether the tiles are 12 inches by 12 inches or 18 inches by 18 inches. 3. The number of tiles needed to cover the area in square feet is displayed.

Case Project 4–4: Math Flash Cards App ★ ★

Requirements Document

Application Title: Math Flash Cards App

Purpose: The Math Flash Cards App is designed for children to practice their basic math skills.

Algorithms:
1. The opening screen requests two integer values.
2. The user can select addition, subtraction, or multiplication.
3. The entire math problem is displayed with the result.

Conditions:
1. The integer values must be between 1 and 20.
2. Use a customized launcher icon.

Case Project 4–5: Currency Conversion App ★ ★ ★

Requirements Document

Application title: Currency Conversion App

Purpose: The Currency Conversion app converts U.S. dollars into euros, Mexican pesos, or Canadian dollars.

Algorithms:
1. The opening screen requests the amount of U.S. dollars to be converted.
2. The user selects euros, Mexican pesos, or Canadian dollars.
3. The conversion of U.S. dollars to the selected currency is displayed.

Conditions:
1. Use *http://xe.com* to locate current conversion rates.
2. The program only converts values below $100,000 U.S. dollars.
3. Use a customized launcher icon.

Case Project 4–6: Average Income Tax by Country App ★ ★ ★

Requirements Document

Application title: Average Income Tax by Country App

Purpose: The Average Income Tax by Country app allows the user to enter the amount of taxable income earned in the past year. The user selects his or her country of residence and the yearly income tax is displayed.

Algorithms:

1. The opening screen requests two integer values.
2. The user can select addition, subtraction, or multiplication.
3. The entire math problem is displayed with the result.

Conditions: The following table displays the annual income tax percentages.

Country	**Average Income Tax**
China	25%
Germany	32%
Sweden	34%
USA	18%

CHAPTER 5

Investigate! Android Lists, Arrays, and Web Browsers

In this chapter, you learn to:

- Create an Android project using a list
- Develop a user interface that uses ListView
- Extend the ListActivity class
- Use an array to create a list
- Code a setListAdapter to display an array
- Design a custom ListView layout with XML code
- Display an image with the ListView control
- Change the default title bar text
- Code a custom setListAdapter for a custom layout
- Call the onListItemClick method when a list item is selected
- Write code using the Switch decision structure
- Call an intent to work with an outside app
- Open an Android Web browser
- Launch a Web site through the use of a URI using an Android browser
- Test an application with multiple decisions

Displaying a list is one of the most common design patterns used in mobile applications. This morning you likely read the news designed as a listing of articles on a phone or tablet. You scrolled down the list of news articles and selected one by tapping the screen to display a full story with text, images, and hyperlinks. As you walked to class today, you probably scrolled a list of songs on a mobile device and listened to your favorite tunes.

From a list, you can open an article, play a song, open a Web site, or even launch a video. A list created with a ListView control may be one of the most important Android design elements because it is used so frequently. To select a list item, a design structure is necessary to route your request to the intended content. In Chapter 4, you learned about the decision structure called an If statement, one of the major control structures used in computer programming. In this chapter, you learn about another decision structure called the Switch statement.

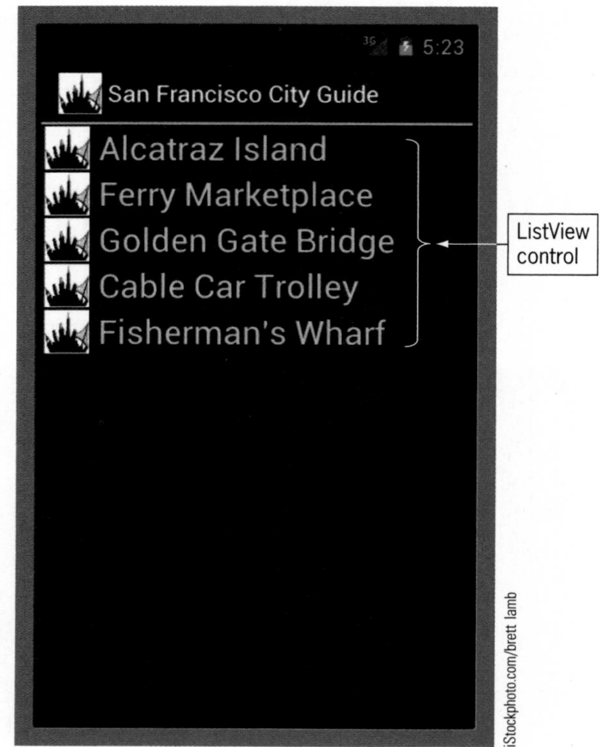

Figure 5-1 The San Francisco City Guide Android app

To demonstrate the process of using a list to navigate to different content, you design a travel city guide for San Francisco, California, highlighting the best attractions the city has to offer. The City Guide application shown in Figure 5-1 provides a list of city attractions. A city guide for a large city can provide easy access to all its sights, activities, and restaurants in one handy guide for your phone.

The Android app in Figure 5-1 could be part of a larger app that displays city maps, detailed site information, and restaurant recommendations. This mobile app provides information about popular places tourists visit in San Francisco. The City Guide app displays five San Francisco attractions. When the user taps one of the attractions, a second window opens displaying either an image or a Web site providing more information about the site or activity. The first two items on the list link to Web sites, as shown in Figure 5-2. A browser opens to display a Web site for Alcatraz Island or Ferry Marketplace. If the user selects Golden Gate Bridge, Cable Car Trolley, or Fisherman's Wharf, an image appears on a second screen, as shown in Figure 5-3.

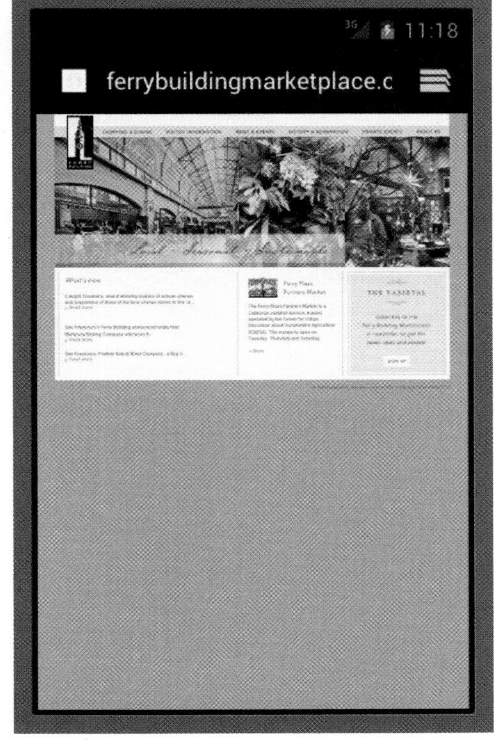

Figure 5-2 Alcatraz and Ferry Marketplace Web sites

iStockphoto.com/DNY59

Erik Patton/Shutterstock.com

Erik Patton/Shutterstock.com

Figure 5-3 San Francisco attractions

IN THE TRENCHES

To see a professional city guide app in action, download a free app created by Trip Advisor, Triposo, or Gowalla.

To create this application, the developer must understand how to perform the following processes, among others:

1. Create a list using a ListView control.
2. Define an array to establish the items of the list.
3. Add the images used in the project.
4. Define an XML file to design the custom list with a leading image.
5. Code a Switch decision structure to handle the selection of items.
6. Open an Android Web browser to display a specified Uniform Resource Identifier (URI).
7. Create multiple classes and XML layout files to display pictures of attractions.

Creating a List

The San Francisco City Guide app begins with a vertical list of attractions on the opening screen, as shown in Figure 5-1. The Java View class creates the list and makes it scrollable if it exceeds the length of the screen. Lists can be used to display a to-do list, your personal contacts, recipe names, shopping items, weekly weather, Twitter messages, and Facebook postings, for example. You use a ListView control to contain the list attraction items. Android also has a TableLayout view that looks similar to a ListView, but a ListView allows you to select each row in the list for further action. Selecting an item opens a Web browser to a related Web page or displays an image of the attraction. You can directly use the ListView control in the Composite category of the Palette in the layout of the emulator (Figure 5-4) as you can with any other user interface component, but coding the list in Java is the preferred method and is used in the chapter project.

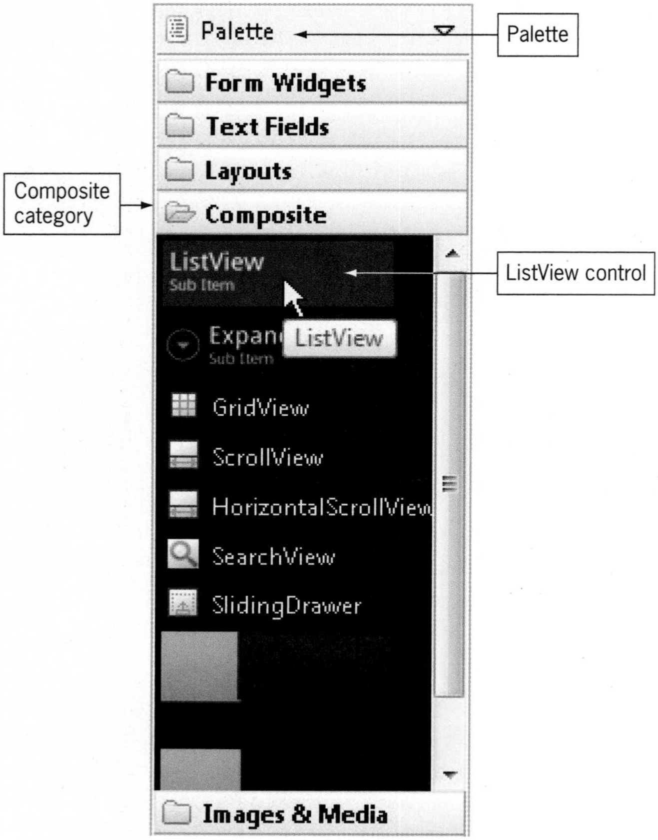

Figure 5-4 ListView control on the Palette

Extending a ListActivity

You begin creating a list by opening Main.java and changing the type of Activity in the code. In the previous chapters, each opening class statement (`public class Main extends Activity`) extended the basic Activity class. If the primary purpose of a class is to display a ListView control, use a class named **ListActivity** instead, which makes it simple to display a list of items within the app. To extend the ListActivity class of Main.java of the City Guide app, follow these steps to begin the application:

1. Open the Eclipse program. Click the New button on the Standard toolbar. Expand the Android folder and select Android Project. Click the Next button. In the New Android Project dialog box, enter the Project Name **City Guide**. To save the project on your USB drive, click to remove the check mark from the Use default location check box. Type **E:\Workspace** (if necessary, enter a different drive letter that identifies the USB drive). Click the Next button. For the Build Target, select Android 4.0, if necessary. Click the Next button. For the Package Name, type **net.androidbootcamp.cityguide**. Enter **Main** in the Create Activity text box.

The new Android City Guide project has a Project Name, a Package Name, and an Activity named Main (Figure 5-5).

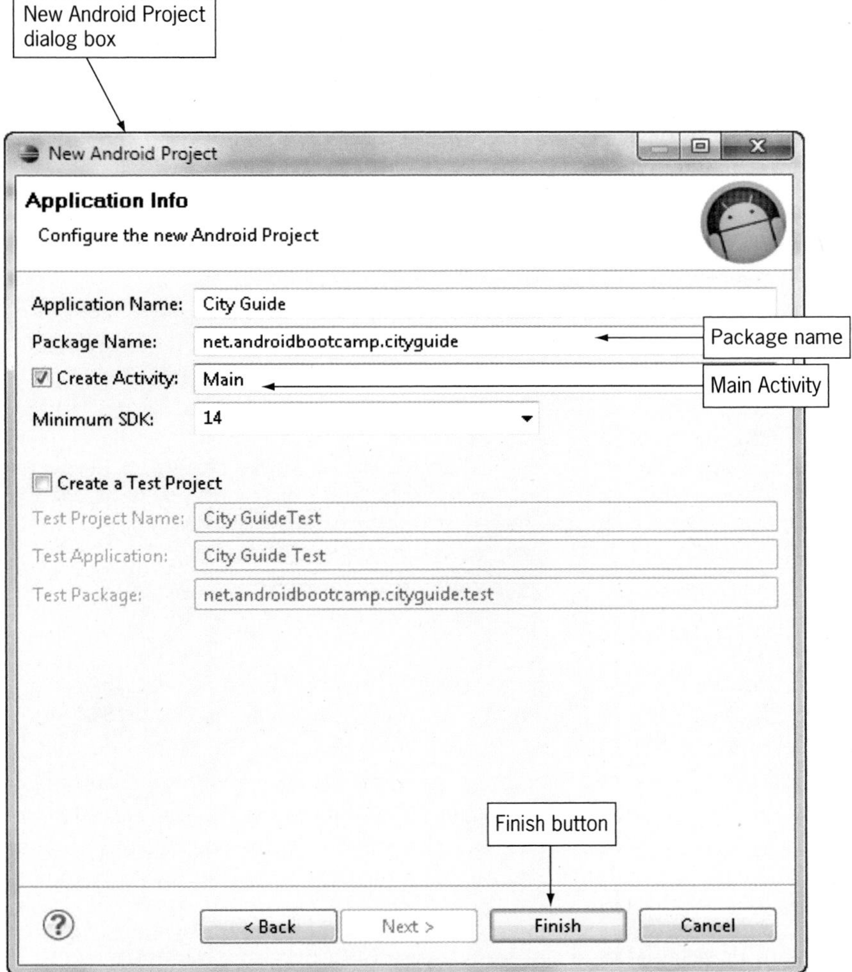

Figure 5-5 Application information for the new Android project

2. Click the Finish button. Expand the City Guide project in the Package Explorer, expand the src and net.androidbootcamp.cityguide folders, and then double-click Main.java to open its code window. Click to the left of *Activity* in the public class Main extends Activity { line, and change Activity to **ListActivity**. Point to ListActivity and click Import 'ListActivity' (android.app). Delete the line import android.app.Activity; and then delete the line *setContentView(R.layout.main);*.

Main extends ListActivity, which contains predefined methods for the use of lists (Figure 5-6).

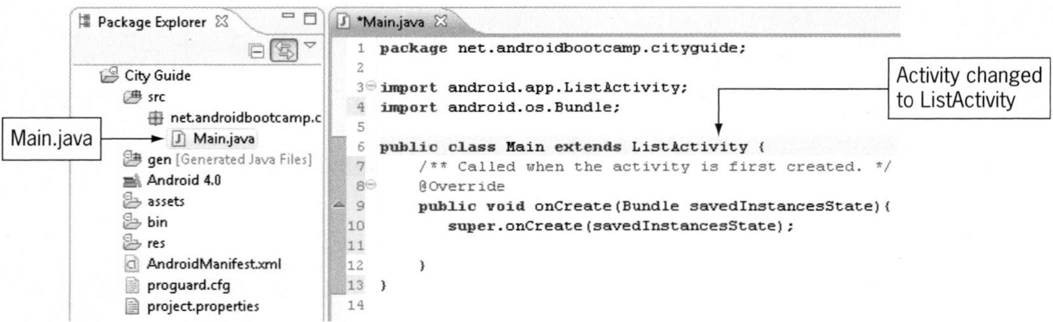

Figure 5-6 Main extends ListActivity

IN THE TRENCHES

Another type of a ListView control is the ExpandableListView, which provides a two-level list. For example, if you were renting a car, a list of all the compact cars would be listed in one category on the top half of your phone and the economy cars in a separate category at the bottom. ExpandableListView provides two separate listings.

Creating an Array

Before the list of attractions can be displayed, the string of attraction names must be declared. By using an **array variable**, which can store more than one value, you can avoid assigning a separate variable for each item in the list. Every application developed thus far involved a limited number of variables. Professional programming applications commonly require much larger sets of data using multiple variables. You learned that data type variables can store only one value at a time. If you changed a variable's value, the previous value was deleted because a typical variable can store only one value at a time. Each individual item in an array that contains a value is called an **element**.

Arrays provide access to data by using a numeric index, or subscript, to identify each element in the array. Using an array, you can store a collection of values of similar data types. For example, you can store five string values without having to declare five different variables. Instead, each value is stored in an individual element of the array, and you refer to each element by its index within the array. The index used to reference a value in the first element within an array is zero. Each subsequent element is referenced by an increasing index value, as shown in Table 5-1.

Element	Value
Attraction[0]	Alcatraz Island
Attraction[1]	Ferry Marketplace
Attraction[2]	Golden Gate Bridge
Attraction[3]	Cable Car Trolley
Attraction[4]	Fisherman's Wharf

Table 5-1 Attraction array with index values

In Table 5-1, an array named Attraction holds five attractions. Each attraction is stored in an array element, and each element is assigned a unique index. The first string is stored in the element with the index of 0. The element is identified by the term attraction [0], pronounced "attraction sub zero."

Declaring an Array

Like declarations for variables of other types, an array declaration has two components: the array's data type and the array's name. You can declare an array containing numeric values as in the following coding example:

```
double[ ] weather={72.3, 65.0, 25.7, 99.5};
```

Declare a String array containing the text values used in the chapter project with the following code:

Code Syntax

```
String[] attraction={"Alcatraz Island", "Ferry Marketplace",
     "Golden Gate Bridge", "Cable Car Trolley", "Fisherman's Wharf"};
```

The attraction list initialized in the array can easily be expanded to include more items at any time. To assign the listing of attractions to the String data type in an array named attraction, follow these steps:

1. After the super.onCreate(savedInstanceState); statement in Main.java, insert a new line and type **String[] attraction={"Alcatraz Island", "Ferry Marketplace", "Golden Gate Bridge", "Cable Car Trolley", "Fisherman's Wharf"};**.

   The String array named attraction is assigned the five attraction locations (Figure 5-7).

```
*Main.java
package net.androidbootcamp.cityguide;

import android.app.ListActivity;

public class Main extends ListActivity {
    /** Called when the activity is first created. */
    @Override
    public void onCreate(Bundle savedInstanceState){
        super.onCreate(savedInstanceState);
        String[] attraction={"Alcatraz Island","Ferry Marketplace",
                "Golden Gate Bridge","Cable Car Trolley","Fisherman's Wharf"};
    }
}
```

Press the Enter key after typing the comma to place statement on two lines

String array initialized

Figure 5-7 String array initialized with attractions

2. Save your work.

GTK

To declare an array without assigning actual values, allocate the size of the array in the brackets to reserve the room needed in memory, as in int[ ] ages = new int[100];. The first number assigned to the ages array is placed in ages [0]. This array holds 101 elements in the array, one more than the maximum index.

Using a setListAdapter and Array Adapter

In the City Guide application, once the array is assigned, you can display an array listing using adapters. An **adapter** provides a data model for the layout of the list and for converting the data from the array into list items. The ListView and adapter work together to display a list. For example, if you want to share an iPad screen with a group, you need an adapter to connect to a projector to display the image on a large screen. Similarly, a **setListAdapter** projects your data to the onscreen list on your device by connecting the ListActivity's ListView object to the array data. A setListAdapter contains the information to connect the onscreen list with the attraction array in the chapter project. Calling a setListAdapter in the Java code binds the elements of the array to a ListView layout. In the next portion of the statement, a ListAdapter called an **ArrayAdapter<String> i** supplies the String array data to the ListView. The three parameters that follow ArrayAdapter refer to the *this* class, a generic layout called simple_list_item_1, and the array named attraction. The following code syntax shows the complete statement:

Code Syntax

```
setListAdapter(new ArrayAdapter<String>(this,
        android.R.layout.simple_list_item_1, attraction));
```

Later in the chapter, instead of using the generic layout called simple_list_item_1, you design an XML layout to customize the layout to include the City Guide's logo. You can change the setListAdapter statement to reference the custom layout when you finish designing it.

Follow these steps to add the setListAdapter that displays the array as a list:

1. After the second line of code initializing the String array, press the Enter key, type **setListAdapter(new ArrayAdapter<String>(this, android.R.layout.simple_list_item_1, attraction));**, and then press the Enter key. Point to ArrayAdapter and click Import 'ArrayAdapter' (android.widget).

   If you are using a Mac, press the Return key instead of the Enter key.

   The setListAdapter displays the attraction array in a generic ListView layout (Figure 5-8).

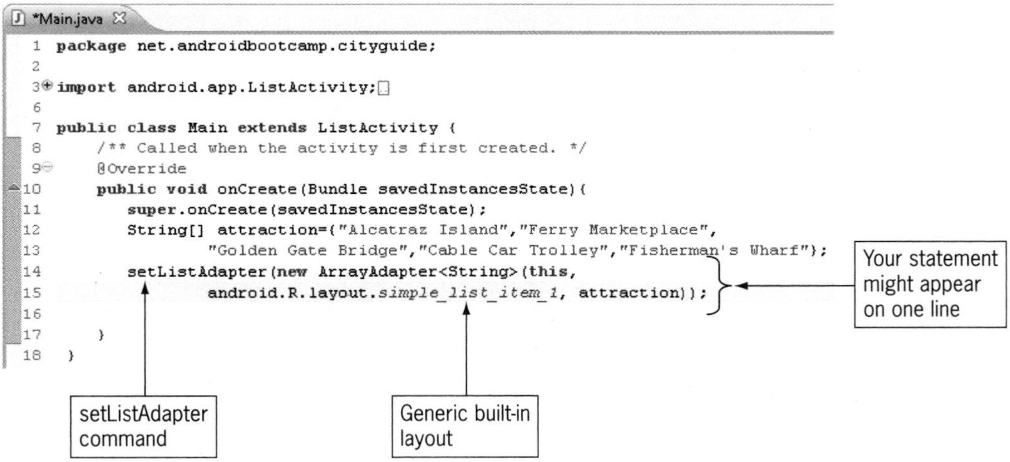

*Main.java

```
package net.androidbootcamp.cityguide;

import android.app.ListActivity;

public class Main extends ListActivity {
    /** Called when the activity is first created. */
    @Override
    public void onCreate(Bundle savedInstancesState){
        super.onCreate(savedInstancesState);
        String[] attraction={"Alcatraz Island","Ferry Marketplace",
                "Golden Gate Bridge","Cable Car Trolley","Fisherman's Wharf"};
        setListAdapter(new ArrayAdapter<String>(this,
                android.R.layout.simple_list_item_1, attraction));

    }
}
```

Your statement might appear on one line

setListAdapter command

Generic built-in layout

Figure 5-8 setListAdapter displays an array

2. To display the attraction list in the generic ListView layout, click Run on the menu bar, and then select Run. Select Android Application and click the OK button. Save Main.java in the next dialog box, if necessary, and unlock the emulator when the app starts.

   The application opens in the emulator window (Figure 5-9).

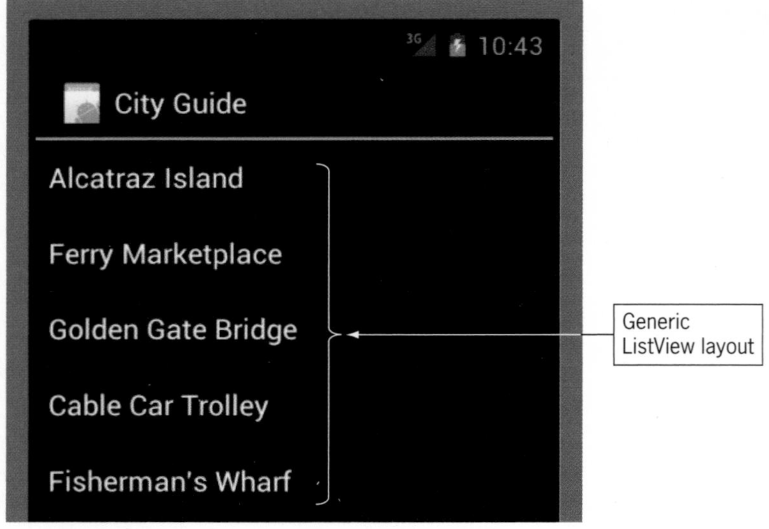

Figure 5-9 ListView built-in layout

3. Close the emulated application window.

GTK
Other generic layouts that you might want to try with ListView include simple_list_item_2, simple_list_item_checked (displays check boxes), and simple_list_item_multiple_choice.

Adding the Images to the Resources Folder

The City Guide application uses several images throughout the app. An icon logo called ic_launcher_sf.png displays the skyline of San Francisco and is used multiple times on the opening screen. Images of the Golden Gate Bridge, Cable Car Trolley, and Fisherman's Wharf appear when the user selects those items from the opening list. To place a copy of the images from the USB drive into the res/drawable-hdpi folder, follow these steps:

1. If necessary, copy the student files to your USB drive. Open the USB folder containing the student files. In the Package Explorer, expand the drawable-hdpi folder in the res folder. Delete the file named ic_launcher.png (the Android logo). To add the four image files to the drawable-hdpi resource folder, drag ic_launcher_sf.png, bridge.png, trolley.png, and wharf.png files to the drawable-hdpi folder until a plus sign pointer appears. Release the mouse button. If necessary, click the Copy files option button, and then click the OK button.

   Copies of the four files appear in the drawable-hdpi folder (Figure 5-10).

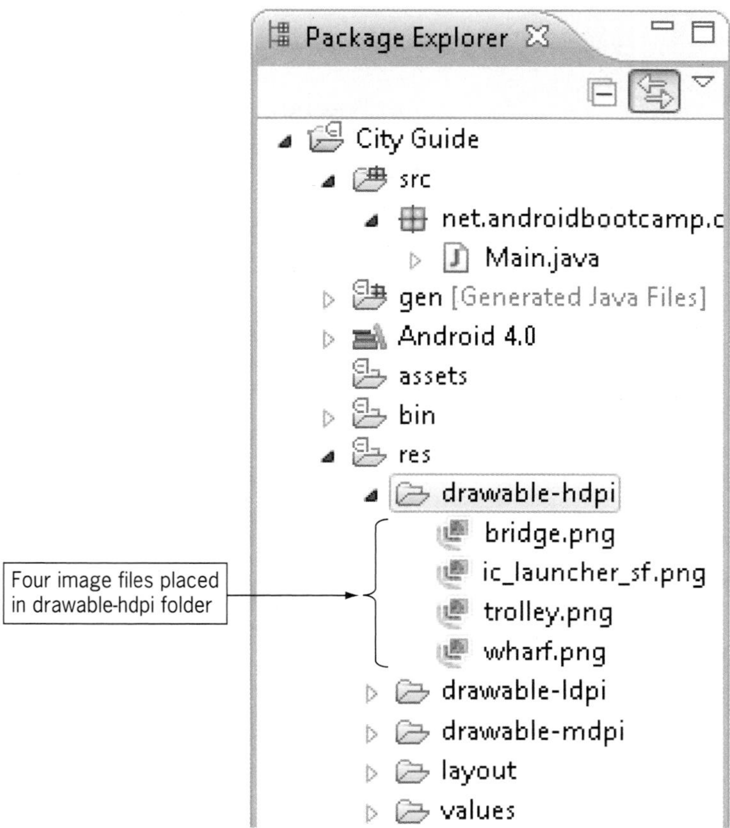

Figure 5-10 Images copied

2. To set the Android Manifest to use the ic_launcher_sf image as the app icon when the application is executed, in the Package Explorer, double-click the AndroidManifest.xml file. Click the AndroidManifest.xml tab at the bottom of the screen. Inside the application code, click in the line android:icon=@"drawable/ic_launcher". Change the filename portion from ic_launcher" to **ic_launcher_sf"**.

   The Android launcher icon is coded in the Android Manifest file (Figure 5-11).

Figure 5-11 Android Manifest code with new Launcher Icon file

3. Click the Save All button on the Standard toolbar to save your work.

IN THE TRENCHES
When publishing apps, you must follow copyright laws relative to copyrighted images used within your Android apps. Copyright is the legal protection extended to the authors or owners of original published and unpublished artistic and intellectual works, and you must seek copyright permissions. However, if the image is accompanied by the statement "This work is dedicated to the public domain," the image is available for fair use in your app.

Creating a Custom XML Layout for ListView

You can design a layout by using the emulator window on the Graphical Layout tab and then drag and drop controls from the Palette, or you can code the main.xml file using XML code. It is easier to use the Palette for a simple layout. However, the opening screen for the City Guide chapter project shown in Figure 5-1 requires a custom layout for the list that includes a San Francisco City Guide logo and unique size and spacing of the attraction names. In the XML code, you must first add an ImageView control to display the ic_launcher_sf image file. The ImageView is named with the id property in the code and resized with the layout_width and layout_height properties, margins are set, and the location source of the file is entered. Next, the code for the TextView control is named, the layout is identified, and the textSize property is set. The text property of android:text="@+id/travel" is used in the setListAdapter and the actual items in the array display instead of the text object named travel. To create a custom XML layout for main.xml, follow these steps:

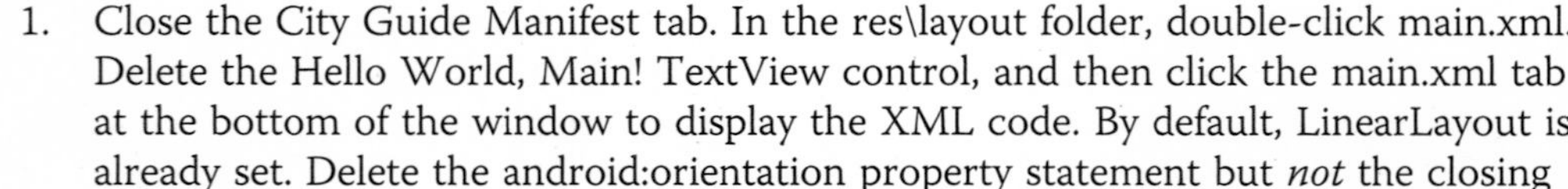

1. Close the City Guide Manifest tab. In the res\layout folder, double-click main.xml. Delete the Hello World, Main! TextView control, and then click the main.xml tab at the bottom of the window to display the XML code. By default, LinearLayout is already set. Delete the android:orientation property statement but *not* the closing

angle bracket (>), and then type **<ImageView** after the closing angle bracket. Press the Enter key. Type the following code using auto-completion as much as possible:

```
    android:id="@+id/ic_launcher_sf"
    android:layout_width="50px"
    android:layout_height="50px"
    android:layout_marginLeft="4px"
    android:layout_marginRight="10px"
    android:layout_marginTop="2px"
    android:src="@drawable/ic_launcher_sf" >
</ImageView>
```

The ImageView control is customized in the main.xml file (Figure 5-12).

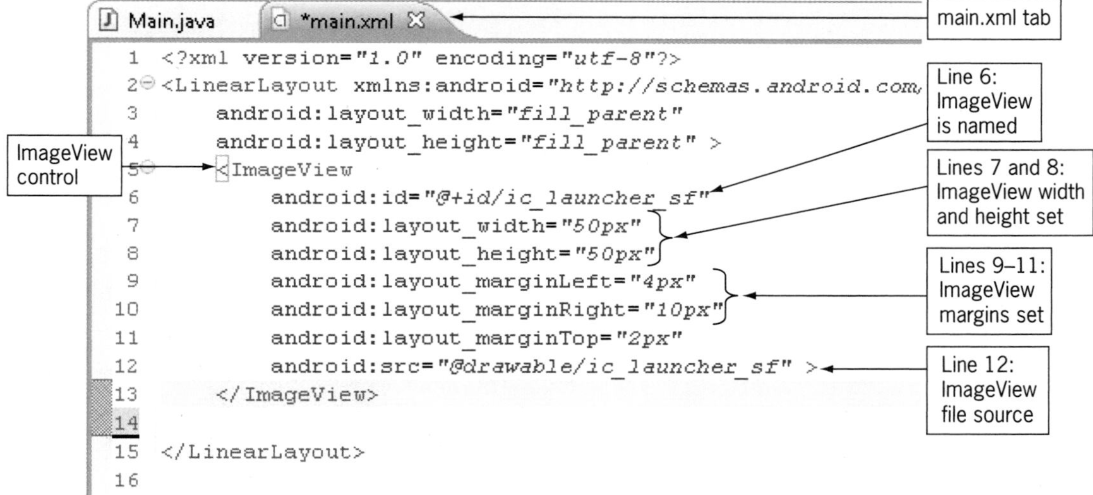

Figure 5-12 ImageView XML code

2. Insert a blank line after the ImageView code and type **<TextView**. Press the Enter key. Type the following code using auto-completion as much as possible:

```
android:id="@+id/travel"
android:layout_width="wrap_content"
android:layout_height="wrap_content"
android:text="@+id/travel"
android:textSize="25sp" >
</TextView>
```

The TextView control is customized in the main.xml file (Figure 5-13).

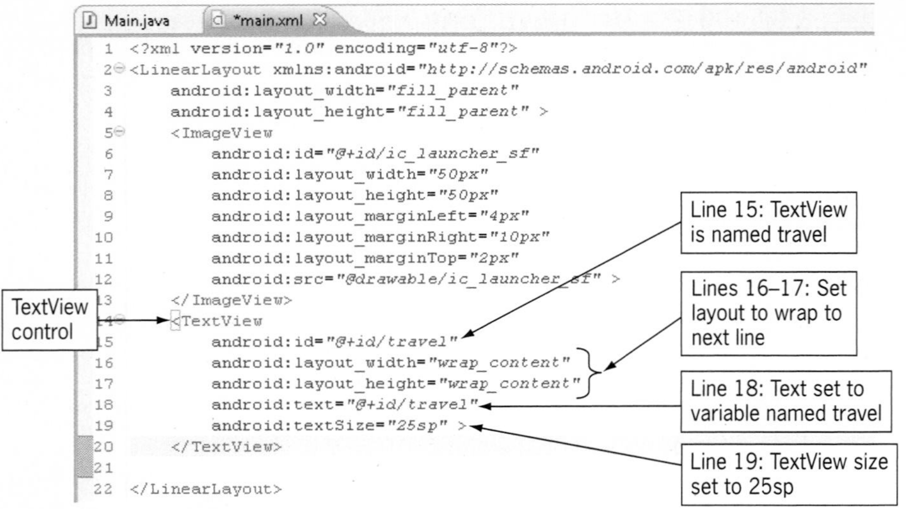

Figure 5-13 TextView XML code

Changing the Title Bar Text

Developers often want a custom title to appear on the title bar at the top of the window instead of the actual application name. A string named app_name in the strings.xml file by default displays the project name. To change the title bar on the opening screen of the City Guide app to *San Francisco City Guide,* follow these steps:

1. Save your work and then close the main.xml window. Expand the res\values folder and double-click the strings.xml file. Click app_name (String) in the Android Resources window. Change the text in the Value text box to **San Francisco City Guide**.

   The app_name value is changed (Figure 5-14).

Figure 5-14 Title bar text is changed from default

2. Save your work.

Coding a setListAdapter with a Custom XML Layout

When the setListAdapter was coded and executed as shown in Figure 5-9, the attractions list was displayed within a built-in layout called simple_list_item_1 in the following statement:

```
setListAdapter(new ArrayAdapter<String>(this,
android.R.layout.simple_list_item_1, attraction));
```

Instead of using a standard layout in the setListAdapter, the custom XML layout you designed in main.xml adds the San Francisco City Guide logo and updates the TextView properties. The syntax changes from the default in two significant ways:

1. The second parameter in the default statement (android.R.layout.*simple_list_item_1*) is changed to R.layout.*main*. The android reference is removed because the Android library default layout is not being used. Instead R.layout.*main* references the main.xml custom layout design for the ImageView and TextView controls.
2. A third parameter is added before the attraction array name to reference the variable travel, which identifies the TextView control created in the main.xml file. The variable is substituted for the actual attraction locations initialized in the attraction array.

The following code syntax shows the code for a custom XML layout:

Code Syntax

```
setListAdapter(new ArrayAdapter<String>(this,
        R.layout.main, R.id.travel, attraction));
```

To edit the setListAdapter to use the custom XML layout, follow these steps:

1. Close the strings.xml window. In the setListAdapter statement of Main.java, click after the comma following the *this* command. Change the android.R.layout.simple_list_item_1, text to **R.layout.main, R.id.travel,** to add the custom layout named main.xml.

   The default setListAdapter is edited to include the custom layout (Figure 5-15).

*Main.java

```
package net.androidbootcamp.cityguide;

import android.app.ListActivity;

public class Main extends ListActivity {
    /** Called when the activity is first created. */
    @Override
    public void onCreate(Bundle savedInstancesState){
       super.onCreate(savedInstancesState);
       String[] attraction={"Alcatraz Island","Ferry Marketplace",
              "Golden Gate Bridge","Cable Car Trolley","Fisherma
       setListAdapter(new ArrayAdapter<String>(this,
              R.layout.main, R.id.travel, attraction));
    }
}
```

Custom layout formatted by main.xml; yours might appear on one line

Figure 5-15 setListAdapter with custom layout for list

2. Run and save the application to view the custom layout of the ListView.

   The emulator displays the opening screen with a custom ListView (Figure 5-16).

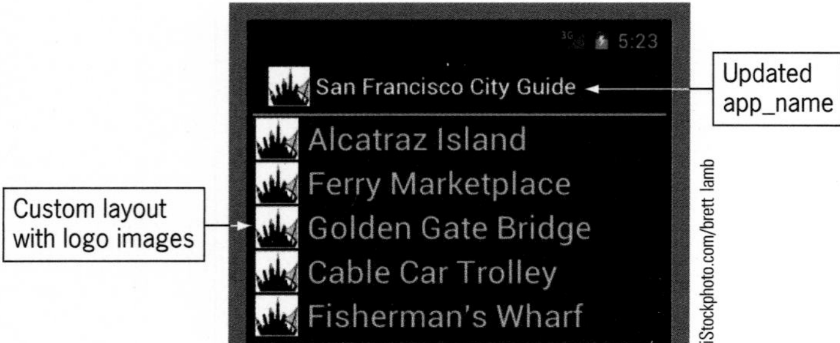

Figure 5-16 ListView custom layout in emulator

3. Close the emulated application window.

Using the onListItemClick Method

The City Guide opening screen has a custom list shown in Figure 5-16. Each of the attractions displayed in the list can be selected by tapping the attraction name on the mobile device. The method **onListItemClick( )** is called when an item in the list is selected. When an attraction in the list is selected, the **position** of the item is passed from the onListItemClick and evaluated with a decision structure, as shown in the following code syntax. If the user selects the first attraction, the position parameter is assigned an integer value of 0. The second item is assigned the position of 1, and so forth.

Code Syntax

```
protected void onListItemClick(ListView l, View v, int position, long id){
}
```

To code the onListItemClick method to respond to the event of the user's selection, follow these steps:

1. In Main.java, press the Enter key after the closing brace of the onCreate method to insert a new line. To respond to the user's selection, type **protected void onListItemClick(ListView l, View v, int position, long id)**. (Be sure to type a lowercase l after ListView, not the number 1.) Type an opening brace after the statement and press the Enter key. A closing brace is automatically placed in the code. After the code is entered to reference the ListView and View, point to the red error line below ListView and select 'Import ListView' (android.widget), and then point to the red error line below View and select 'Import View' (android.view).

The onListItemClick method detects the selection's position (Figure 5-17).

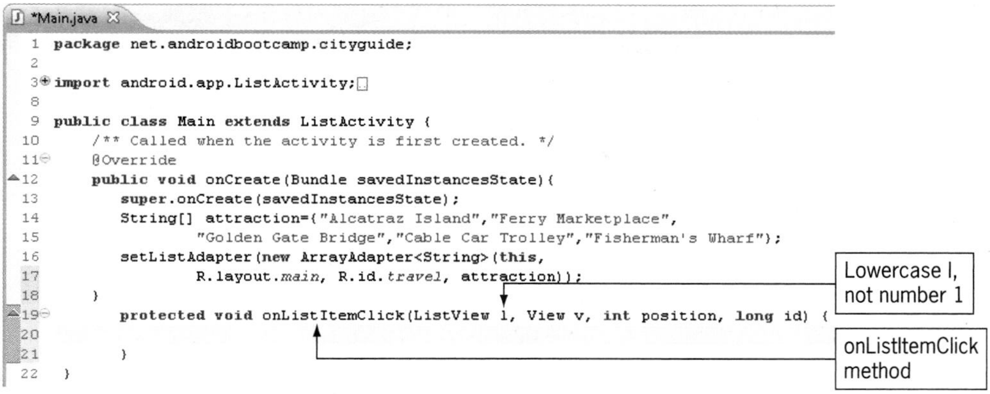

*Main.java

```
package net.androidbootcamp.cityguide;

import android.app.ListActivity;

public class Main extends ListActivity {
    /** Called when the activity is first created. */
    @Override
    public void onCreate(Bundle savedInstancesState){
        super.onCreate(savedInstancesState);
        String[] attraction={"Alcatraz Island","Ferry Marketplace",
                "Golden Gate Bridge","Cable Car Trolley","Fisherman's Wharf"};
        setListAdapter(new ArrayAdapter<String>(this,
                R.layout.main, R.id.travel, attraction));
    }
        protected void onListItemClick(ListView l, View v, int position, long id) {

        }
}
```

Lowercase l, not number 1

onListItemClick method

Figure 5-17 onListItemClick method

2. Save your work.

Decision Structure—Switch Statement

Each item in the list produces a different result when selected, such as opening a Web browser or displaying a picture of the attraction on a second screen. In Chapter 4, If statements evaluated the user's selection and the decision structure determined the results. You can use another decision structure called a Switch statement with a list or menu. The **Switch** statement allows you to choose from many statements based on an integer or char (single character) input. The switch keyword is followed by an integer expression in parentheses, which is followed by the cases, all enclosed in braces, as shown in the following code syntax:

Code Syntax

```
switch(position){
    case 0:
         //statements that are executed if position == 0
    break;
    case 1:
          //statements that are executed if position == 1
    break;
    default:
         //statements that are executed if position != any of the cases
}
```

The integer named *position* is evaluated in the Switch statement and executes the corresponding case. The **case** keyword is followed by a value and a colon. Typically the statement within a case ends with a **break** statement, which exits the Switch decision structure and continues with the next statement. Be careful not to omit the break statement or the subsequent case statement is executed as well. If there is no matching case value, the default option is executed. A default statement is optional. In the chapter project, a default statement is not necessary because the user must select one of the items in the list for an action to occur.

In the City Guide app, five attractions make up the list, so the following positions are possible for the Switch statement: case 0, case 1, case 2, case 3, and case 4. To code the Switch decision structure, follow these steps:

1. Within the braces of the onListItemClick method, type **switch(position){** and press the Enter key.

   The Switch decision structure is coded within the onListItemClick method (Figure 5-18).

```
protected void onListItemClick(ListView l, View v, int position, long id) {
  switch(position){
  
  }
}
```

Beginning of Switch statement decision structure

Figure 5-18 Switch statement

2. Within the braces of the Switch statement, add the case integer options. Type the following code, inserting a blank line after each case statement:

```
case 0:

        break;
case 1:

        break;
case 2:

        break;
case 3:

        break;
case 4:

        break;
```

   The case statements for the five selections from the attractions list each are coded (Figure 5-19).

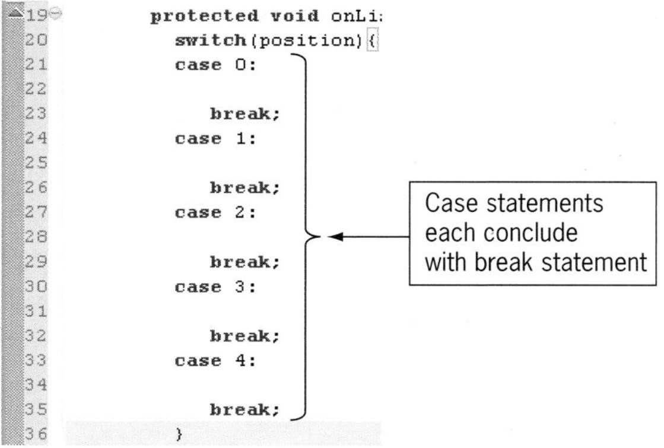

protected void onLi
switch(position){
case 0:
break;
case 1:
break;
case 2:
break;
case 3:
break;
case 4:
break;
}
Case statements each conclude with break statement

Figure 5-19 Case statements

3. Save your work.

GTK
Switch statements do not allow ranges such as 10–50. Use If statements when evaluating a range or strings.

Android Intents

When the user selects one of the first two list items in the project, Alcatraz Island or Ferry Marketplace, a built-in Android browser launches a Web site about each attraction. A browser is launched with Android code using an intent. Android intents send and receive activities and services that include opening a Web page in a browser, calling a phone number, locating a GPS position on a map, posting your notes to a note-taking program such as Evernote, opening your contacts list, sending a photo, or even posting to your social network. Additional Android intents are explored throughout the rest of this book. Android intents are powerful features that allow apps to talk to each other in a very simple way.

To better understand an intent, imagine a student sitting in a classroom. To ask a question or make a request, the student raises a hand. The teacher is alerted to the hand and responds to the student. An intent works the same way. Your app raises its hand and the other apps state that they are ready to handle your request. When the chapter project sends an intent, the browser app handles the request and opens the Web site.

IN THE TRENCHES
Android platform devices have many options for supported browsers. Popular Android browsers include Opera Mini Web, Dolphin, Skyfire, Mozilla Firefox, and Miren.

Launching the Browser from an Android Device

Android phones have a built-in browser with an intent filter that accepts intent requests from other apps. The intent sends the browser a **URI** (Uniform Resource Identifier), a string that identifies the resources of the Web. You might already be familiar with the term **URL** (Uniform Resource Locator), which means a Web site address. A URI is a URL with additional information necessary for gaining access to the resources required for posting the page. Depending on the lists of browsers installed on an Android device, Android selects a suitable browser (usually a user-set preferred browser), which accepts the action called ACTION_VIEW (must be in caps) and displays the site. **ACTION_VIEW** is the most common action performed on data. It is a generic action you can use to send any request to get the most reasonable action to occur. As shown in the following code syntax, a startActivity statement informs the present Activity that a new Activity is being started and the browser opens the Web site:

Code Syntax

```
startActivity(new Intent(Intent.ACTION_VIEW,
        Uri.parse("http://alcatrazcruises.com/")));
```

When the user selects the Alcatraz Island item from the attractions list, the Switch statement sends a zero integer value to the case statements. The case 0: statement is true, so the program executes the startActivity statement, which sends the browser a parsed string containing the URI Web address. The browser application then launches the Alcatraz Web site. When you click the Back button in some browser windows or the left arrow to the right of the menu button on the right side of the emulator, the previous Activity opens. In the chapter project, the attractions list ListView activity is displayed again. To code the startActivity that launches a Web site in an Android browser, follow these steps:

1. In Main.java, click the blank line after the line containing case 0: inside the Switch decision structure. Type **startActivity(new Intent(Intent.ACTION_VIEW, Uri.parse("http://alcatrazcruises.com/")));**. Point to Intent and click Import 'Intent' (android content). Point to Uri and Import 'Uri' (android.net).

   The startActivity code launches the Alcatraz Web site when the user selects the first list item (Figure 5-20).

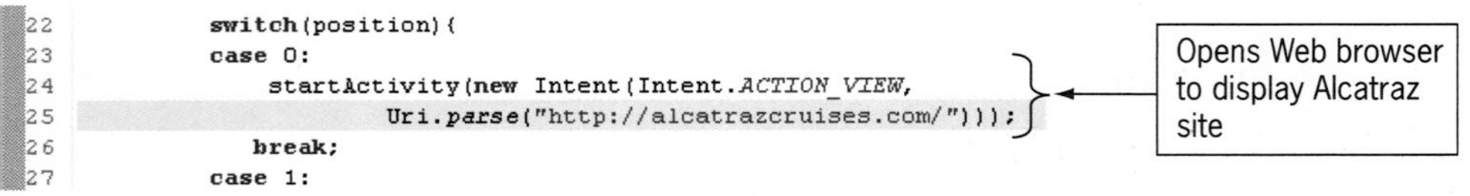

Figure 5-20 Code for launching the Alcatraz Web site

2. In Main.java, click the blank line after the line containing case 1:. Type **startActivity(new Intent(Intent.ACTION_VIEW, Uri.parse("http://ferrybuildingmarketplace.com")));**.

The startActivity code launches the Ferry Marketplace Web site when the user selects the second list item (Figure 5-21).

```
        case 0:
            startActivity(new Intent(Intent.ACTION_VIEW,
                    Uri.parse("http://alcatrazcruises.com/")));
            break;
        case 1:
            startActivity(new Intent(Intent.ACTION_VIEW,
                    Uri.parse("http://ferrybuildingmarketplace.com")));
            break;
```

Opens Web browser to display Ferry Marketplace site

Figure 5-21 Code for launching the Ferry Marketplace Web site

3. To display the Alcatraz Island Web site in the browser, click Run on the menu bar, and then select Run. Select Android Application and click the OK button. Save all the files in the next dialog box, if necessary, and unlock the emulator. Select the Alcatraz Island list item.

   The first item is selected from the list in the emulator and the Android browser displays the Alcatraz Island Web site. The site loads slowly in the emulator. Some Web sites are especially designed for mobile devices (Figure 5-22).

Android browser displays Alcatraz Web site in emulator

Figure 5-22 Browser opens in the emulator

4. Close the emulated application window.

IN THE TRENCHES

Be sure to test any links within your Android apps often. If you have hundreds of links, verifying Web links can be simple in concept but very time consuming in practice. A good place to start is with the World Wide Web Consortium's free Web Site Validation Service (*http://validator.w3.org*).

Designing XML Layout Files

The last three case statements open a second screen that displays a picture of the selected attraction. Three XML layout files must be designed to display an ImageView control with an image source file. To create an XML layout file, follow these steps:

1. In the Package Explorer, right-click the layout folder. On the shortcut menu, point to New and then click Other. In the New dialog box, click Android XML Layout File, and then click the Next button. In the New Android Layout XML File dialog box, type **bridge.xml** in the File text box to name the layout file. In the Root Element list, select LinearLayout. Click the Finish button. The emulator window opens. In the Images & Media category in the Palette, drag the ImageView control to the emulator. The Resource Chooser dialog box opens. Select bridge, and then click the OK button. Resize the image to fill the entire window.

   The bridge XML file is designed with an image of the Golden Gate Bridge (Figure 5-23).

Figure 5-23 bridge.xml layout file

2. Close the bridge.xml file tab and save your work. Right-click the layout folder, point to New on the shortcut menu, and then click Other. In the New dialog box, click Android XML Layout File, and then click the Next button. In the New Android Layout XML File dialog box, type **trolley.xml** in the File text box to name the layout file. In the Root Element list, select LinearLayout. Click the Finish button. The emulator window opens. In the Images & Media category in the Palette, drag the ImageView control to the emulator. The Resource Chooser dialog box opens. Select trolley, and then click the OK button. Resize the image to fill the entire window.

   The trolley XML file is designed with an image of the cable car trolley (Figure 5-24).

Figure 5-24 trolley.xml layout file

3. Close the trolley.xml file tab and save your work. Right-click the layout folder, point to New on the shortcut menu, and then click Other. In the New dialog box, click Android XML Layout File, and then click the Next button. In the New Android Layout XML File dialog box, type **wharf.xml** in the File text box to name the layout file. In the Root Element list, select LinearLayout. Click the Finish button. The emulator window opens. In the Images & Media category in the Palette, drag the ImageView control to the emulator. The Resource Chooser dialog box opens. Select wharf, and then click the OK button. Resize the image to fill the entire window.

   The wharf XML file is designed with an image of the Fisherman's Wharf (Figure 5-25).

Figure 5-25 wharf.xml layout file

Adding Multiple Class Files

The three XML files are displayed in three Java class files. Multiple classes are needed to launch the XML layout files that each display an image when the user selects Golden Gate Bridge, Cable Car Trolley, or Fisherman's Wharf. An onCreate method requests that the user interface opens to display an image of the attraction. Remember, each time you add a class to an application, the class must be referenced in the Android Manifest file. To add a class file to launch the XML layout file and add those files to the Android Manifest file, follow these steps:

1. Close the wharf.xml file tab and save your work. To create a second class, right-click the src\net.androidbootcamp.cityguide folder, point to New on the shortcut menu, and then click Class. Type **Bridge** in the Name text box to create a second class that will define the bridge Activity. Click the Superclass Browse button. Type **Activity** in the Choose a type text box. As you type, matching items are displayed. Click Activity – android.app and then click the OK button to extend the Activity class. Click the Finish button. To launch the Activity, in the Bridge.java file, click inside the braces and type **oncreate** and then press Ctrl+spacebar to display an auto-complete listing. Double-click the first onCreate method in the auto-complete listing. Click at the end of Line 10 and then press the Enter key to insert a blank line. Type **setContentView(R.** to display an auto-complete listing. Double-click layout. Type a period. Another auto-complete listing requests the XML layout file you intend to display. Double-click bridge : int. Type a right closing parenthesis if one does not appear automatically. Type a semicolon after the parenthesis to complete the statement.

A new class named Bridge that launches bridge.xml is created (Figure 5-26).

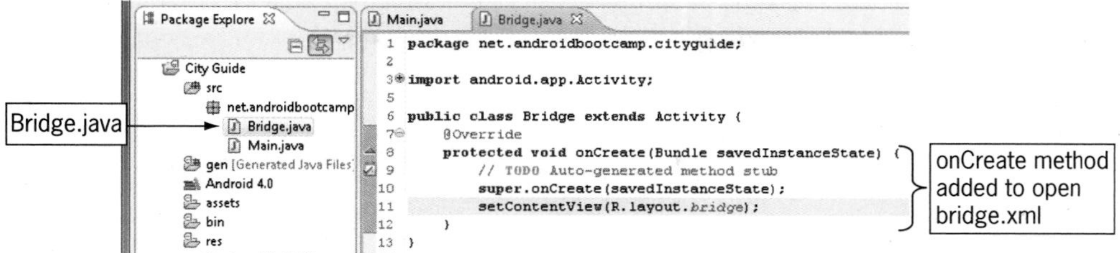

Figure 5-26 Complete code for Bridge.java class

2. Close the Bridge.java file tab and save your work. To create a third class, right-click the src\net.androidbootcamp.cityguide folder, point to New on the shortcut menu, and then click Class. Type **Trolley** in the Name text box to create a third class that will define the trolley Activity. Click the Superclass Browse button. Type **Activity** in the Choose a type text box. As you type, matching items are displayed. Click Activity – android.app and then click the OK button to extend the Activity class. Click the Finish button. To launch the Activity, click inside the braces in the Trolley.java file, type **oncreate** and then press Ctrl+spacebar. Double-click the first onCreate method in the auto-complete listing. Click at the end of the line containing *super.onCreate(savedInstanceState);* and then press the Enter key to insert a blank line. Type **setContentView(R.** to display an auto-complete listing. Double-click layout. Type a period. Another auto-complete listing requests the XML layout file you intend to display. Double-click trolley : int. A right closing parenthesis appears. Type a semicolon after the parenthesis to complete the statement.

   A new class named Trolley is created that launches trolley.xml (Figure 5-27).

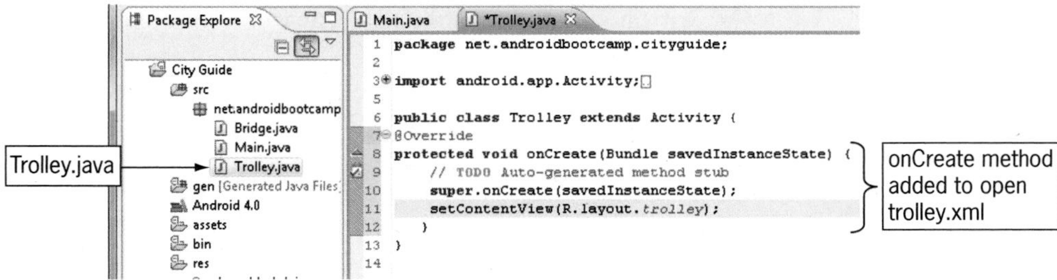

Figure 5-27 Complete code for Trolley.java class

3. Close the Trolley.java file tab and save your work. To create a fourth class, right-click the src\net.androidbootcamp.cityguide folder, point to New on the shortcut menu, and then click Class. Type **Wharf** in the Name text box to create a fourth class that

will define the wharf Activity. Click the Superclass Browse button. Type **Activity** in the Choose a type text box. Click Activity – android.app in the matching items, and then click the OK button to extend the Activity class. Click the Finish button. To launch the Activity, in the Wharf.java file click inside the braces, type **oncreate** and then press Ctrl+spacebar. Double-click the first onCreate method in the auto-complete listing. Click at the end of Line 10 and then press the Enter key to insert a blank line. Type **setContentView(R.** to display an auto-complete listing. Double-click layout. Type a period. Another auto-complete listing requests the XML layout file you intend to display. Double-click wharf : int. A right closing parenthesis appears. Type a semicolon after the parenthesis to complete the statement.

A new class named Wharf is created that launches wharf.xml (Figure 5-28).

Figure 5-28 Complete code for Wharf.java class

4. Close the Wharf.java file tab and save your work. To add the reference to these Java class files in the Android Manifest file, in the Package Explorer, double-click the AndroidManifest.xml file. Click the Application tab at the bottom of the City Guide Manifest page. Scroll down to display the Application Nodes section. Click the Add button. Select Activity in the Create a new element at the top level, in Application dialog box. Click the OK button. The Attributes for Activity section opens in the Application tab. In the Name text box, type the class name preceded by a period (**.Bridge**) to add the Bridge Activity. Click the Add button again. Click the first radio button (Create a new element at the top level, in Application) and select Activity. Click the OK button. In the Name text box, type the class name preceded by a period (**.Trolley**) to add the Trolley Activity. Click the Add button again. Click the first radio button (Create a new element at the top level, in Application) and select Activity. Click the OK button. In the Name text box, type the class name preceded by a period (**.Wharf**) to add the Wharf Activity. Save your work.

   The AndroidManifest.xml file includes the three Activities (Figure 5-29).

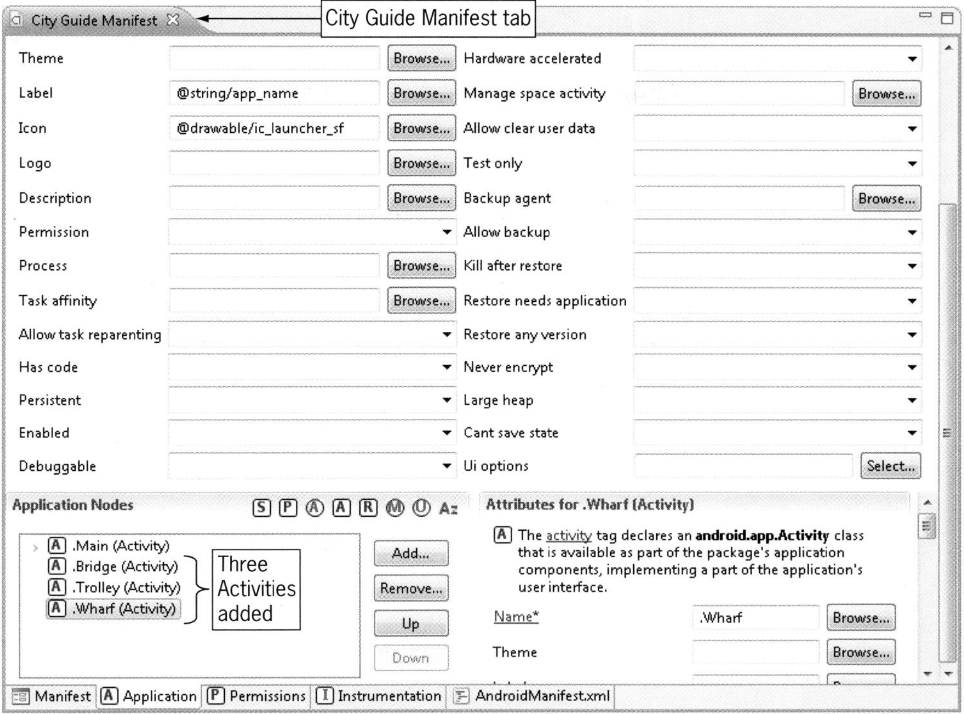

Figure 5-29 City Guide Android Manifest

Opening the Class Files

The last step in the development of the San Francisco City Guide app is to open the class files when the user selects Golden Gate Bridge (case 2), Cable Car Trolley (case 3), or Fisherman's Wharf (case 4). A startActivity method opens the next Activity, which in turn launches the appropriate XML layout displaying an image of the attraction. To code the remaining case statement within the Switch decision structure that starts each of the Activities, follow these steps:

1. Close the City Guide Manifest tab. In Main.java, click the blank line below the one containing case 2: and type **startActivity(new Intent(Main.this, Bridge.class));**. Click the blank line below the one containing case 3: and type **startActivity(new Intent(Main.this, Trolley.class));**. Click the blank line below the one containing case 4: and type **startActivity(new Intent(Main.this, Wharf.class));**.

   The case statements 2 through 4 are coded with a startActivity that executes the appropriate class (Figure 5-30).

```
Main.java
package net.androidbootcamp.cityguide;

import android.app.ListActivity;

public class Main extends ListActivity {
    /** Called when the activity is first created. */
    @Override
    public void onCreate(Bundle savedInstancesState){
       super.onCreate(savedInstancesState);
       String[] attraction={"Alcatraz Island","Ferry Marketplace",
               "Golden Gate Bridge","Cable Car Trolley","Fisherman's Wharf"};
       setListAdapter(new ArrayAdapter<String>(this,
               R.layout.main, R.id.travel, attraction));
    }
       protected void onListItemClick(ListView l, View v, int position, long id) {
         switch(position){
         case 0:
             startActivity(new Intent(Intent.ACTION_VIEW,
                     Uri.parse("http://alcatrazcruises.com/")));
            break;
         case 1:
            startActivity(new Intent(Intent.ACTION_VIEW,
                    Uri.parse("http://ferrybuildingmarketplace.com")));
            break;
         case 2:
            startActivity(new Intent(Main.this, Bridge.class));
            break;
         case 3:
            startActivity(new Intent(Main.this, Trolley.class));
             break;
         case 4:
            startActivity(new Intent(Main.this, Wharf.class));
            break;
         }
       }
  }
```

Figure 5-30 Complete code for Main.java

2. Compare your code to Figure 5-30, make changes as necessary to match the code in the figure, and then save your work.

Running and Testing the Application

As you save and run the San Francisco City Guide application, be sure you test every option of this app. Before publishing to the Android Market, it is critical to make sure all the fields can gracefully handle any click or any value entered in any Android app. Click Run on the menu bar, and then select Run to save and test the application in the emulator. A dialog box requesting how you would like to run the application opens the first time the application is executed. Select Android Application and click the OK button. Save all the files in the next dialog box, if necessary, and unlock the emulator. The application opens in the emulator window where you can test each list item in the San Francisco City Guide app, as shown in Figure 5-1, Figure 5-2, and Figure 5-3.

IN THE TRENCHES

Testing an Android app is called usability testing. In addition to the traditional navigation and ease of use, Section 508 compliance is a third component to be tested. The 1998 Amendment to Section 508 of the Rehabilitation Act spells out accessibility requirements for individuals with certain disabilities. For more details, refer to *www.section508.gov*.

Wrap It Up—Chapter Summary

This chapter described the steps to create a list with items users select to launch Web sites and XML layouts through the use of a Switch decision structure in the City Guide program. The introduction of intents to outside services such as a Web browser begins our adventure of many other intent options used throughout the rest of this book.

- The Java View class creates a list and makes it scrollable if it exceeds the length of the screen. To contain the list items, use a ListView control, which allows you to select each row in the list for further action, such as displaying an image or Web page.
- Instead of extending the basic Activity class in Main.java by using the `public class Main extends Activity` opening class statement, when you want to display a ListView control, extend the ListActivity class in Main.java with the statement `public class Main extends ListActivity`.
- Before you can specify the items in a list, declare the item names using an array variable, which can store more than one value of similar data types. For example, you can store five string values in an array without having to declare five variables.
- Arrays provide access to data by using a numeric index to identify each element in the array. Each value is stored in an element of the array, which you refer to by its index. The index for the first element in an array is zero. For example, attraction [0] is the first element in the Attraction array.
- To declare an array, specify the array's data type and name followed by the values in braces, as in String[ ] attraction={"Alcatraz Island", "Ferry Marketplace", "Golden Gate Bridge", "Cable Car Trolley", "Fisherman's Wharf"};.
- You can display the values in an array using an adapter, which provides a data model for the layout of the list and for converting the array data into list items. A ListView control is the container for the list items, and an adapter such as the setListAdapter command connects the array data to the ListView control so the items are displayed on the device screen. In other words, calling a setListAdapter in the Java code binds the elements of an array to a ListView layout.
- To design a simple layout, you drag controls from the Palette to the emulator on the Graphical Layout tab. To design a custom layout, you add code to the main XML file for the application, such as main.xml.

- By default, the application name is displayed in an app's title bar. To display text other than the application name, change the app_name value in the strings.xml file.
- A setListAdapter statement has three parameters: One refers to the *this* class, the second refers to the layout used to display the list, and the third refers to the array containing the list values to display. For the second parameter, setListAdapter can use a standard layout, as in android.R.layout.*simple_list_item_1*, which specifies the built-in simple_list_item_1 layout to display the list. To use a custom layout instead, replace the name of the standard layout with the name of the custom layout, as in R.layout.*main*, which references a custom layout named main.xml. You also remove the *android* reference because you are no longer using an Android library default layout.
- To have an app take action when a user selects an item in a list, you code the onListItemClick method to respond to the event of the user's selection.
- You can use the Switch decision structure with a list or menu. In a Switch statement, an integer or character variable is evaluated and the corresponding case is executed. Each case is specified using the *case* keyword followed by a value and a colon. For example, if a list contains five items, the Switch statement will have five cases, such as case 0, case 1, case 2, case 3, and case 4. End each case with a break statement to exit the Switch decision structure and continue with the next statement.
- Android intents send and receive activities and services, including opening a Web page in a browser. An intent can use the ACTION_VIEW action to send a URI to a built-in Android browser and display the specified Web site.
- As you develop an application, you must test every option and possible user action, including incorrect values and selections. Thoroughly test an Android app before publishing to the Android Market.

Key Terms

ACTION_VIEW—A generic action you can use to send any request to get the most reasonable action to occur.

adapter—Provides a data model for the layout of a list and for converting the data from the array into list items.

array variable—A variable that can store more than one value.

ArrayAdapter<String> i—A ListAdapter that supplies string array data to a ListView object.

break—A statement that ends a case within a Switch statement and continues with the statement following the Switch decision structure.

case—A keyword used in a Switch statement to indicate a condition. In a Switch statement, the case keyword is followed by a value and a colon.

element—A single individual item that contains a value in an array.

ListActivity—A class that displays a list of items within an app.

onListItemClick( )—A method called when an item in a list is selected.

position—The placement of an item in a list. When an item in a list is selected, the position of the item is passed from the onListItemClick method and evaluated with a decision structure. The first item is assigned the position of 0, the second item is assigned the position of 1, and so forth.

setListAdapter—A command that projects your data to the onscreen list on your device by connecting the ListActivity's ListView object to array data.

Switch—A type of decision statement that allows you to choose from many statements based on an integer or char input.

URI—An acronym for Uniform Resource Identifier, a URI is a string that identifies the resources of the Web. Similar to a URL, a URI includes additional information necessary for gaining access to the resources required for posting the page.

URL—An acronym for Uniform Resource Locator, a URL is a Web site address.

Developer FAQs

1. Which Android control displays a vertical listing of items?
2. When does a scroll bar appear in a list?
3. Typically in an Android .java file, the class extends Activity. When the primary purpose of the class is to display a list, what is the opening Main class statement?
4. Initialize an array named lotteryNumbers with the integers 22, 6, 38, 30, and 17.
5. Answer the following questions about the following initialized array:

   ```
   String[] toppings = new String[12];
   ```

   a. What is the statement to assign pepperoni to the first array location?
   b. What is the statement to assign green peppers to the fourth location in the array?
   c. How many toppings can this array hold?
   d. Rewrite this statement to initially be assigned the following four toppings only: extra cheese, black olives, mushrooms, and bacon.
6. Write a line of code that assigns the values Samsung, Creative, Sony, Motorola, and Asus to the elements in the array phoneBrands.
7. Fix this array statement:

   ```
   doubles { } driveSize = ["32.0", "64.0", "128.0"]
   ```

8. Write two lines of code that assign an array named languages with the items Java, C#, Python, Visual Basic, and Ruby and display this array as a generic list.

9. Which type of pictures can be used for free fair use without copyright?
10. What does URI stand for?
11. Write a statement that opens the Android Help Site: *http://developer.android.com*.
12. Write a single line of XML code that changes the size of the text of a TextView control to 35 scaled-independent pixels.
13. Write a single line of XML code that changes the height of an image to 100 pixels.
14. Write a Switch decision structure that tests the user's age in an integer variable named teenAge and assigns the variable schoolYear as in Table 5-2.

Age	High School Year
14	Freshman
15	Sophomore
16	Junior
17	Senior
Any other age	Not in High School

Table 5-2

15. Change the following If decision structure to a Switch decision structure:

```
if (count == 3) {
      result = "Password incorrect";
} else {
     result = "Request password";
}
```

16. What is the purpose of a default statement in a decision structure?
17. Name two decision structures.
18. What happens when the Web page opens in the emulator and the Back button is clicked in the chapter project?
19. What does the "R" in R.id.travel stand for?
20. Write a startActivity statement that launches a class named Car.

Beyond the Book

Using the Internet, search the Web for the answers to the following questions to further your Android knowledge.

1. Create a five-item list array program of your own favorite hobby and test out three types of built-in Android list formats. Take a screen shot comparing the three layouts identified by the layout format.
2. Compare four different Android browsers. Write a paragraph about each browser.
3. Research the 508 standards for Android app design. Create a list of 10 standards that should be met while designing Android applications.
4. Besides the 508 standards, research the topic of Android usability testing. Write one page on testing guidelines that assist in the design and testing process.

Case Programming Projects

Complete one or more of the following case programming projects. Use the same steps and techniques taught within the chapter. Submit the program you create to your instructor. The level of difficulty is indicated for each case programming project.

Easiest: ⋆

Intermediate: ⋆⋆

Challenging: ⋆⋆⋆

Case Project 5–1: Italian Restaurant App ★

Requirements Document

Application title: Italian Restaurant App

Purpose: An Italian restaurant named La Scala would like an app that displays the specials of the day on a list. As each special is selected, an image is displayed.

Algorithms:

1. The opening screen displays a list of today's specials (Figure 5-31):

   Appetizer Special – Antipasto

   Main Course – Spaghetti and Clams

   Dessert Special – Tiramisu

   La Scala Full Web Site

2. When the user selects an item from the list, a full-screen image of the item is displayed (Figure 5-32). The fourth option opens the Web site *http://www.lascaladining.com*.

Conditions:

1. The pictures of the three specials are provided with your student files (antipasto.png, clams.png, and tiramisu.png).
2. Use the built-in layout *simple_list_item_1*.
3. Use the Switch decision structure.

6:22
La Scala Italian Restaurant
Appetizer Special - Antipasto
Main Course - Spaghetti and Clams
Dessert Special - Tiramisu
La Scala Full Web Site

Figure 5-31

Igor Dutina/Shutterstock.com

Francesco83/Shutterstock.com

erwinova/Shutterstock.com

Figure 5-32

Case Project 5–2: Box Office App ★

Requirements Document

Application title:	Box Office App
Purpose:	The top 10 grossing movies of all time are placed on a list in the Box Office App. As each movie is clicked, the list link opens the Internet Movie Database site for that movie.
Algorithms:	1. The opening screen displays the top 10 movie apps on a custom layout with a movie icon (Figure 5-33). 2. When the user selects one of the top 10 box office hits, the Web site that corresponds to each movie on *www.imdb.com* opens.
Conditions:	1. The movie icon is provided with your student files. 2. Design a custom layout similar to Figure 5-33.

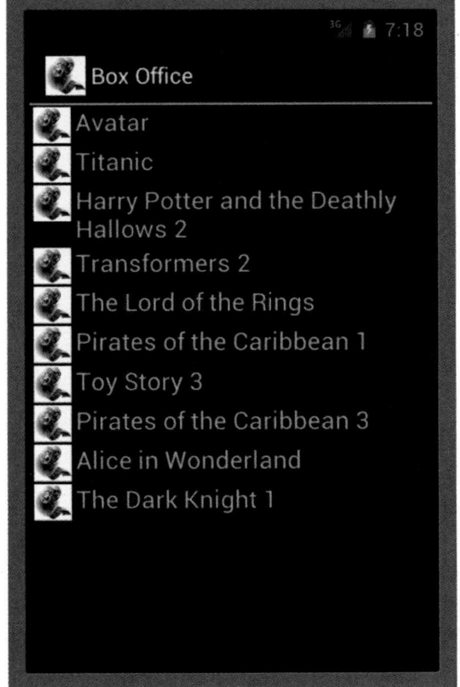

iStockphoto.com/Viktor Chornobay

Figure 5-33

Case Project 5–3: Rent a Car App ★★

Requirements Document

Application title: Rent a Car App

Purpose: A rental car app provides a listing of six nationally known car rental companies. By selecting a car company, a car rental site opens.

Algorithms:

1. An opening screen displays an image of a car and a button.
2. The second screen displays a listing of six car rental companies. This screen also contains a custom icon and layout.
3. Each car rental agency can be selected to view a Web site of the corresponding company.

Conditions:

1. Select your own images.
2. Create a custom layout for the list.

Case Project 5–4: Coffee Finder App ★★

Requirements Document

Application title: Coffee Finder App

Purpose: This Coffee Finder App locates four places in your town or city to get a great cup of joe.

Algorithms:

1. The opening screen displays the name of four coffee shops.
2. When the user selects a coffee shop, a second screen displays the name and address of the selected coffee shop with a picture or logo for the coffee shop.

Conditions:

1. Select your own images.
2. Create a custom layout for the list.

Case Project 5–5: Tech Gadgets App ★★★

Requirements Document

Application title: Tech Gadgets App

Purpose: The Tech Gadgets app shows the top five technology gifts on your wish list.

Algorithms:

1. The opening screen displays names of five technology gadgets of your own choosing.
2. If you select any of the gadgets, a second screen opens that has an image and a button. If the user clicks the button, a Web page opens that displays more information about the tech gadget.

Conditions:

1. Select your own images.
2. Create a custom layout for the list.

Case Project 5–6: Create Your Own App ★★★

Requirements Document

Application title: Create Your Own App

Purpose: Get creative! Create an app with five to eight list items with a custom layout and a custom icon that links to Web pages and other XML layout screens.

Algorithms:

1. Create an app on a topic of your own choice. Create a list.
2. Display XML layout pages as well as Web pages on different list items.

Conditions:

1. Select your own images.
2. Use a custom layout and icon.

CHAPTER 6

Jam! Implementing Audio in Android Apps

In this chapter, you learn to:

- Create an Android project using a splash screen
- Design a TextView control with a background image
- Pause the execution of an Activity with a timer
- Understand the Activity life cycle
- Open an Activity with onCreate( )
- End an Activity with finish( )
- Assign class variables
- Create a raw folder for music files
- Play music with a MediaPlayer method
- Start and resume music playback using the start and pause methods
- Change the Text property of a control
- Change the visibility of a control

Playing music on a smartphone is one of the primary uses of a mobile device, especially as MP3 players are losing popularity. The most common phone activities include texting, talking, gaming, and playing music. Talking and texting continue to be mainstream communication channels, but the proportion of users taking advantage of apps, games, and multimedia on their phones is growing. The principal specification when purchasing a smartphone is typically the amount of memory it has. Consumers often purchase a phone with more memory so they can store music.

To demonstrate playing music through an Android built-in media player, the Chapter 6 project is named Eastern Music and opens with an image and the text "Sounds of the East." This opening screen (Figure 6-1), also called a splash screen, is displayed for approximately five seconds, and then the program automatically opens the second window. The Eastern Music application (Figure 6-2) plays two songs: Bamboo, a Far East song from the ancient Orient, and Palace, a Turkish folk song. If the user selects the first button, the Bamboo song plays until the user selects the first button again to pause the Bamboo song. If the user selects the second button, the Palace song plays until the user selects the second button again. The emulator plays the music through your computer's speakers.

turtix/Shutterstock.com

Figure 6-1 Eastern Music Android app

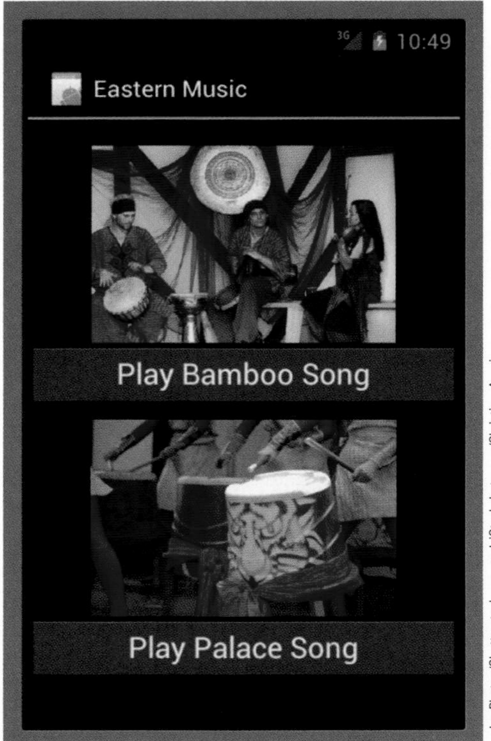

LouLouPhotos/Shutterstock.com and iStockphoto.com/Christian Araujo

Figure 6-2 Music played in the Android app

IN THE TRENCHES

Android music apps can play music on the memory card, download music available for purchase or free from music-sharing sites, tune into Internet-based radio stations, or connect to music saved in a cloud service.

To create this application, the developer must understand how to perform the following processes, among others:

1. Create a splash screen with a timer.
2. Design a TextView control with a background image.
3. Initialize a TimerTask and a timer.
4. Launch a second Activity.
5. Design a second XML layout.
6. Add music files to the raw folder.
7. Initialize the MediaPlayer class.
8. Play and pause music with a Button control.

Creating a Splash Screen

The Eastern Music app opens with a window that is displayed for approximately five seconds before automatically launching the next window. Unlike the project in Chapter 2 (Healthy Recipes), which required a button to be tapped to begin a click event that opened a second screen, this program does not require user interaction to open the second Activity class. Many Android applications on the market show splash screens that often include the name of the program, display a brand logo for the application, or identify the author. A splash screen opens as you launch your app, providing time for Android to initialize its resources. Extending the length of time that your splash screen is displayed enables your app to load necessary files.

In the Eastern Music app, instead of using Main as the name of the initial Activity, the opening Activity shown in Figure 6-3 is named Splash. A second .java file named Main.java is added later in the chapter. The Main Activity is responsible for playing the two songs. To start the Eastern Music application with a splash screen, complete the following step:

1. Open the Eclipse program. Click the New button on the Standard toolbar. Expand the Android folder, if necessary, and select Android Project. Click the Next button. In the New Android Project dialog box, enter the Project Name **Eastern Music**. To save the project on your USB drive, click to remove the check mark from the Use default location check box. Type **E:\Workspace** (if necessary, enter a different drive letter that identifies the USB drive). Click the Next button. For the Build Target, select Android 4.0, if necessary. Click the Next button. For the Package Name, type **net.androidbootcamp.easternmusic**. Enter **Splash** in the Create Activity text box.

The new Android Eastern Music project has an application name, a package name, and a Splash Activity (Figure 6-3).

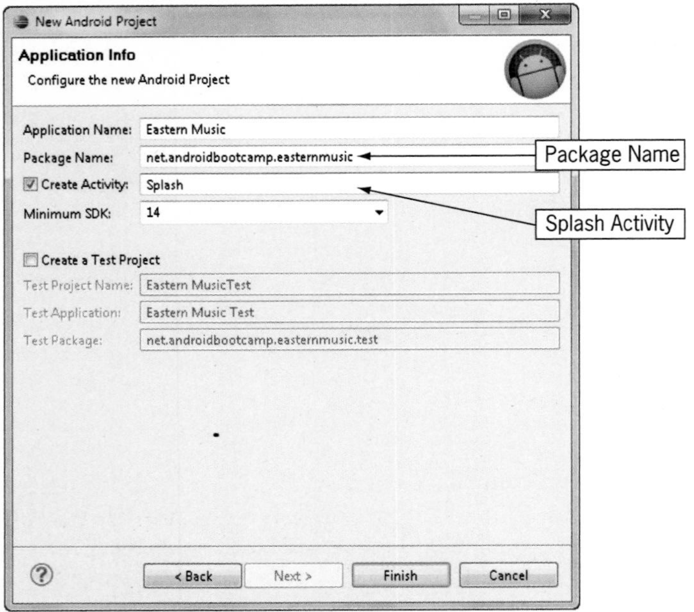

Figure 6-3 Setting up the Splash Activity in the Eastern Music project

Adding a Background Image to a TextView Widget

On the splash screen in Figure 6-1, an image with the text "Sounds of the East" is displayed. This image is not an ImageView widget, but instead a TextView widget with a background image. You use a TextView property named background to specify the image. The image is first placed in the drawable-hdpi folder and then referenced in the TextView background. The TextView background can display an image or a solid-color fill such as the hexadecimal color #0000FF for blue. The margins and gravity properties are used to place the text in the location of your choice. To add the images for this project and a splash.xml file with a TextView widget that contains a background image, follow these steps:

1. Click the Finish button in the New Android Project dialog box. Expand the Eastern Music project in the Package Explorer. Open the USB folder containing the student files. In the Package Explorer pane, expand the res folder. To add the three image files to the drawable-hdpi resource folder, drag band.png, bell.png, and drums.png to the drawable-hdpi folder until a plus sign pointer appears. Release the mouse button. If necessary, click the Copy files option button, and then click the OK button.

   Copies of the three image files appear in the drawable-hdpi folder (Figure 6-4).

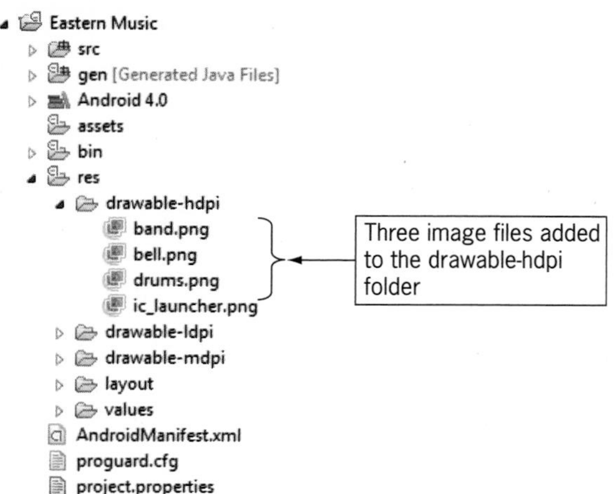

Figure 6-4 Image files in the drawable-hdpi folder

2. To add a splash.xml file, right-click the layout folder. On the shortcut menu, point to New and then click Other. In the New dialog box, click Android XML Layout File, and then click the Next button. In the New Android Layout XML File dialog box, type **splash.xml** in the File text box to name the layout file. In the Root Element list, select LinearLayout. Click the Finish button. The emulator window opens. In the Form Widgets category in the Palette, drag the TextView control to the emulator. To open the Properties pane, right-click the emulator window, point to Show In on the shortcut menu, and then click Properties. With the TextView control selected, change the Text property to **Sounds of the East** and type **#000000** for the Text color property. Set the Text size property to **20sp**. Click to the right of the Text style property, click the ellipsis button, and then select bold. Click the OK button. Click to the right of the Gravity property, click the ellipsis button, and then select center_horizontal. Click the OK button. In the Background property, click the ellipsis button. In the Reference Chooser dialog box, expand the Drawable folder and then click bell. Click the OK button. Resize the image to fit the emulator window.

   A TextView image with an image background is displayed in the splash.xml file (Figure 6-5).

Figure 6-5 splash.xml displays a TextView control

3. Close the splash.xml tab and save your work.

Creating a Timer

When most Android apps open, a splash screen is displayed for a few seconds, often preloading database files and information behind the scenes in large-scale applications. In the Eastern Music app, a timer is necessary to display the splash.xml file for approximately five seconds before the Main Activity intent is called. A **timer** in Java executes a one-time task, such as displaying an opening splash screen, or performs a continuous process, such as a morning wake-up call set to run at regular intervals.

Timers can be used to pause an action temporarily or to time dependent or repeated activities such as animation in a cartoon application. The timer object uses milliseconds as the unit of time. On an Android device, 1,000 milliseconds is equivalent to about one second. This fixed period of time is supported by two Java classes, namely **TimerTask** and **Timer**. To create a timer, the first step is to create a TimerTask object, as shown in the following syntax:

Code Syntax

```
TimerTask task = new TimerTask() {

}
```

GTK

Each time a timer runs its tasks, it executes within a single thread. A **thread** is a single sequential flow of control within a program. Java allows an application to have multiple threads of execution running concurrently. You can assign multiple threads so they occur simultaneously, completing several tasks at the same time. For example, a program could display a splash screen, download files needed for the application, and even play an opening sound at the same time.

A TimerTask invokes a scheduled timer. A timer may remind you of a childhood game called hide-and-seek. Do you remember covering your eyes and counting to 50 while your friends found a hiding spot before you began searching for everyone? A timer might only count to five seconds (5,000 milliseconds), but in a similar fashion, the application pauses while the timer counts to the established time limit. After the timed interval is completed, the program resumes and continues with the next task.

After entering the TimerTask code, point to the red error line under the TimerTask( ) to add the run( ) method, an auto-generated method stub, as shown in the following code syntax. Any statements within the braces of the run( ) method are executed after the TimerTask class is invoked.

Code Syntax

```
TimerTask task = new TimerTask() {
      @Override
     public void run() {
     // TODO Auto-generated method stub
}
```

The TimerTask must implement a run method that is called by the timer when the task is scheduled for execution. To add a TimerTask class to the Splash Activity, follow these steps:

1. In the Package Explorer, expand the src folder, expand net.androidbootcamp.easternmusic, and then double-click Splash.java to open the code window. To set the splash.xml layout as the opening window, change setContentView (R.layout.*main*) to **setContentView(R.layout.*splash*);**. Press the Enter key to insert a new line, and then type **TimerTask task = new TimerTask( )** { to add the TimerTask. Point to the red error line below TimerTask( ).

   The setContentView method is updated to display the splash.xml file and the TimerTask class is initiated (Figure 6-6).

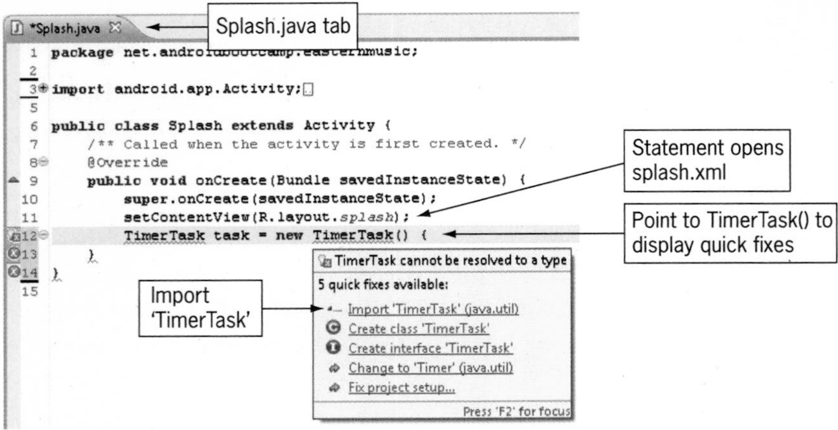

Figure 6-6 setContentView and TimerTask statements

2. First add the import statement by clicking Import 'TimerTask' (java util). Point to TimerTask( ) again to view the quick fix. Select Add unimplemented methods to add the auto-generated method stub for the run method. To complete the stub, click to right of } at the end of the stub, press the Enter key, and then type **};** to close the class.

   The auto-generated stub for the run method is created automatically (Figure 6-7).

*Splash.java

```
package net.androidbootcamp.easternmusic;

import java.util.TimerTask;

public class Splash extends Activity {
    /** Called when the activity is first created. */
    @Override
    public void onCreate(Bundle savedInstanceState) {
        super.onCreate(savedInstanceState);
        setContentView(R.layout.splash);
        TimerTask task = new TimerTask() {

            @Override
            public void run() {
                // TODO Auto-generated method stub

            }
        };
    }
}
```

run( ) method stub

Semicolon ends stub

Figure 6-7 run( ) method

IN THE TRENCHES

Timers can also be used to display updates of how long an installation is taking by displaying a countdown, monitor what a user is doing, or execute other routines while an Activity is running.

Scheduling a Timer

After including a reference to the TimerTask class, a timer must be scheduled for the amount of time that the splash screen is displayed. The Timer class shown in the following code syntax creates a timed event when the schedule method is called. A delay timer is scheduled in milliseconds using the Timer class. Delay schedules simply prompt an event to occur once at a specified time.

Code Syntax

```
Timer opening = new Timer();
opening.schedule(task,5000);
```

In the first line of the code syntax, the object named opening initializes a new instance of the Timer class. When the schedule method of the Timer class is called in the second line, two arguments are required. The first parameter (task) is the name of the variable that was initialized for the Timer class. The second parameter represents the number of milliseconds (5,000 milliseconds = 5 seconds). Follow these steps to add the scheduled timer:

1. In the code on the Splash.java tab, after the closing braces for the TimerTask class and the semicolon, insert a new line and then type **Timer opening = new Timer();**. Point to Timer and click Import 'Timer' (java.util).

   An instance of the Timer class is created named opening (Figure 6-8).

*Splash.java

```
package net.androidbootcamp.easternmusic;

import java.util.Timer;

public class Splash extends Activity {
    /** Called when the activity is first created. */
    @Override
    public void onCreate(Bundle savedInstanceState) {
        super.onCreate(savedInstanceState);
        setContentView(R.layout.splash);
        TimerTask task = new TimerTask() {

            @Override
            public void run() {
                // TODO Auto-generated method stub

            }
        };
        Timer opening = new Timer();
    }
}
```

Instance of Timer

Figure 6-8 Timer class

2. To schedule a timer using the schedule method from the Timer class to pause for five seconds, press the Enter key to insert a new line, and then type **opening.schedule (task,5000);**.

   The timer lasting five seconds is scheduled (Figure 6-9).

Splash.java

```
1  package net.androidbootcamp.easternmusic;
2
3  import java.util.Timer;
7
8  public class Splash extends Activity {
9      /** Called when the activity is first created. */
10     @Override
11     public void onCreate(Bundle savedInstanceState) {
12         super.onCreate(savedInstanceState);
13         setContentView(R.layout.splash);
14         TimerTask task = new TimerTask() {
15
16             @Override
17             public void run() {
18                 // TODO Auto-generated method stub
19
20             }
21         };
22         Timer opening = new Timer();
23         opening.schedule(task,5000);
24     }
25 }
```

Timer scheduled for 5 seconds

Figure 6-9 Timer scheduled

IN THE TRENCHES

Be careful not to code excessively long timers that waste the time of the user. A user-friendly program runs smoothly without long delays.

Life and Death of an Activity

In Line 12 of the Eastern Music app, as shown in Figure 6-9, the Splash Activity begins its life in the Activity life cycle with the onCreate( ) method. Each Activity has a **life cycle**, which is the series of actions from the beginning of an Activity to its end. Actions that occur during the life cycle provide ways to manage how users interact with your app. Each Activity in this book begins with an onCreate( ) method. The onCreate( ) method initializes the user interface with an XML layout; the life of the Activity is started. As in any life cycle, the opposite of birth is death. In this case, an **onDestroy( ) method** is the end of the Activity. The onCreate( ) method sets up all the resources required to perform the Activity, and onDestroy( ) releases those same resources to free up memory on your mobile device. The life cycle of the Splash Activity also begins with onCreate( ) and ends with onDestroy( ). Other actions can take place during the life of the Activity. For example, when the scheduled timer starts (Line 23 in Figure 6-9), the Splash Activity is paused. If you open multiple apps on a smartphone and receive a phone call, you must either pause or terminate the other apps to secure enough available memory to respond to the incoming call. To handle the life cycle actions between onCreate( ) and onDestroy( ), you use methods such as onRestart( ), onStart( ), onResume( ), onPause( ), and onStop( ). Each of these methods changes the state of the Activity. The four **states** of an Activity determine whether the activity is active, paused, stopped, or dead. The life cycle of an application affects how an app works and how the different parts are being orchestrated. Table 6-1 shows the development of an Activity throughout its life cycle.

Method	Description
onCreate( )	The onCreate( ) method begins each Activity. This method also provides a Bundle containing the Activity's previously frozen state, if it had one.
onRestart( )	If the Activity is stopped, onRestart( ) begins the Activity again. If this method is called, it indicates your Activity is being redisplayed to the user from a stopped state. The onRestart( ) method is always followed by onStart( ).
onStart( )	If the Activity is hidden, onStart( ) makes the Activity visible.
onResume( )	The onResume( ) method is called when the user begins interacting with the Activity. The onResume( ) method is always followed by onPause( ).
onPause( )	This method is called when an Activity is about to resume.
onStop( )	This method hides the Activity.
onDestroy( )	This method destroys the Activity. Typically, the finish( ) method (part of onDestroy( )) is used to declare that the Activity is finished; when the next Activity is called, it releases all the resources from the first Activity.

Table 6-1 Methods used in the life cycle of an Activity

When an Activity is launched using onCreate( ), the app performs the actions in the Activity. In other words, the Activity becomes the top sheet of paper on a stack of papers. When the methods shown in Table 6-1 are used between the onCreate( ) and onDestroy( ) methods, they shuffle the order of the papers in that stack. When onDestroy( ) is called, imagine that the pile of papers is thrown away. The finish( ) method is part of the onDestroy( ) method and is called when the Activity is completed and should be closed. Typically, the finish( ) method occurs directly before another Activity is launched. As an Android developer, you should be well acquainted with the life cycle of Activities because an app that you publish in the Android market must "play" well with all the other apps on a mobile device. For example, your Android app must pause when a text message, phone call, or other event occurs.

The diagram in Figure 6-10 shows the life cycle of an Activity. The rectangles represent methods you can implement to perform operations when the Activity moves between states. The colored ovals are the possible major states of the Activity.

Activity starts

onCreate()

User navigates back to the Activity

onStart()

onRestart()

Process is killed

onResume()

Activity is running

The Activity comes to the foreground

Another Activity comes in front of the Activity

The Activity comes to the foreground

Other applications need memory

onPause()

The Activity is no longer visible

onStop()

onDestroy()

Activity is shut down

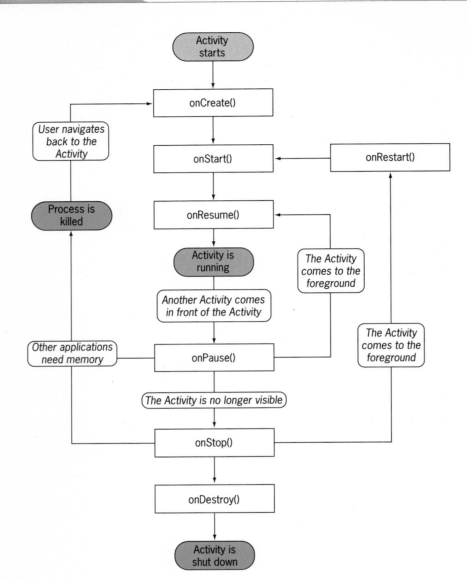

Figure 6-10 Activity life cycle

As an example of the Activity life cycle, the native Android application designed for taking a picture using the built-in camera transitions through each stage in the life cycle. When the user launches the camera app, the camera Activity executes the onCreate( ) method to display the opening screen and the image captured through the camera lens. The user taps a Button control to take a picture. The onStop( ) method is called to hide the live image displayed after the picture is taken. The onRestart( ) method is called after the picture is taken to restart the rest of the app. The onStart( ) method is called to display the picture that was just taken. If the user taps the screen to upload the image to Facebook, the onPause( ) method is called to pause operations of the camera app while the image is uploaded. The onResume( ) method is launched after the picture is uploaded to reactivate the camera. The user can choose to take another image, which repeats the process, or to exit the camera app. If the user selects the exit option, onDestroy( ) or finish( ) frees the saved resources from the temporary memory of the device and closes the camera application.

In the Eastern Music application, after the timer pauses the program temporarily, the Splash Activity should be destroyed with onDestroy( ) before launching the second Activity. The app should call the onDestroy( ) method from within the run method of the timer task that was invoked by TimerTask. Doing so guarantees that the ongoing task execution is the last task this timer performs. To close the Splash Activity, follow these steps:

1. In Splash.java, click inside the run( ) auto-generated method stub in the blank line under the comment // TODO Auto-generated method stub and type **finish( );**.

   The finish( ) statement releases the resources that were created for the Splash Activity and closes the Activity (Figure 6-11).

Splash.java

```
package net.androidbootcamp.easternmusic;

import java.util.Timer;

public class Splash extends Activity {
    /** Called when the activity is first created.
    @Override
    public void onCreate(Bundle savedInstanceState)
        super.onCreate(savedInstanceState);
        setContentView(R.layout.splash);
        TimerTask task = new TimerTask(){

            @Override
            public void run() {
                // TODO Auto-generated method stub
                finish();
            }
        };
        Timer opening = new Timer();
        opening.schedule(task,5000);
    }
}
```

finish( ) method

Figure 6-11 finish( ) method called

2. Save your work.

Launching the Next Activity

After the Activity for the splash screen is destroyed, an intent must request that the next Activity is launched. An XML layout named main.xml already exists as the default layout. A second class named Main must be created before the code can launch this Java class. You must update the Android Manifest file to include the Main Activity. The Main Activity is responsible for playing music. To create a second class and launch the Main Activity, follow these steps:

1. In the Package Explorer, right-click the net.androidbootcamp.easternmusic folder, point to New on the shortcut menu, and then click Class. Type **Main** in the Name text box. Click the Superclass Browse button. Type **Activity** in the Choose a type text box. Click Activity – android.app and then click the OK button to extend the Activity class. Click the Finish button to finish creating the Main class.

   A second class named Main is created (Figure 6-12).

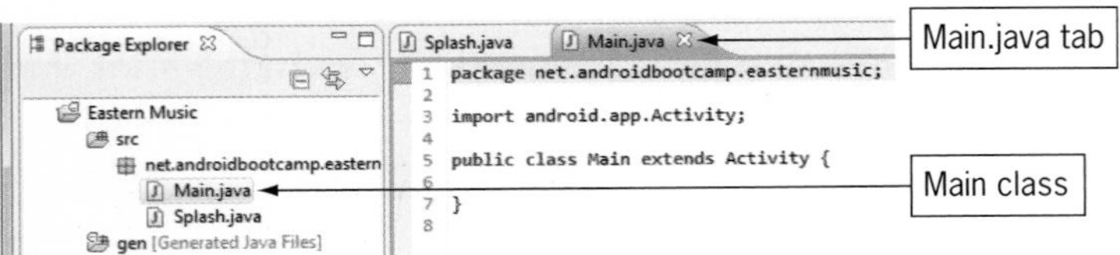

Figure 6-12 Main class created

2. In the Package Explorer, double-click the AndroidManifest.xml file. To add the Main class to the Android Manifest, click the Application tab at the bottom of the Eastern Music Manifest page. Scroll down to display the Application Nodes section. Click the Add button. Select Activity in the Create a new element at the top level, in Application dialog box. Click the OK button. The Attributes for Activity section opens in the Application tab. In the Name text box in this section, type **.Main**.

   The .Main class is added to the Android Manifest file (Figure 6-13).

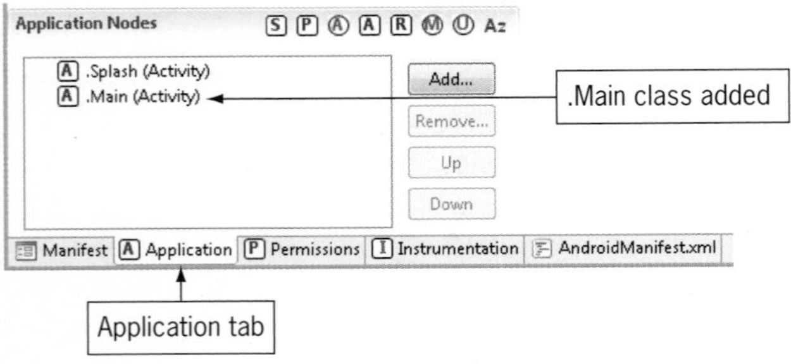

Figure 6-13 Adding the Main Activity

3. Close the Eastern Music Manifest tab and save the changes. To launch the second Activity, display Splash.java, insert a new line in the run( ) auto-generated method stub after the finish( ); statement, and then type **startActivity(new Intent(Splash.**

this, Main.class));. Point to the red error line below Intent and select 'Import Intent' (android.content). Save your work.

The second Activity named Main is launched with an Intent statement (Figure 6-14).

Splash.java

```
package net.androidbootcamp.easternmusic;

import java.util.Timer;

public class Splash extends Activity {
    /** Called when the activity is first created. */
    @Override
    public void onCreate(Bundle savedInstanceState) {
        super.onCreate(savedInstanceState);
        setContentView(R.layout.splash);
        TimerTask task = new TimerTask(){

            @Override
            public void run() {
                // TODO Auto-generated method stub
                finish();
                startActivity(new Intent(Splash.this, Main.class));
            }
        };
        Timer opening = new Timer();
        opening.schedule(task,5000);
    }
}
```

Opens the Main Activity

Figure 6-14 Intent statement

Designing the main.xml File

In the Eastern Music app, after the first Activity displaying the splash screen finishes and the second Activity named Main is launched, a second XML layout file is displayed when the onCreate( ) method is called within the Main.java file. The Main.java file uses the default Linear layout with two ImageView and Button controls. To design the XML layout for main.xml, follow these steps:

1. Close the Splash.java tab. In the res/layout folder, right-click main.xml, point to Open With on the shortcut menu, and then click Android Layout Editor. Delete the default Hello World, Splash! control. Drag an ImageView control from the Images & Media category of the Palette to the emulator window. In the Resource Chooser dialog box, click the first option button if necessary, click band, and then click the OK button. With the band.png image selected, change the Layout height in the Properties pane to **150dp**, the Layout margin top to **20dp**, and the Layout width to **320dp**. Drag a Button from the Form Widgets category of the Palette and place it below the image. Set the Button Id property to **@+id/btnBamboo**. Change the Text property to **Play Bamboo Song**. Set the Text size to **22sp** and the Layout margin bottom to **10dp**. Set the Layout width to **320dp**. Save your work.

   The image and button to select the first song named Bamboo are designed in main.xml (Figure 6-15).

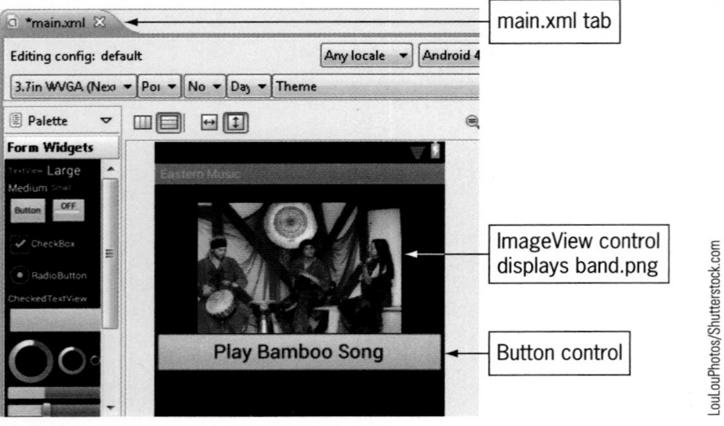

Figure 6-15 ImageView and Button controls in main.xml

2. Drag another ImageView control to the emulator window. In the Resource Chooser dialog box, click drums, and then click the OK button. With the drums.png image selected, change the Layout height in the Properties pane to **150dp**, the Layout margin top to **20dp**, and the Layout width to **320dp**. Drag a Button from the Form Widgets category of the Palette and place it below the image. Set the Button Id property to **@+id/btnPalace**. Change the Text property to **Play Palace Song**. Set the Text size to **22sp** and the Layout margin bottom to **10dp**. Set the Layout width to **320dp**. Save your work.

   The image and button to select the second song named Palace are designed in main.xml (Figure 6-16).

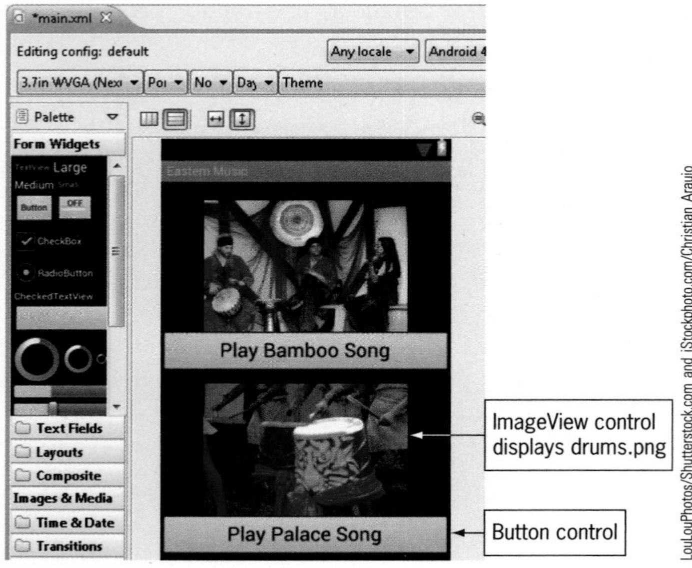

Figure 6-16 main.xml layout complete

Class Variables

In the coding examples used thus far in this book, variables have been local variables. **Local variables** are declared by variable declaration statements within a method, such as a primitive integer variable within an onCreate( ) method. The local variable effectively ceases to exist when the execution of the method is complete. The **scope** of a variable refers to the variable's visibility within a class. Variables that are accessible only to a restricted portion of a program such as a single method are said to have local scope. Variables that are accessible from anywhere in a class, however, are said to have global scope. If a variable is needed in multiple methods within a class, the global variable is assigned at the beginning of a class, not within a method. This global scope variable is called a **class variable** in Java, and can be accessed by multiple methods throughout the program. In the chapter project, the Button, MediaPlayer (necessary for playing sound), and an integer variable named playing are needed in the onCreate( ) method and within both onClick( ) methods for each Button control. To keep the value of these variables throughout multiple classes, the variables are defined as class variables that cease to exist when their class or activity is unloaded.

After class variables are defined in Main.java, the onCreate( ) method opens the main.xml layout and defines the two Button controls. The Activity waits for the user to select one of the two buttons, each of which plays a song. If a button is clicked twice, the music pauses. Each button must have a setOnClickListener that awaits the user's click. After the user taps a button, the setOnClickListener method implements the Button.OnClickListener, creating an instance of the OnClickListener and calling the onClick method. The onClick method responds to the user's action. For example, in the chapter project, the response is to play a song. The onClick method is where you place the code to handle playing the song. To code the class variables, display the main.xml layout, reference the two Button controls, and set an onClickListener, follow these steps:

1. Close the main.xml window and save your work. In Main.java, after the public class Main extends Activity statement, create two blank lines. On the second line, type **Button btBamboo, btPalace;** to create a class variable reference. Point to Button and click 'Import Button' (android widget). Insert a new line, and then type **MediaPlayer mpBamboo, mpPalace;** to create a class variable reference for the media player. Point to MediaPlayer and click 'Import MediaPlayer' (android.media). Insert a new line, and then type **int playing;** to create a primitive class variable named playing, which keeps track of whether a song is playing.

   Class variables that can be accessed by the rest of the program are initialized (Figure 6-17).

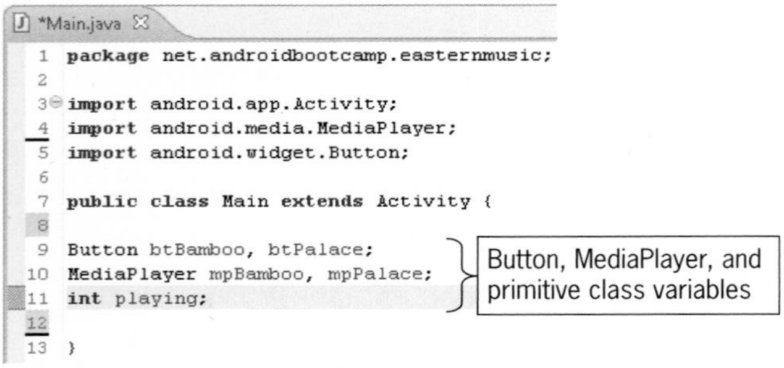

```
*Main.java

package net.androidbootcamp.easternmusic;

import android.app.Activity;
import android.media.MediaPlayer;
import android.widget.Button;

public class Main extends Activity {

Button btBamboo, btPalace;
MediaPlayer mpBamboo, mpPalace;
int playing;

}
```

Button, MediaPlayer, and primitive class variables

Figure 6-17 Class variables

2. Press the Enter key twice, type **oncreate**, and then press Ctrl+spacebar. Double-click the first onCreate method in the auto-complete listing to generate the method structure. Click after the semicolon, press the Enter key, and then type **setContentView(R.** to display an auto-complete listing. Double-click layout. Type a period. Double-click main: int—R layout. Type **);** to complete the statement.

   The onCreate method displays the main.xml file (Figure 6-18).

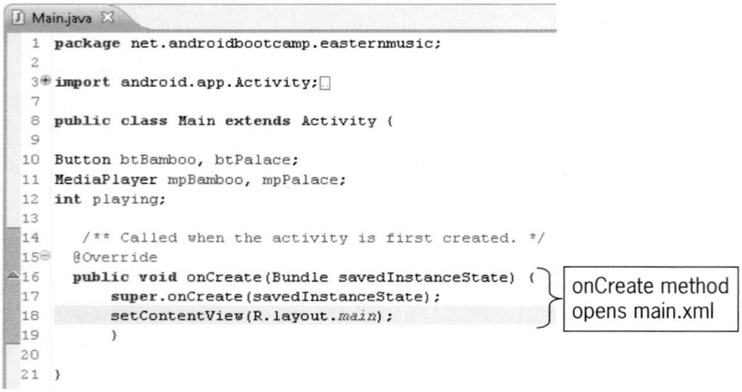

```
Main.java

package net.androidbootcamp.easternmusic;

import android.app.Activity;

public class Main extends Activity {

Button btBamboo, btPalace;
MediaPlayer mpBamboo, mpPalace;
int playing;

   /** Called when the activity is first created. */
  @Override
  public void onCreate(Bundle savedInstanceState) {
      super.onCreate(savedInstanceState);
      setContentView(R.layout.main);
      }

}
```

onCreate method opens main.xml

Figure 6-18 onCreate method

3. Both Button references were made as class variables. To create an instance of each Button control, press the Enter key and type **btBamboo = (Button)findViewById(R.id.btnBamboo);**. Press the Enter key and then type **btPalace = (Button)findViewById(R.id.btnPalace);**.

   The Button controls named btnBamboo and btnPalace are referenced in Main.java (Figure 6-19).

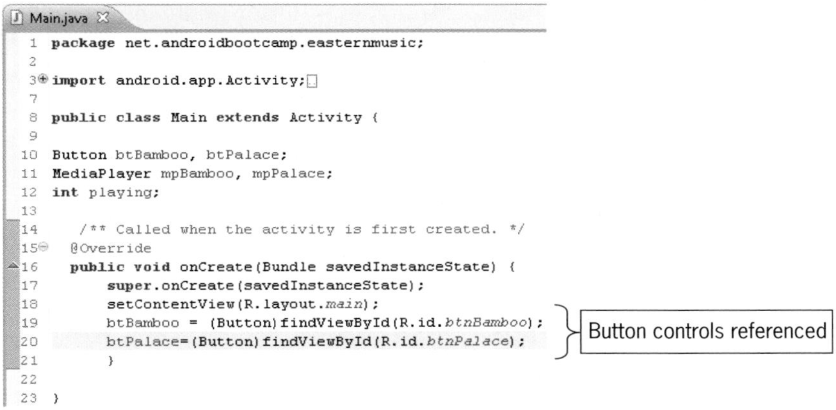

Main.java

```
package net.androidbootcamp.easternmusic;

import android.app.Activity;

public class Main extends Activity {

Button btBamboo, btPalace;
MediaPlayer mpBamboo, mpPalace;
int playing;

    /** Called when the activity is first created. */
   @Override
   public void onCreate(Bundle savedInstanceState) {
       super.onCreate(savedInstanceState);
       setContentView(R.layout.main);
       btBamboo = (Button)findViewById(R.id.btnBamboo);
       btPalace=(Button)findViewById(R.id.btnPalace);
       }

}
```

Button controls referenced

Figure 6-19 Button controls referenced

4. To create a setOnClickListener method so the btBamboo Button waits for the user's click, press the Enter key and type **btBamboo.setOnClickListener(bBamboo);**. To create an instance of the Button OnClickListener, click between the two ending braces and type **Button.OnClickListener bBamboo = new Button.OnClickListener() {** and then press the Enter key. Place a semicolon after the closing brace. This onClickListener is designed for a class variable for a Button. Point to the red error line below Button.OnClickListener and select Add unimplemented methods to add the quick fix.

   An OnClickListener auto-generated stub appears in the code for the first button (Figure 6-20).

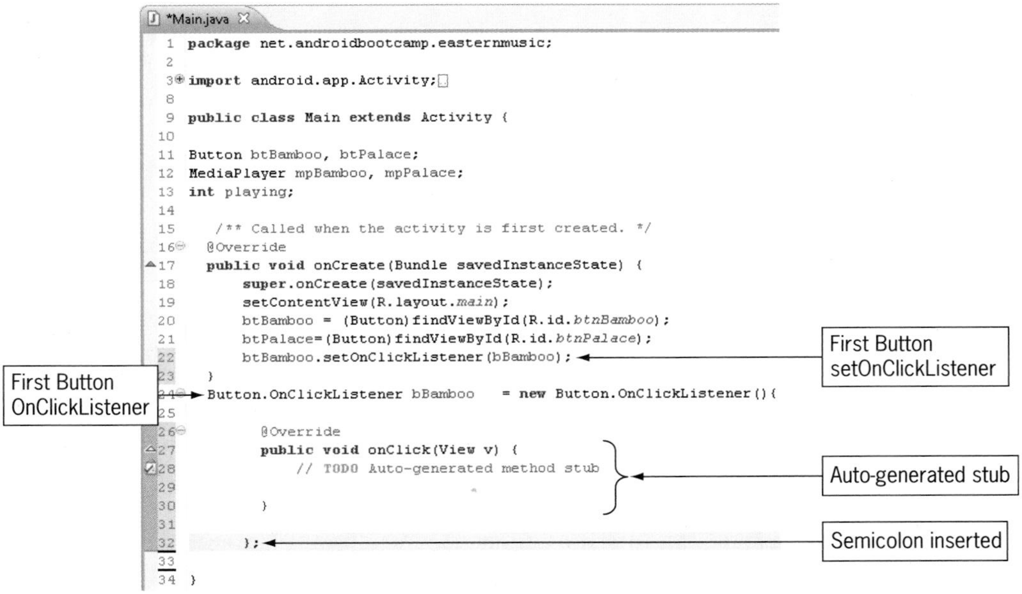

*Main.java

```
package net.androidbootcamp.easternmusic;

import android.app.Activity;

public class Main extends Activity {

Button btBamboo, btPalace;
MediaPlayer mpBamboo, mpPalace;
int playing;

    /** Called when the activity is first created. */
   @Override
   public void onCreate(Bundle savedInstanceState) {
       super.onCreate(savedInstanceState);
       setContentView(R.layout.main);
       btBamboo = (Button)findViewById(R.id.btnBamboo);
       btPalace=(Button)findViewById(R.id.btnPalace);
       btBamboo.setOnClickListener(bBamboo);
   }
   Button.OnClickListener bBamboo    = new Button.OnClickListener(){

        @Override
        public void onClick(View v) {
            // TODO Auto-generated method stub

        }

   };

}
```

First Button setOnClickListener

First Button OnClickListener

Auto-generated stub

Semicolon inserted

Figure 6-20 Inserting the first Button OnClickListener stub

5. To create a setOnClickListener method so the btPalace Button waits for the user's click, click after the btBamboo.setOnClickListener(bBamboo); statement, press the Enter key, and then type **btPalace.setOnClickListener(bPalace);**. To create an instance of the btnPalace button OnClickListener, click after the brace with the semicolon at the end of the code, press the Enter key, type **Button.OnClickListener bPalace = new Button.OnClickListener() {** and then press the Enter key to create the closing brace. Place a semicolon after this closing brace. Point to the red error line below Button.OnClickListener and select Add unimplemented methods to add the quick fix. Save your work.

   An OnClickListener auto-generated stub appears in the code for the second button (Figure 6-21).

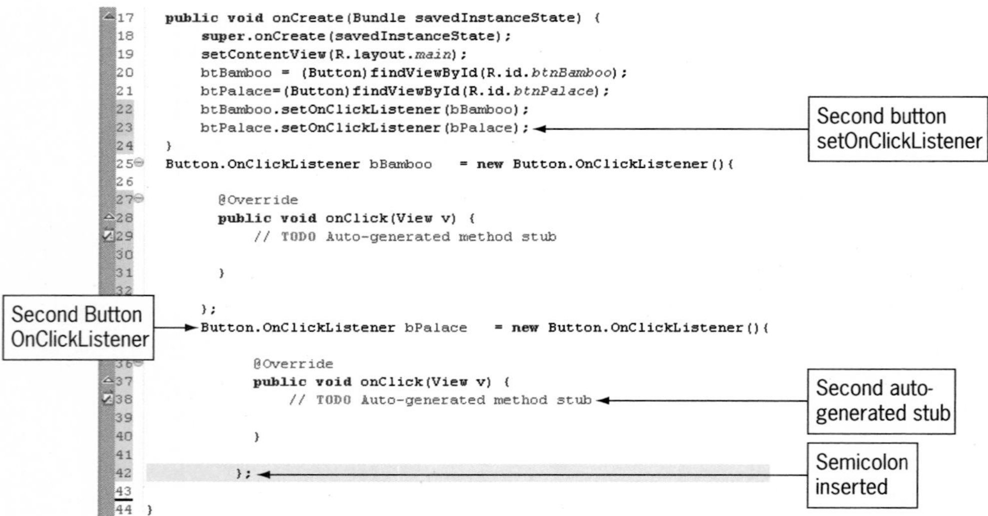

Figure 6-21 Inserting the second Button OnClickListener stub

Playing Music

Every Android phone and tablet includes a built-in music player where you can store your favorite music. You can also write your own applications that offer music playback capabilities. To enable the Eastern Music chapter project to play two songs, Android includes a MediaPlayer class that can play both audio and music files. Android lets you play audio and video from several types of data sources. You can play audio or video from media files stored in the application's resources (a folder named raw), from stand-alone files in the Android file system of the device, from an SD (Secure Digital) memory card in the phone itself, or from a data stream provided through an Internet connection. The most common file type of media supported for audio playback with the MediaPlayer class is .mp3, but other audio file types such as .wav, .ogg, and .midi are typically supported by most Android hardware. The Android device platform supports a wide variety of media types based on the codecs included in the device by the manufacturer. A **codec** is a computer technology used to compress and decompress audio and video files.

IN THE TRENCHES

The Android platform provides a class to record audio and video, where supported by the mobile device hardware. To record audio or video, use the MediaRecorder class. The emulator does not provide the capability to capture audio or video, but an actual mobile device can record media input, accessible through the MediaRecorder class.

Creating a Raw Folder for Music Files

In an Android project, music files are typically stored in a subfolder of the res folder called raw. In newer versions of Android, the raw folder must be created before music files can be placed in that folder. The two .mp3 files played in the Eastern Music app are named bamboo.mp3 and palace.mp3, and should be placed in the raw folder. To create a raw folder that contains music files, follow these steps:

1. In the Package Explorer, right-click the res folder. Point to New on the shortcut menu, and then click Folder. The New Folder dialog box opens. In the Folder name text box, type **raw**.

   A folder named raw is created using the New Folder dialog box (Figure 6-22).

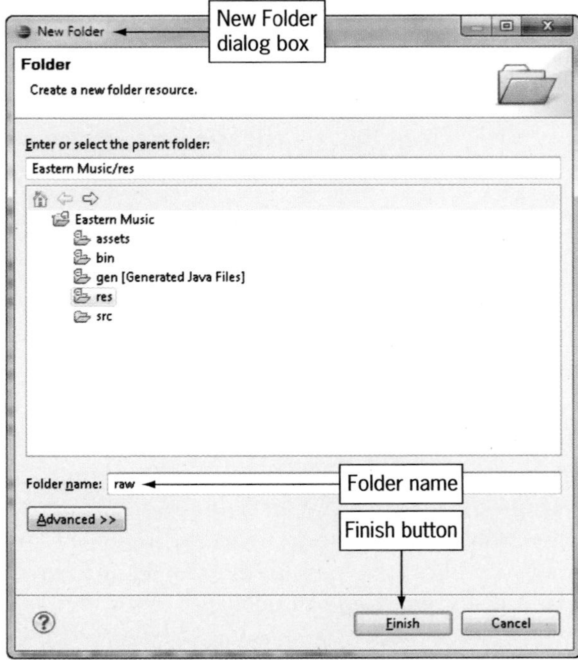

Figure 6-22 New Folder dialog box

2. Click the Finish button. To add the project music files to the raw folder, open the USB folder containing your student files. To add the two music files to the raw resource folder, select bamboo.mp3 and palace.mp3, and then drag the files to the raw folder until a plus sign pointer appears. Release the mouse button. If necessary, click the Copy files option button, and then click the OK button. Expand the raw folder.

   Copies of the music files appear in the raw folder (Figure 6-23).

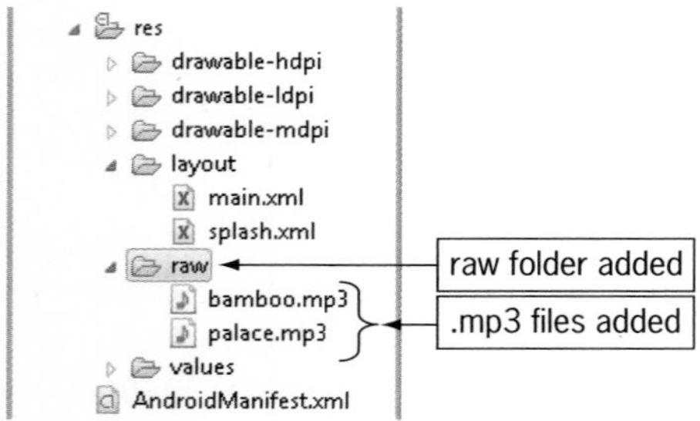

Figure 6-23 Music files in the raw folder

Using the MediaPlayer Class

The **MediaPlayer class** provides the methods to control audio playback on an Android device. At the beginning of the Main.java code, two MediaPlayer class variables are declared. After the variables are declared, an instance of the MediaPlayer class is assigned to each variable. In the following code syntax, mpBamboo is assigned to an instance of the MediaPlayer class that accesses the bamboo music file in the raw folder.

Code Syntax

```
MediaPlayer mpBamboo = MediaPlayer.create(this, R.raw.bamboo);
```

The class variables mpBamboo and mpPalace are assigned the music files from the raw folder. To declare an instance of the MediaPlayer class, follow this step:

1. In Main.java, press the Enter key after the btPalace.setOnClickListener(bPalace); statement to create a new line. Type **mpBamboo = new MediaPlayer();** to create a new instance of MediaPlayer. Insert a new line and type **mpBamboo = MediaPlayer.create(this, R.raw.bamboo);** to assign the first song to mpBamboo. Press the Enter key. Type **mpPalace = new MediaPlayer();** to add an instance for the second MediaPlayer variable. Insert a new line and type **mpPalace = MediaPlayer.create(this, R.raw.palace);** to assign the second song to mpPalace.

   The two class variables are assigned an instance of the MediaPlayer class (Figure 6-24).

```
*Main.java

package net.androidbootcamp.easternmusic;

import android.app.Activity;

public class Main extends Activity {

Button btBamboo, btPalace;
MediaPlayer mpBamboo, mpPalace;
int playing;

    /** Called when the activity is first created. */
    @Override
    public void onCreate(Bundle savedInstanceState) {
        super.onCreate(savedInstanceState);
        setContentView(R.layout.main);
        btBamboo = (Button)findViewById(R.id.btnBamboo);
        btPalace = (Button)findViewById(R.id.btnPalace);
        btBamboo.setOnClickListener(bBamboo);
        btPalace.setOnClickListener(bPalace);
        mpBamboo = new  MediaPlayer();
        mpBamboo = MediaPlayer.create(this, R.raw.bamboo);
        mpPalace = new MediaPlayer();
        mpPalace = MediaPlayer.create(this, R.raw.palace);

    }
    Button.OnClickListener bBamboo    = new Button.OnClickListener(){

```

MediaPlayer statements

Figure 6-24 MediaPlayer instance statements

GTK

Music can be used in many ways throughout Android apps. Music can provide sound effects to inform the user of a recent e-mail or to praise you when you reach the winning level on your favorite game. Background music is often used as a soundtrack to create a theme in an adventure game.

The MediaPlayer State

Android uses the MediaPlayer class to control the playing of the audio file. Whether the music file is playing is called the state of the MediaPlayer. The three common states of the audio file include when the music starts, when the music pauses, and when the music stops. The state of the music is established by the MediaPlayer's temporary behavior. Table 6-2 provides an example of the most common MediaPlayer states.

Method	Purpose
start( )	Starts media playback
pause( )	Pauses media playback
stop( )	Stops media playback

Table 6-2 Common MediaPlayer states

In the Eastern Music project, the user first taps a button to start the music playing. The start( ) method is used to begin the playback of the selected music file. When the user taps the same button again, the music temporarily pauses the music file by calling the pause( ) method. To restart the song, the start( ) method must be called again. To determine the state of MediaPlayer, the code must assess if this is the first time the user is tapping the button to start the song or if the user is tapping the same button twice to pause the song. The user can tap the button a third time to start the song again. This cycle continues until the user exits the project. In the chapter project, an integer variable named playing is initially set to zero. Each time the user taps the button, the playing variable changes value. The first time the user taps the button, the variable is changed to the value of 1 to assist the program in determining the state of the MediaPlayer. If the user taps the same button again to pause the song, the variable changes to the value of 0. Android does not have a method for determining the present state of the MediaPlayer, but by using this simple primitive variable, you can keep track of the state of the music. A Switch decision structure uses the variable named playing to change the state of the music. The onClick( ) method is called every time the user selects a button. To initiate the variable used to determine the state of MediaPlayer and to code a Switch decision structure to determine the state, follow these steps:

1. In Main.java, press the Enter key after the mpPalace = MediaPlayer.create(this, R.raw.palace); statement to create a new line. Type **playing = 0;** to initialize the variable named playing as the value 0. When the user clicks a button, the Switch statement follows the path of case 0, which begins the audio playback of one of the songs.

   The variable named playing is initialized as the value 0 (Figure 6-25).

Main.java

```
package net.androidbootcamp.easternmusic;

import android.app.Activity;

public class Main extends Activity {

Button btBamboo, btPalace;
MediaPlayer mpBamboo, mpPalace;
int playing;

    /** Called when the activity is first created. */
    @Override
    public void onCreate(Bundle savedInstanceState) {
        super.onCreate(savedInstanceState);
        setContentView(R.layout.main);
        btBamboo = (Button)findViewById(R.id.btnBamboo);
        btPalace= (Button)findViewById(R.id.btnPalace);
        btBamboo.setOnClickListener(bBamboo);
        btPalace.setOnClickListener(bPalace);
        mpBamboo = new  MediaPlayer();
        mpBamboo = MediaPlayer.create(this, R.raw.bamboo);
        mpPalace= new MediaPlayer();
        mpPalace = MediaPlayer.create(this, R.raw.palace);
        playing=0;

    }
    Button.OnClickListener bBamboo    = new Button.OnClickLis

        @Override
        public void onClick(View v) {
            // TODO Auto-generated method stub
```

Variable that changes as the state of the music changes

Figure 6-25 The *playing* variable is set to 0

2. Inside the braces of the first onClick method (after the // TODO comment), type the following Switch decision structure that is used to determine the state of the music:

```
switch(playing) {
        case 0:
              mpBamboo.start();
              playing = 1;
              break;
        case 1:
              mpBamboo.pause();
              playing = 0;
              break;
   }
```

The Switch decision structure that determines the state of the music is coded for the first onClick method (Figure 6-26).

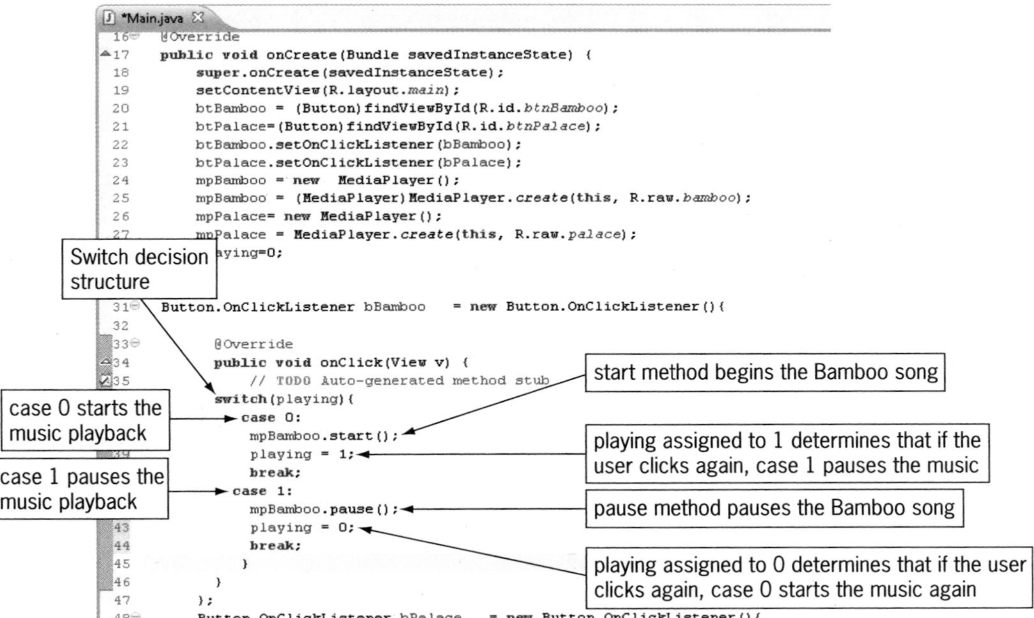

Figure 6-26 Switch statements for both onClick methods

IN THE TRENCHES

Music playback control operation may fail due to various reasons, such as unsupported audio/video format, poorly interleaved audio/video, file size overwhelming memory capabilities, or a streaming timeout on the Internet.

Changing the Text Property Using Code

When the user selects a song to play, the Button control with the text "Play Bamboo Song" is tapped. To pause the song, the user must tap the same button, but the text should be changed to a more fitting action, such as "Pause Bamboo Song." A property can initially be entered in the XML layout or coded in Java. In Chapter 4, the setText( ) method displays text in the TextView control. To change the Text property for a Button control using Java code, the control name and the SetText( ) method are separated by a period that precedes a string of text within parentheses, as shown in the following code syntax:

Code Syntax

```
btBamboo.setText("Pause Bamboo Song");
```

The btBamboo Button control displays the text "Pause Bamboo Song." If the user wants to restart the song, a second setText( ) method changes the text back to "Play Bamboo Song." To change the text on the Button control for the first button, follow these steps:

1. In Main.java in the first onClick( ) method, press the Enter key after the statement playing = 1; in case 0. Type **btBamboo.setText("Pause Bamboo Song");** to change the text displayed on the Button control. To change the text back to the original text if the user restarts the music, in case 1 of the Switch decision structure, press the Enter key after the statement playing = 0;. Type **btBamboo.setText("Play Bamboo Song");** to change the text displayed on the Button control.

   The first button changes text while the music is paused or restarted (Figure 6-27).

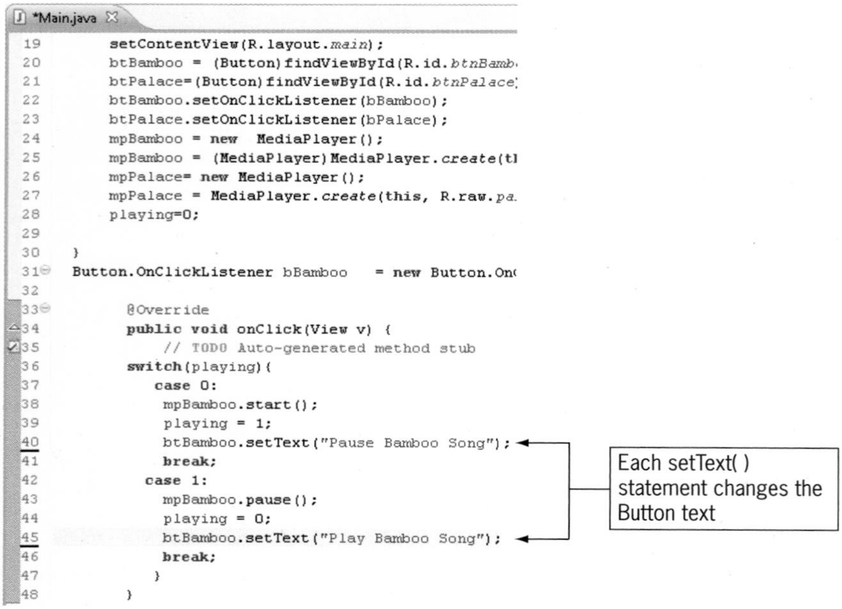

```
*Main.java
        setContentView(R.layout.main);
        btBamboo = (Button)findViewById(R.id.btnBamb
        btPalace=(Button)findViewById(R.id.btnPalace
        btBamboo.setOnClickListener(bBamboo);
        btPalace.setOnClickListener(bPalace);
        mpBamboo = new  MediaPlayer();
        mpBamboo = (MediaPlayer)MediaPlayer.create(t
        mpPalace= new MediaPlayer();
        mpPalace = MediaPlayer.create(this, R.raw.pa
        playing=0;

    }
    Button.OnClickListener bBamboo    = new Button.On

          @Override
          public void onClick(View v) {
              // TODO Auto-generated method stub
          switch(playing){
             case 0:
              mpBamboo.start();
              playing = 1;
              btBamboo.setText("Pause Bamboo Song");
              break;
            case 1:
              mpBamboo.pause();
              playing = 0;
              btBamboo.setText("Play Bamboo Song");
              break;
             }
          }
```

Each setText( ) statement changes the Button text

Figure 6-27 The setText( ) method changes the button control in both case statements

2. To test the music and text on the first Button control, save and run the program. The second Button control has not been coded yet.

   When you tap the first Button control, the Bamboo song plays and the Button text is changed. You can restart or pause the music by pressing the button again (Figure 6-28).

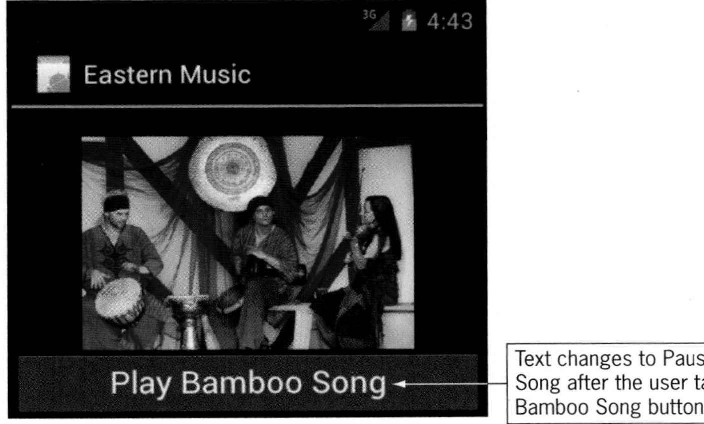

Figure 6-28 Music plays and the button text is changed

Changing the Visibility Property Using Code

When the program is complete, the user can select the button that plays the Bamboo song or the Palace song. One issue that must be resolved is that it is possible to tap the Bamboo song button and then tap the Palace button, playing both songs at once. To resolve this problem, when the user selects one of the songs, the button to the other song can be coded to disappear until the user has paused the current song from playing. The Java property that controls whether a control is displayed on the emulator is the **Visibility property**. By default, the Visibility property is set to display any control you place on the emulator when the program runs. To cause the control not to appear, you must code the setVisibility property to change the view to invisible. To change the visibility of the button to reappear, the setVisibility property is changed to visible, as shown in the following code syntax:

Code Syntax

```
To hide the control:    btBamboo.setVisibility(View.INVISIBLE);
To display the control: btBamboo.setVisibility(View.VISIBLE);
```

To set the setVisibility property for the Bamboo button control to change the view to invisible and to copy and paste the code for the first onClick code to create a Switch decision structure for the second button, you can complete the following steps:

1. In Main.java in the first onClick( ) method in the case 0 option, press the Enter key after the statement btBamboo.setText("Pause Bamboo Song");. Type **btPalace.setVisibility(View.INVISIBLE);** to hide the Palace button when the Bamboo song is playing. When the music is paused, the Palace button should be visible again. In the case 1 option, press the Enter key after the statement btBamboo.setText("Play Bamboo Song");. Type **btPalace.setVisibility(View.VISIBLE);** to change the visibility of the Palace button.

   The Palace button hides when the music plays and displays when the music stops (Figure 6-29).

```
Main.java
20        btBamboo = (Button)findViewById(R.id.btnBamboo
21        btPalace=(Button)findViewById(R.id.btnPalace);
22        btBamboo.setOnClickListener(bBamboo);
23        btPalace.setOnClickListener(bPalace);
24        mpBamboo = new  MediaPlayer();
25        mpBamboo = MediaPlayer.create(this, R.raw.bamb
26        mpPalace= new MediaPlayer();
27        mpPalace = MediaPlayer.create(this, R.raw.pala
28        playing=0;
29
30    }
31    Button.OnClickListener bBamboo   = new Button.OnCl
32
33        @Override
34        public void onClick(View v) {
35            // TODO Auto-generated method stub
36        switch(playing){
37           case 0:
38            mpBamboo.start();
39            playing = 1;
40            btBamboo.setText("Pause Bamboo Song");
41            btPalace.setVisibility(View.INVISIBLE);
42            break;
43          case 1:
44            mpBamboo.pause();
45            playing = 0;
46            btBamboo.setText("Play Bamboo Song");
47            btPalace.setVisibility(View.VISIBLE);
48            break;
49          }
50      }
51    };
52    Button.OnClickListener bPalace   = new Button.
```


Figure 6-29 The setVisibility( ) method changes the visibility of the Button control

2. To code the second onClick( ) method for Palace button, select and copy Lines 36–48 in Figure 6-29 by clicking Edit on the menu bar and then clicking Copy. Click Line 57 inside the second onClick( ) method, click Edit on the menu bar, and then click Paste. Change every reference of mpBamboo to **mpPalace**. Change every reference of btBamboo to **btPalace** or vice versa. Change the setText messages to read **Pause Palace Song** and **Play Palace Song**. You might need to add **};** as the second-to-last line of code. Compare your code with the complete code, making changes as necessary.

   The second onClick( ) method is coded using a Switch decision structure (Figure 6-30).

Main.java

```
package net.androidbootcamp.easternmusic;

import android.app.Activity;

public class Main extends Activity {

Button btBamboo, btPalace;
MediaPlayer mpBamboo, mpPalace;
int playing;

    /** Called when the activity is first created. */
   @Override
   public void onCreate(Bundle savedInstanceState) {
       super.onCreate(savedInstanceState);
       setContentView(R.layout.main);
       btBamboo = (Button)findViewById(R.id.btnBamboo);
       btPalace=(Button)findViewById(R.id.btnPalace);
       btBamboo.setOnClickListener(bBamboo);
       btPalace.setOnClickListener(bPalace);
       mpBamboo = new  MediaPlayer();
       mpBamboo = MediaPlayer.create(this, R.raw.bamboo);
       mpPalace= new MediaPlayer();
       mpPalace = MediaPlayer.create(this, R.raw.palace);
       playing=0;

   }
   Button.OnClickListener bBamboo   = new Button.OnClickListener(){

         @Override
         public void onClick(View v) {
             // TODO Auto-generated method stub
         switch(playing){
            case 0:
             mpBamboo.start();
             playing = 1;
             btBamboo.setText("Pause Bamboo Song");
             btPalace.setVisibility(View.INVISIBLE);
             break;
           case 1:
             mpBamboo.pause();
             playing = 0;
             btBamboo.setText("Play Bamboo Song");
             btPalace.setVisibility(View.VISIBLE);
             break;
            }
         }
       };
       Button.OnClickListener bPalace    = new Button.OnClickListener(){

             @Override
             public void onClick(View v) {
                 // TODO Auto-generated method stub
             switch(playing){
             case 0:
              mpPalace.start();
              btPalace.setText("Pause Palace Song");
              btBamboo.setVisibility(View.INVISIBLE);
              playing = 1;
              break;
             case 1:
              mpPalace.pause();
              btPalace.setText("Play Palace Song");
              btBamboo.setVisibility(View.VISIBLE);
              playing = 0;
              break;
             }
         };
     };
 }
```

Bamboo button is coded

Palace button is coded

Semicolon ends the second onClickListener

Figure 6-30 Complete code for Main.java

Running and Testing the Application

Your first experience with media in an Android application is complete. Click Run on the menu bar, and then select Run to save and test the application in the emulator. Select Android Application and click the OK button. Save all the files in the next dialog box, if necessary, and unlock the emulator. The application opens in the emulator window, as shown in Figure 6-1 and Figure 6-2. The splash screen opens for five seconds. The main screen opens next, requesting your button selection to play each of the songs. Test both buttons and make sure your speakers are on so you can hear the Eastern music play.

Wrap It Up—Chapter Summary

In this chapter, the Android platform created a memorable multimedia experience with the sounds of Eastern music. A splash screen provided time to load extra files if needed and displayed an initial logo for brand recognition. Methods such as setText( ) and setVisibility( ) helped to create an easy-to-use Android application that was clear to the user. The state of music using the start and pause methods of MediaPlayer filled your classroom or home with the enjoyment of music.

- An Android application can show a splash screen that displays the name of the program, a brand logo for the application, or the name of the author. The splash screen opens as you launch your app, providing time for Android to initialize its resources.
- A TextView widget can display a background color or image stored in one of the project's drawable folders.
- A timer in Java executes a one-time task such as displaying an opening splash screen, or it performs a continuous process such as a wake-up call that rings each morning at the same time. Timers can be used to pause an action temporarily or to time dependent or repeated activities. The timer object uses milliseconds as the unit of time.
- After including a reference to the TimerTask class in your code, schedule a timer for the amount of time that an event occurs, such as a splash screen being displayed.
- Each Activity has a life cycle, which is the series of actions from the beginning of an Activity to its end. An Activity usually starts with the onCreate( ) method, which sets up all the resources required to perform the Activity. An Activity usually ends with the onDestroy( ) method, which releases those same resources to free up memory on the mobile device. Other actions can take place during the life of the Activity, including onRestart( ), onStart( ), onResume( ), onPause( ), and onStop( ).
- Local variables are declared by variable declaration statements within a method. The local variable effectively ceases to exist when the execution of the method is complete.

- The scope of a variable refers to the variable's visibility within a class. Variables that are accessible only to a restricted portion of a program such as a single method have local scope. Variables that are accessible from anywhere in a class, however, have global scope. If a variable is needed in multiple methods within a class, the global variable is assigned at the beginning of a class, not within a method. This global scope variable is called a class variable in Java and can be accessed by multiple methods throughout the program.
- Every Android phone and tablet includes a built-in music player where you can store music. You can also write applications that offer music playback capabilities. The media types an Android device platform supports are determined by the codecs the manufacturer included in the device. A codec is a computer technology used to compress and decompress audio and video files.
- In an Android project, music files are typically stored in the res\raw subfolder. In newer versions of Android, you must create the raw subfolder before storing music files.
- The MediaPlayer class provides the methods to control audio playback on an Android device. First declare the MediaPlayer class variables, and then assign an instance of the MediaPlayer class to each variable. Whether the music file is playing is called the state of the MediaPlayer. The three common states of the audio file include when the music starts, when the music pauses, and when the music stops.
- The Java property that controls whether a control is displayed on the emulator is the Visibility property. By default, the Visibility property is set to display any control you place on the emulator when the program runs. To cause the control not to appear, you must code the setVisibility property in Java to change the view to invisible. To change the visibility of the button to reappear, change the setVisibility property to visible.

Key Terms

class variable—A variable with global scope; it can be accessed by multiple methods throughout the program.

codec—A computer technology used to compress and decompress audio and video files.

life cycle—The series of actions from the beginning, or birth, of an Activity to its end, or destruction.

local variable—A variable declared by a variable declaration statement within a method.

MediaPlayer class—The Java class that provides the methods to control audio playback on an Android device.

onDestroy( ) method—A method used to end an Activity. Whereas the onCreate( ) method sets up required resources, the onDestroy( ) method releases those same resources to free up memory.

scope—The scope of a variable refers to the variable's visibility within a class.

state—A stage in an Activity's life cycle that determines whether the Activity is active, paused, stopped, or dead.

thread—A single sequential flow of control within a program.

Timer—A Java class that creates a timed event when the schedule method is called.

timer—A tool that performs a one-time task such as displaying an opening splash screen, or performs a continuous process such as a morning wake-up call set to run at regular intervals.

TimerTask—A Java class that invokes a scheduled timer.

Visibility property—The Java property that controls whether a control is displayed on the emulator.

Developer FAQs

1. What is the name of the initial window that typically displays a company logo for a few seconds?
2. Which property of TextView displays a solid color behind the text?
3. Which property of TextView displays an image as a backdrop behind the text?
4. Write a line of code that creates an instance of the TimerTask class with the object named welcome.
5. Write a line of code that creates an instance of the Timer class with the object named stopwatch.
6. Write a line of code that would hold the initial opening screen for four seconds. The Timer object is named stopwatch and the TimerTask object is named welcome.
7. How long (identify units) does this statement schedule a pause in the execution?

   ```
   logo.schedule(trial, 3);
   ```
8. Write a line of code that closes the resources of the existing Activity.
9. Typically, which method begins an Activity?
10. Typically, which method releases the resources used within an Activity and ends the Activity?
11. What are the four states of an Activity?
12. Which method follows an onPause( ) method?

13. Write two statements that initialize the media player necessary to create an instance of a file named blues residing in your raw folder. Name the variable mpJazz.
14. Write a statement that is needed to begin the song playing from question 13.
15. Write a statement that is needed to pause the song playing from question 14.
16. Write a statement that is needed to change the text on a button named btJazz to the text Pause Unforgettable.
17. Write a statement that hides the button in question 16.
18. What is the name of the folder that typically holds media files in the Android project?
19. Why are class variables sometimes used instead of local variables?
20. What is the most common extension for a song played on an Android device?

Beyond the Book

Using the Internet, search the Web for the answers to the following questions to further your Android knowledge.

1. Research the four most common music file types played on an Android device. Write a paragraph about each music file type. Compare the file size, music quality, and usage of each file type.
2. Using a typical weather app as an example, describe the Android life cycle using each of the methods and a process that happens within the weather app. (*Hint*: See the example using the camera app in the chapter.)
3. At the Android Market, research five music apps. Write a paragraph on the name, features, and purpose of each app.
4. The MediaPlayer class has a method named seekTo( ). Research the purpose of this method.

Case Programming Projects

Complete one or more of the following case programming projects. Use the same steps and techniques taught within the chapter. Submit the program you create to your instructor. The level of difficulty is indicated for each case programming project.

Easiest: ★

Intermediate: ★★

Challenging: ★★★

Case Project 6–1: Rhythm of the Strings App ★

Requirements Document

Application title: Rhythm of the Strings App

Purpose: A music app compares the music types of different string instruments.

Algorithms:

1. A splash screen opens displaying the strings.png image with the title "Rhythm of the Strings" for four seconds (Figure 6-31).
2. Two types of string music are available in this app. A country song named country.mp3 can be played while displaying an image of a banjo. A second selection of a violin plays sonata.mp3 while displaying an image of a violin (Figure 6-32).

Conditions:

1. The pictures of the two string instruments (banjo and violin) and the two music files are provided with your student files.
2. The music should be played and paused by a button control. When a song is playing, the other button should not be displayed.

iStockphoto.com/Brian Sweeney

Figure 6-31

iStockphoto.com/Richard Rudisill and iStockphoto.com/Floriano Rescigno

Figure 6-32

Case Project 6–2: Guitar Solo App ★

Requirements Document

Application title:	Guitar Solo App
Purpose:	A new guitar performance artist needs an Android app to demo her talent.
Algorithms:	1. The opening screen displays the text “Solo Guitar Demo” and an image of a guitar (Figure 6-33). 2. A second screen displays the guitar image and a button. When the user selects the Play Guitar Solo button, a guitar solo plays.
Conditions:	1. The opening screen is displayed for three seconds. 2. Design a layout similar to Figure 6-34. 3. The song can be paused by the user and restarted.

iStockphoto.com/Marek Mnich

Figure 6-33

iStockphoto.com/Marek Mnich

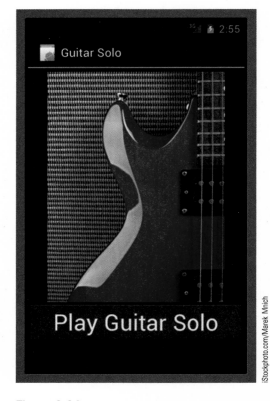

Figure 6-34

Case Project 6–3: Serenity Sounds App ★★

Requirements Document

Application title: Serenity Sounds App

Purpose: A relaxation app provides songs to allow you to breathe deeply and meditate.

Algorithms:

1. An opening screen displays an image of a relaxing location.
2. The second screen displays two song names with a description about each song. A button is available that plays each song or pauses each song.

Conditions:

1. An opening image is provided named relax.png in the student files.
2. Listen to each song and create your own description of each song.
3. When a song is playing, the other button should not be displayed. Each song can play and pause on the user's selection.

Case Project 6–4: Sleep Machine App ★★

Requirements Document

Application title: Sleep Machine App

Purpose: The Sleep Machine app plays sounds of the ocean and a babbling brook to help you sleep.

Algorithms:

1. The opening screen displays an image and the title Sleep Machine for four seconds.
2. The second screen displays two buttons with two images that allow the user to select ocean sounds or babbling brook sounds for restful sleeping.

Conditions:

1. Select your own images and sound effects located on free audio Web sites.
2. When a sound effect is playing, the other button should not be displayed. Each sound effect can play and pause on the user's selection.

Case Project 6–5: Ring Tones App ★★★

Requirements Document

Application title: Ring Tones App

Purpose: The Ring Tones app allows you to listen to three different ring tones available using RadioButton controls for selection.

Algorithms:

1. Create an app that opens with a mobile phone picture and a title for three seconds.
2. The second screen shows three RadioButton controls displaying different ring tone titles and a description of each ring tone.

Conditions:

1. Select your own images and free ring tones available by searching the Web.
2. When a ring tone is playing, the other buttons should not be displayed. Each ring tone can play and pause on the user's selection.

Case Project 6–6: Your Personal Playlist App ★★★

Requirements Document

Application title: Your Personal Playlist App

Purpose: Get creative! Play your favorite three songs on your own personal playlist app.

Algorithms:

1. Create an app that opens with your own picture and a title for six seconds.
2. The second screen shows three buttons displaying different song titles and an image of the artist or group.

Conditions:

1. Select your own images and music files.
2. When a song is playing, the other buttons should not be displayed. Each song can play and pause on the user's selection.

Glossary

ACTION_VIEW A generic action you can use to send any request to get the most reasonable action to occur.

Activity An Android component that represents a single screen with a user interface.

adapter Provides a data model for the layout of a list and for converting the data from the array into list items.

Android 4.0 Library A project folder that contains the android.jar file, which includes all the class libraries needed to build an Android application for the specified version.

Android Manifest A file required in every Android application with the filename AndroidManifest.xml. This file provides essential information to the Android device, such as the name of your Java application and a listing of each Activity.

Android Market An online store that sells programs written for the Android platform.

AndroidManifest.xml A file containing all the information Android needs to run an application.

array variable A variable that can store more than one value.

ArrayAdapter<String> i A ListAdapter that supplies string array data to a ListView object.

assets folder A project folder containing any asset files that are accessed through classic file manipulation.

break A statement that ends a case within a Switch statement and continues with the statement following the Switch decision structure.

case A keyword used in a Switch statement to indicate a condition. In a Switch statement, the case keyword is followed by a value and a colon.

Change Gravity A tool that changes the linear alignment of a control, so that it is aligned to the left, center, right, top, or bottom of an object or the screen.

class A group of objects that establishes an introduction to each object's properties.

class variable A variable with global scope; it can be accessed by multiple methods throughout the program.

codec A computer technology used to compress and decompress audio and video files.

compound condition More than one condition included in an If statement.

DecimalFormat A class that provides patterns for formatting numbers in program output.

decision structure A fundamental control structure used in computer programming that deals with the different conditions that occur based on the values entered into an application.

element A single individual item that contains a value in an array.

Entries A Spinner property that connects a string array to the Spinner control for display.

equals method A method of the String class that Java uses to compare strings.

event handler A part of a program coded to respond to the specific event.

final A type of variable that can only be initialized once; any attempt to reassign the value results in a compile error when the application is executed.

gen folder A project folder that contains automatically generated Java files.

GetSelectedItem( ) A method that returns the text of the selected Spinner item.

GetText( ) A method that reads text stored in an EditText control.

hexadecimal color code A triplet of three colors using hexadecimal numbers, where colors are specified first by a pound sign followed by how much red (00 to FF), how much green (00 to FF), and how much blue (00 to FF) are in the final color.

hint A short description of a field that appears as light text in a Text Field control.

If Else statement A statement that executes one set of instructions if a specified condition is true and another set of instructions if the condition is false.

If statement A statement that executes one set of instructions if a specified condition is true and takes no action if the condition is not true.

ImageView control A control that displays an icon or a graphic from a picture file.

import To make the classes from a particular Android package available throughout the application.

import statement A statement that makes more Java functions available to a program.

instantiate To create an object of a specific class.

intent Code in the Android Manifest file that allows an Android application with more than one Activity to navigate between Activities.

isChecked( ) method A method that tests a checked property to determine if a RadioButton object has been selected.

item In a Spinner control, a string of text that appears in a list for user selection.

Java An object-oriented programming language and a platform originated by Sun Microsystems.

launcher icon An icon that appears on the home screen to represent the application.

layout A container that can hold widgets and other graphical elements to help you design an interface for an application.

life cycle The series of actions from the beginning, or birth, of an Activity to its end, or destruction.

Linear layout A layout that arranges components in a vertical column or horizontal row.

ListActivity A class that displays a list of items within an app.

local variable A variable declared by a variable declaration statement within a method.

localization The use of the String table to change text based on the user's preferred language.

margin Blank space that offsets a control a certain amount of density independent pixels (dp) on each of its four sides.

MediaPlayer class The Java class that provides the methods to control audio playback on an Android device.

method A set of Java statements that can be included inside a Java class.

nest To place one statement, such as an If statement, within another statement.

object A specific, concrete instance of a class.

object-oriented programming language A type of programming language that allows good software engineering practices such as code reuse.

onDestroy( ) method A method used to end an Activity. Whereas the onCreate( ) method sets up required resources, the onDestroy( ) method releases those same resources to free up memory.

onListItemClick( ) A method called when an item in a list is selected.

Open Handset Alliance An open-source business alliance of 80 firms that develop open standards for mobile devices.

Package Explorer A pane on the left side of the Eclipse program window that contains the folders for the current project.

Parse A class that converts a string into a number data type.

position The placement of an item in a list. When an item in a list is selected, the position of the item is passed from the onListItemClick method and evaluated with a decision structure. The first item is assigned the position of 0, the second item is assigned the position of 1, and so forth.

prompt Text that displays instructions at the top of the Spinner control.

RadioGroup A group of RadioButton controls; only one RadioButton control can be selected at a time.

Relative layout A layout that arranges components in relation to each other.

res folder A project folder that contains all the resources, such as images, music, and video files, that an application may need.

scope The scope of a variable refers to the variable's visibility within a class.

setContentView The Java code necessary to display the content of a specific screen.

setListAdapter A command that projects your data to the onscreen list on your device by connecting the ListActivity's ListView object to array data.

smartphone A mobile phone with advanced computing ability and connectivity features.

soft keyboard An onscreen keyboard positioned over the lower part of an application's window.

sp A unit of measurement that stands for scaled-independent pixels.

Spinner control A widget similar to a drop-down list for selecting a single item from a fixed listing.

src folder A project folder that includes the Java code source files for the project.

state A stage in an Activity's life cycle that determines whether the Activity is active, paused, stopped, or dead.

string A series of alphanumeric characters that can include spaces.

strings.xml A default file that is part of every Android application and holds commonly used strings in an application.

stub A piece of code that serves as a placeholder to declare itself, containing just enough code to link to the rest of the program.

Switch A type of decision statement that allows you to choose from many statements based on an integer or char input.

Text property A property that changes the text written within a control.

Text size property A property that sets the size of text in a control.

theme A style applied to an Activity or an entire application.

thread A single sequential flow of control within a program.

Timer A Java class that creates a timed event when the schedule method is called.

timer A tool that performs a one-time task such as displaying an opening splash screen, or performs a continuous process such as a morning wake-up call set to run at regular intervals.

TimerTask A Java class that invokes a scheduled timer.

toast notification A message that appears as an overlay on a user's screen, often displaying a validation warning.

URI An acronym for Uniform Resource Identifier, a URI is a string that identifies the resources of the Web. Similar to a URL, a URI includes additional information necessary for gaining access to the resources required for posting the page.

URL An acronym for Uniform Resource Locator, a URL is a Web site address.

variable A name used in a Java program to contain data that changes during the execution of the program.

Visibility property The Java property that controls whether a control is displayed on the emulator.

widget A single element such as a TextView, Button, or CheckBox control, and is also called an object.

XML An acronym for Extensible Markup Language, a widely used system for defining data formats. XML assists in the layout of the Android emulator.

Index

L

M

N

O

P

Q